Unfolding State

The Transformation of

Bangladesh

Unfolding State

The Transformation of

Bangladesh

Ali Riaz

de Sitter Publications

LIBRARY AND ARCHIVES CANADA CATALOGUING IN PUBLICATION

Unfolding state : the transformation of Bangladesh / Ali Riaz.

Includes index.

ISBN 1-897160-10-0

    1. Bangladesh--Politics and government--1971-. 2. Bangladesh-- Social conditions. 3. Bangladesh--History. I. Unfolding state.

DS395.5.R53 2005   954.9205   C2005-905472

Cover design: de Sitter Publications

de Sitter Publications
104 Consumers Dr., Whitby, ON,
L1N 1C4, Canada

http://www.desitterpublications.com
sales@desitterpublications.com

To Safuran Ara
My sister

Contents

List of Tables

ACKNOWLEDGEMENTS

Books evolve as much as they are written. At least that has happened with this book. My interactions with friends, colleagues, government officials, private citizens, researchers on Bangladesh, and students over a long period of time and through various means—in person, via e-mail, over the telephone, and at conferences—have helped to develop the ideas, questions, and arguments that constitute the core of the book. These exchanges occurred in various places and under different circumstances; some of them were formal but many were informal. Each encounter had its role in the creation of this book. I thank them all for their contributions. The names are too many to be mentioned individually. Some of them, however, must be acknowledged personally and with profound gratitude.

First, I thank Professor Sankran Krishna and Professor Farideh Farhi of the University of Hawaii who, during my graduate school years, encouraged my interest in the state. As such, the genesis of this book lies in their courses and the discussions I had with them and my resulting dissertation. I am deeply indebted to them.

My former colleagues at the British Broadcasting Corporation (BBC), especially Dr. Peter Mangold, Dr. Syed Mahmud Ali, Manoshi Barua, Kazi Jawad, Ghulam Quader, Masud Hasan Khan, Kamal Ahmed, and Urbi Basu, deserve special thanks. Over a period of five years, and on many occasions, they challenged my assumptions and ideas and forced me to question myself. Two documentary series on Bangladesh that I produced for the BBC—one in 1996 on the occasion of the silver jubilee of Bangladesh and the other in 2000 on the political changes of 1975—helped me to gather additional information for the book. For the latter I thank Kadir Kallol, a BBC reporter in Dhaka who worked tirelessly to arrange many interviews in early 2000. These discussions with political leaders, former military officials, and bureaucrats clarified and helped contextualize the events. These interviews would have been difficult to conduct without the help of Kadir. The interviewees, Tofail Ahmed of the Awami League, Colonel (Rtd.) Oli Ahmed of the BNP, Hasanul Huq Inu of the JSD, former cabinet secretary Mujibul Huq, former bureaucrat Abul Mal Abdul

Muhith, former Chief of Staff of the Bangladesh Army General (Rtd.) Shafiullah, Colonel (Rtd.) Abdul Hamid, former activist Professor Anwar Hossain, and journalists Reazuddin Ahmed and Iqbal Sobhan Chowdhury provided helpful information and valuable insights. I thank all of them. Eminent lawyer and former Law Minister Dr. Kamal Hossain talked to me on several occasions. His insights have helped me in many ways.

My sincere thanks go to Dr. Marina Carter, who has read the manuscript twice, suggested changes to make my arguments intelligible, and copyedited with the utmost care. The perceptive comments of Professor Mehnaaz Momen of Texas A&M International University and Professor Harry Vanden of Florida State University enriched my understanding of the state-formation process. I have benefited immensely from the comments of Professor Subir Sinha of SOAS, London University. My colleague at Illinois State University Professor Julie Webber has been a constant source of inspiration. Her comments on a chapter led to another revision and improved the clarity of meaning. Thanks are also due to Professor Subho Basu for his encouragement. Professor Jamal Nassar, chair of the Department of Politics and Government at ISU, has been most helpful and was always there to provide support whenever I needed it.

A number of libraries in Dhaka allowed me to use their collections on more than one occasion. These include the Dhaka University Library, the Bangladesh Institute of Development Studies (BIDS) Library, and the Central Public Library. The collections of the British Library in London were also helpful. During my research trips to Dhaka, a number of officials at the Bangladesh Secretariat extended their cooperation on the condition of anonymity. Anonymous they will remain to others, but I know how helpful they were to me. During the data gathering phase, Zillur Rahman, S. Reza, and Nayeemul Islam Khan were my first ports of call. They extended their support as much possible. I could not ask for more. Among my research assistants Mina Aitelhadj deserves special thanks for her help in compiling the bibliography.

I am grateful to Rowman and Littlefield for permitting me to use some materials from my book *God Willing: The Politics of Islamism in Bangladesh*, and the Regents of the University of California for their permission to use parts of my article "Bangladesh in 2004: The Politics of

Vengenance and the erosion of Democracy" published in the *Asian Survey* (45:1).

Thanks to Shivu Ishwaran of de Sitter Publications for taking an interest in this book, for being patient and supportive, and for making the publication process smooth. I am greatly indebted to Jody Yvonne of de Sitter Publications for being so meticulous with the manuscript. It is because of his attention to details that a number of mistakes were identified before the typesetting. His suggestions were also helpful in bringing clarity to some ideas.

The last though most important expression of my gratitude goes to my wife Shagufta Jabeen and our daughter Ila Sruti. Their enthusiasm was contagious and that is what kept me going. Whenever I was writing something, Ila asked me whether it was "something for the book." For me, this was a reminder of the work yet to be done.

I am grateful to everyone who helped me gather information and write the book, but I alone am responsible for the facts, their interpretation, and the conclusions that appear in the book.

Introduction

Understanding the State Transformation

In 1971, in the eastern province of Pakistan, a movement for political autonomy turned into a secessionist movement after the Pakistani military cracked down on the ethnic Bengali community, the majority population of the country. After nine months of war, millions of deaths, the rapes of hundreds of thousands of women, and the displacement of more than ten million people, a nation-state emerged: Bangladesh. Born out of the first successful secessionist movement since the Second World War in a land ravaged by the war and impoverished by lack of resources, the Bangladeshi state began its journey with high ideals—the ideals of egalitarianism, of secularism, and of democracy. The emergence of the state brought to power the social classes who had been politically marginalized within the Pakistani polity and kindled hope for an ethnic group subjected to economic marginalization for almost a quarter of a century; but it also sounded warning bells for the institutions of the world capitalist system, and the United States.

The regime began implementing some of these ideals of social-democratic secularism, but before long had reneged on its promises. The ideals of egalitarianism, described as socialism in the constitution, gave way before the demands of private entrepreneurship; the mode of governance drifted toward authoritarianism at the expense of democracy, and religious idiom soon found its way back to the political discourse undermining the principles of secularism. Three and a half years after independence came the most dramatic event: the military intervened in politics killing the founding leaders of the nation. This was the beginning of the final act of the transformation of the state. The process continued in various forms under different military rulers until 1990, when a popular uprising ousted the extant military regime. It was described as "the second liberation" by the popular press. The events rekindled hope and raised the possibility of change in the Bangladeshi polity. But the Bangladeshi state had by then become deeply integrated within the international economic system and was being ruled by a new alliance of classes. The civilian regimes have since alternated between two major political parties and have maintained the status quo. The transformation looks to be irreversible. There is no going back.

The present book is about this transformation process—the spectacular unfolding of a state. It is an account of how and why the Bangladeshi state changed to an "administrative state" dominated by a nascent bourgeoisie, bureaucrats, and the military from an "intermediate state" dominated by the middle classes. Obvious questions are: what prompted the transformation? And, how has the state been transformed?

This book is also about the state in peripheral societies: an investigation into the formation and transformation processes of states—questions largely ignored by existing theories of the state. Although the book is empirical in nature and focuses on one country, it has conceptual implications that may contribute to the debate on the state in general and particularly on state capitalism, class formation in developing societies, the state-society relationship, and the intricate relationship between exogenous and endogenous factors in effecting social change. Discussions on the state abound in the fields of political theory and international relations, but they have largely focused on the advanced capitalist state rather than on states in peripheral societies, because "those engaged in the debate are trained almost exclusively on the advanced industrialized economies" (Phillips 2004:14). This is not to say that there has not been any deliberation on third world states, but these have been largely in the context of development.

One can find three representations of third world states in social science discourse: the first is in the context of globalization wherein third world states are considered in decline under the pervasive powers of globalization (Strange 1995), a dying breed making their last gasp. The second representation centers on governance issues, or more specifically on the "governance problem." Capacity, or the lack of capacity, of the state in the third world is the "problem" and therefore begs a solution, and it is the effort to find the right prescription to "fix" the problem that drives this strand. The third approach looks at the state in relation to society and attempts to analyze their relationship. Within this third strand one can find acknowledgements of how the state in peripheral societies demands closer scrutiny, as an institution, as an actor, and as an arena of conflict of contending forces. But this strand remains weak to date, and on the margin of discussions on the state *per se*. Mindful of this lacuna, the present book attempts to insert the peripheral state into the debate. It raises two fundamental questions: what determines the nature of the state? And, how does the nature of the state change?

Through an examination of the Bangladeshi state, characterized by its historical specificity (i.e., post-colonial) and its position within the global capitalist system (i.e., peripheral), this book intends to demonstrate that domestic imperatives and external compulsions play pivotal roles while structural and conjunctural factors facilitate the transformation process. An analysis of the causes of, and conditions for, the meteoric rise and dramatic fall of an "intermediate state" in Bangladesh will help us understand the complexity of the phenomenon and various modes of interactions of state and social classes. I also intend to show how the global capitalist system influences the formation and transformation processes of the state in societies located on the periphery.

The objective of this book is, therefore, two-fold: first, it seeks to offer an alternative framework of analysis for understanding the state in post-colonial/peripheral societies; and, secondly, it strives to combine theoretical analysis with a macro-level case study. To achieve the first objective, a reexamination and revision of some fundamental theoretical categories such as the state and class is required. This is because "the study of capitalism outside the advanced industrialized democracies need[s] to dispense with restrictive assumptions about the nature of the states, classes, labor, and so on, and [seek] to understand the articulation of capitalist development in systems not characterized by the institutional and societal attributes found in the customary models" (Phillips 2004:15). The second objective is dealt with using a historical-structural approach that attempts to "disclose 'deep structures' which underline and produce directly observable phenomena of social life" (Bottomore 1983:471) and emphasize the historical transformation of structures by conflicts, movements, class struggles, and individuals.

I am well aware that terminology such as "periphery" is not in vogue, especially at a time when "globalization" has become such a buzz word. As such, some readers may find the use of "peripheral" in identifying the location of the Bangladeshi state within the global system uncomfortable and may feel that it gestures toward a certain structural, already assigned location of Bangladesh in the global political economy. Yet, it is my contention, notwithstanding the limitations of the term, that its analytical value cannot be undermined. Those countries that are not members of the advanced capitalist community and did not belong to the socialist bloc are referred to by various titles, such as "developing," "less-developed," "underdeveloped," "Global South," and so on. Although these titles have some validity, they are obviously identified with an ideological position and are often misleading (for example, "the Global South," even though one cannot discount that at least three major "developed" countries are also geographically located in the Southern Hemisphere). Additionally, the principal weakness of these concepts is their vagueness in terms of the relations of production and exchange that characterize these countries. The concept of "peripheral formations" used by world-system analysts like Samir Amin and Immanuel Wallerstein cannot claim to be completely free from such limitations, yet, in my view, are more successful in helping us understand the production relations of the countries in question better than other terms.

In the context of this book, the concept of the periphery is interpreted within the Marxian reproduction scheme. In the classical reproduction scheme, production is divided between two departments: the means of production (Department I) and the means of reproduction of the labor force (Department II). The former refers to the capital goods and joint inputs that are used by both Departments, while the latter refers to wage goods and wage services for the workers employed in them. In the case of a peripheral economy, Department I is either absent or incomplete. Thus, peripheral formations are characterized by disarticulation between economic sectors. Additionally, the full circuit of capital cannot take place within the countries themselves. The concept of a peripheral formation also refers to a particular structure of unequal relationships on a global scale, which emerged as a result of a process lasting some four centuries. The "capitalist world-system" that had emerged in an almost complete form by 1914, and has continued to develop since then, "integrated" a large number of countries within the capitalist system in the name of "developmentalist" ideology and produced the conditions now commonly termed "underdevelopment." The need of Western capitalism to expand the scale of its accumulation and the continuation of that accumulation changed the patterns of class formation, class relations, and forms of state in the peripheral societies.

While the Bangladeshi state is characterized by its peripheral position within the global capitalist system, its historical specificity—post-coloniality—has its mark all over state formation processes. Therefore, understanding state transformation demands that we contemplate and analyze both of these elements.

My aim in this chapter is to introduce the central concepts or, in other words, the building blocs of the proposed analytical framework, followed by the details of the framework. In the final section, I provide a summary of my arguments, which are elaborated throughout the book with historical evidence and empirical precision, in the context of Bangladesh.

The Building Blocs

State-formation, interchangeable with "state-building" and "state-making," is commonly understood to be the processes that lead to the centralization of political power over a well-defined territory, and with a monopoly of the means of coercion. Studies that identify the main elements of these processes can be grouped into four strands: capitalist dynamics and class conflict explanations, statist explanations, world system analyses, and geopolitical analyses. The first two strands emphasize internal factors, while the latter two highlight external factors, as the driving forces behind state formation processes. The logic of, and contradictions in, productive systems and economic modes of production within the state are seen as key elements by the capitalist dynamics and class conflict explanations. The statist explanations focus on consequences of events within the state such as governability crises. The world system analyses, on the contrary, examine the logic of the capitalist world economy and the place of the state within that world economy. The geopolitical analyses insist that interstate forces have a determining influence on state formation processes (Schwarz 2004:3). These explanations, especially their differences in focus, not only reflect what Colin Hay (2002:257) has called "disciplinary parochialism," between International Political Economy (IPE) and Comparative Political Economy (CPE), but also show a false dichotomy between exogenous and endogenous factors. Understanding state formation processes in peripheral

6

societies requires us to dispense with this false dichotomy. What is essential is engagement with, and deployment of, conceptual frameworks from both strands, and a meshing of their perspectives and approaches.

The available literature on state formation is fraught with another problem that we need to be aware of and address at the outset. Barnett (2002:105) has alluded to this as an inclination toward "mono-causality"; that is to say, the frameworks of earlier studies have attempted to find *a* modal process, *a* master variable. This tendency has resulted in understanding the development of the modern nation state as a linear, step-wise process with a clearly identifiable end. But history has shown us that "there are many paths towards state formation" (Barnett 2002:105). And, of course, there is no finality to the process—the state remains open to potential changes all the time.

These shortcomings make it imperative that we choose a different point of departure and conceptualize the building blocs differently in order to understand state formation processes. The key concepts around which this study is built are intermediate classes, hegemony, and the relative autonomy of the state. These concepts and categories are used throughout the study to explain different social conditions and phenomena. I have no intention of providing any final definitions of these concepts, because of their essentially contested nature, but in this section I will simply furnish the meaning as imparted in this study.

Intermediate Classes

The notion of "intermediate class" was advanced by Gramsci (1979)[1] and later developed by Kalecki (1972) in a general way as being relevant to many developing countries. In the Indian context, K. N. Raj (1973:1191) saw it as the most appropriate category for explaining Indian politics while Namboodripad (1973) and Byers (1996) fiercely contested the notion, especially its appropriateness. According to Gramsci, peripheral countries are comprised of a broad spectrum of classes between the polar classes (i.e., proletariat and the bourgeoisie). Kalecki (1972) suggests that rich peasants, petty traders and businessmen, urban professionals and intellectuals all belong to an intermediate class and share some common aspirations.

7

Ahmad, who explored the idea of intermediate classes further, defined them as follows:

> Small landowners, rich and middle peasants, the merchants of rural and semi-rural townships, small-scale manufacturers, retailers, and so on, are included here among the intermediate and auxiliary classes. The professional petty bourgeoisie has arisen mainly from these classes and shares many of the same interests and attitudes (Ahmad 1985:44).

Ahmad also argues that these intermediate classes have their own political projects and that they tend to establish their dominance over the state apparatuses, as well as over the proletariat and propertied classes.

Although this study will employ the description provided by Ahmad, it is necessary to keep in mind two important points. Firstly, in this study class is understood as a relational category, i.e., classes are determined by their relationship to one another within a system of social production. Secondly, the Marxian presupposition that each society has two fundamental classes is misleading for peripheral societies and should be avoided.

What I am suggesting with the first point is that social relations of production are the key to understanding class. Here, social relations of production primarily refer to (1) the relation to the means or forces of production, and (2) the form of surplus product (value) appropriation. These two elements essentially form the material basis of class and define, very broadly, class interests. Given that class is a historically contingent entity, the specific historical situation of the society needs to be considered while contemporary class formations and class relations are discussed.

The second point indicates that the concept of class is based on the understanding that in a given society at a given time some classes have a disproportionate share of assets (ranging from income to wealth and social status) than other social classes, and there exists a hierarchy among these classes. According to a Marxist interpretation, in a capitalist social formation one social class establishes its control over the means of production and by virtue of its economic position dominates and controls all aspects of

8

social life. This class is referred to as the "dominant class." The "dominant class" is, therefore, the class that has a disproportionate share of economic and political power and, hence, much freer access to the state and an ability to direct the rules of the power game in its favor. The Marxist notion of class always suggests that in each mode of production there are two fundamental classes—the class of exploited producers and the exploiting classes. Thus, in a capitalist society there exist two fundamental classes: the bourgeoisie and the proletariat. This oversimplified and bipolar division of social classes may have some relevance to mature and advanced capitalist societies, but it has not proved very useful in understanding peripheral societies. As Roxborough (1982) noted, referring to the Third World in general, "the class structures of the Third World differ from those of the advanced nations in two principal ways: they are more complex, and classes themselves are usually much weaker." Furthermore, "not only are the class structures of the underdeveloped nations complex and weak, they are frequently 'incomplete' [sic] in the sense that the dominant class, or one fraction of the dominant class, is absent" (Roxborough 1982:72-73). The Marxian notion of a dominant class is problematic and misleading in peripheral societies as it implies a direct relationship between the state apparatus and a specific class. In the capitalist periphery, where historical origins and the formation of the state and social classes are different, the relationship of the social classes is more nuanced and mediated by a power bloc, which gives a particular shape to the relationship. It is in this context that the term "dominant class" is avoided in the present study and the term "prominent classes" is used to describe the classes that appear as important and significant in the capitalist periphery. Thus, the term refers to the class or classes who have gained prominence in politics, with or without the economic leverage commonly associated with a dominant class.

Hegemony

The term "hegemony" is used according to its Gramscian connotations. As defined by Gramsci, it is characterized by "the 'spontaneous' consent given by the great masses of the population to the general direction imposed on social life by the dominant fundamental group; the consent is 'historically' caused by the prestige (and consequent confidence) which the dominant group enjoys because of its position and function in the world of production" (Gramsci 1971:12). The question of hegemony, however, is not merely material, it is also a politics of moral and intellectual leadership. To assert its hegemony, the ruling class must be able to defend its own corporate interests by universalizing them, by ensuring that these interests can at least apparently "become the interests of the...subordinate groups" (Gramsci 1971:181). To this extent, hegemony implies consent rather than domination, integration rather than exclusion, and co-optation rather than suppression.

From this point of view, a ruling class is hegemonic when it establishes both material dominance and intellectual and moral leadership over society and when it succeeds in persuading subaltern classes that positions of subordination and superordination are just, proper, and legitimate. This requires that the ruling class be prepared to make certain concessions, which, while not fundamental, contribute to the political co-optation of popular sectors and the progressive expansion of the productive process. In this instance, as Gramsci points out, the ruling class "really cause(s) the entire society to move forward, not merely satisfying its own existential requirements, but continuously augmenting its cadres for the conquest of ever new spheres of economic and productive activity" (Gramsci 1971:60). This is the moment of "historic unity," when the ruling class has established its material, ethical, and political leadership over society and when relationships of superordination and subordination are accepted by all as organic and not contradictory, as legitimate and not exploitative. When such a situation crystallizes, the ruling class achieves what might be called *paradigmatic hegemony*.

Relative Autonomy of the State

As the debate on "state failures" in developing countries gained salience since the early 1990s, the issue of state formation and the transformation of state forms came to the forefront in various social science disciplines. This is, in some ways, a reincarnation of the debate in the 1970s when discussions about the capitalist state proliferated. One of the most significant consequences of that debate was the recognition of the omnipresence of the state in our lives. Evans (1995:5) succinctly describes this realization:

> From the poorest countries of the Third World to the most advanced exemplars of welfare capitalism, one of the few universals in the history of the twentieth century is the increasingly pervasive influence of the state as an institution and social actor.

However, the concept of the state is one of the most problematic in politics. It has been variously conceptualized. These conceptualizations are based upon some combinations of its functions, purposes, activities, personnel, organizational contours, legitimacy, legal norms, rules and machinery, sovereignty, coercive monopoly, and territorial control. Thus, any definition of the relative autonomy of the state demands a clarification of our understanding of it and a review of state theories, especially Marxist theories of the state.

In this study, the concept of "state" is meant to convey a differentiated set of institutions and personnel which have a legitimate monopoly on authoritative rule-making, backed up by a monopoly on the means of physical violence, within a territorially demarcated area (Mann 1986:112; Rueschmeyer and Evans 1985:45-6). The concept implicitly incorporates three aspects of the state: apparatus, power, and authority. State apparatus, in this context, means the complex set of institutions staffed by a professional bureaucracy and armed forces, specialized to some degree or other, which together ensure the formulation and execution of policies. Secondly, the state represents a concentration of economic and political power. In most cases, it is the biggest single such concentration in a particular social formation. Thirdly, it also represents a concentration of authority. Which means, in the ideological sense, it is able to give legitimacy to the actions of those who act in its name, or at least claims such.

In terms of the constitutive elements of the state, we can broadly group them into three sets: the regime (mostly armed with legislative power, and having limited capacity for implementation); the executives (or, in other words, the bureaucracy and attendant organizations which have immense control over the implementation process); and the military (along with other paramilitary forces that have a monopoly over legitimate coercion).

However, the state, be it in the periphery or in an advanced capitalist society, should not be viewed as only the conglomeration of these elements. Rather, it should be understood as the balance between them. At a given moment of time and in a given social formation, it is the relationship and balance between these elements that determines the nature of state. The other equally important aspect is the relationship between these institutions and the society where it is located.

It is in the context of this relationship between the constitutive elements of the state and between the state and society that the concept of relative autonomy of the state emerged. It owes a great deal to Marxist and neo-Marxist theories of the state. The primary view of the state reflected in the general theory of politics in Marx's writings asserts that the form and functions of the state reflect, and are largely determined by, the economic base of the society. Given that the ownership of material and mental production lies with the bourgeoisie in the capitalist mode of production, the state becomes the repressive machinery of the bourgeoisie.[2]

Marx (1974), however, maintained that there are exceptions, one example being Louis Bonaparte's regime (1852-1870, he was commonly known as Napoleon III) in France. In a special historical situation where no class had enough power to rule through the state, the state did not function as the direct instrument of any class. Engels holds the same opinion: in all but exceptional situations, the state acts in a fairly uncomplicated way as the direct spokesman and protector of the exploiting class. The state, Engels writes, is "normally the state of the most powerful, economically dominant class, which by its means becomes also the politically dominant class and so acquires new means of holding down and exploiting the oppressed class" (Engels 1975:231). Yet, Engels notes, "exceptional periods occur when the warring classes are so nearly equal in forces that the state power, as apparent mediator, acquires for the moment a certain independence in relation to both" (Engels 1975:231).

Marxists and neo-Marxists subsequently elaborated the concept of the relative autonomy of the state. Authors who have taken part in the debate and significantly contributed to reshaping the Marxist concept of

12

state include Miliband (1969, 1973), Poulantzas (1973, 1973a, 1975, 1976, 1976a), Anderson (1974), Therborn (1978), Offe (1975), Block (1987), and Skocpol (1985). Non-Marxist scholars like Krasner (1978), Stepan (1978), Trimberger (1978), Hamilton (1982), and Nordlinger (1981) have also examined the question of the state at length. These authors have approached the issue from different perspectives and advanced a number of definitions of "relative autonomy" of the state. They are, however, primarily concerned with developed capitalist states and with formulating abstract theories. Their studies pay little attention to peripheral societies, although Skocpol's analysis included countries like China. Alavi, in his seminal work on the post-colonial state, underscored the importance of the concept of relative autonomy in peripheral societies. Kohli (1987) and Bardhan (1984) utilized this concept in their studies on India, but in a different manner.

Nevertheless, instead of viewing autonomy as an exceptional situation or aberration, a number of scholars have suggested that the state can possess relative autonomy in a normal situation, and that autonomy is not just a transitional phenomenon as hinted by Marx and Engels. Referring to the tensions and conflicts that arise between the capitalist state and the bourgeoisie, even on a long-term basis, Marxist authors insist that an antagonistic relationship can and does exist between the bourgeoisie and the state. In making this claim, they quite explicitly draw a firm conceptual distinction between power as embodied in the state and power originating in social classes.

Antonio Gramsci first pointed to the distinction between class power and state power. He understood the state in capitalist societies as being essential to maintaining the dominance of the bourgeoisie, securing its long-term interests, and unification. The state, according to Gramsci, embodies two modalities of class domination: the use of force and also the exercise of "hegemony"; that is, the active consent of the ruled. Here, "hegemony" is not simply a matter of installing "false consciousness"; rather, it requires concessions to popular interests and an appeal to "national" objectives that apparently transcend class interests. Carnoy (1984) explains: "Hegemony, in Gramscian terms, meant the ideological predominance of bourgeois values and norms over the subordinate classes" (Carnoy 1984:66). From this interpretation, the question of the state becomes a primary one in understanding capitalist society. According to Gramsci, "the State is the entire complex of practical and theoretical activities with which the ruling class not only justifies and maintains the domination, but manages to win the active consent of those over whom it rules" (Gramsci 1971:244).

It is necessary, here, to understand that Gramsci does not view the state as merely the coercive machinery of the bourgeoisie. He contends that although the ultimate aim of the state is to ensure the domination of the bourgeoisie, it tends to incorporate the interests of all classes and in doing so sometimes transcends class interests.

The distinction between state power and class power, and the relative autonomy of the state, was further emphasized by Miliband (1973:88):

> One of the main reasons for stressing the notion of the relative autonomy of the state is that *there is a basic distinction to be made between class power and state power*, and that the analysis of the meaning and implications of that notion of relative autonomy must indeed focus on the forces which causes it to be greater or lesser, the circumstances in which is exercised, and so on. The blurring of the distinction between class power and state power ... makes any such analysis impossible. (Emphasis added)

It is indeed true that the notion of the relative autonomy of the state discussed so far is primarily conceived in the context of advanced capitalist states, but its importance in understanding the peripheral capitalist state is significant for two reasons. Firstly, it emphasizes the need for a distinction between state power and class power. Secondly, it recognizes that the state does act on its own in many different situations.

A significant shift in the understanding of "state autonomy" has taken place since Peter Evans introduced the concept of "embedded autonomy." Evans classified Third World states into two categories: predatory and developmental (1995:12) and went on to say that "embedded autonomy is...key to the developmental state's effectiveness" (Evans 1995:50). He defined embedded autonomy as "Weberian bureaucratic insulation with intense connection to the surrounding social structure" (Evans 1995:50).

For Evans, autonomy means autonomy/independence from "vested interests," "special interest groups," "distribution coalition," and "rent-seekers" who, in more favorable conditions, would be able to influence public policy to their own advantage. He insists that autonomy makes the state capable of constructing long-term projects of social change that transcend the short-term interests of a specific group. However, a state cannot be heavily insulated from the society, hence the need for "embeddedness"—a dense tie with the domestic productive class. This notion of a contradictory combination of embededdness and autonomy, as Evans's own study has shown, can only be applied to "developmental" states (e.g., Korea), and has little relevance to "predatory" states (e.g., Zaire). Evans notes "embeddedness is as important as autonomy," and yet he underscores the significance of embeddedness further, adding "the embeddedness of the developmental state represents something more specific than the fact that the state grows out of its social milieu" (Evans 1995:59). Although the notion of embedded autonomy has drawn a lot of attention, especially in explaining the efficacy of the newly industrialized countries, its usefulness in understanding the complexity of post-colonial states remains questionable on several counts. In societies where the domestic productive class is either absent or weak, the state can gain little from weaving networks of intense connection. Mutual acceptance of different actor's authority and legitimacy is a necessary condition for embeddedness. But it remains absent in fractious politics and the economies of post-colonial societies. Thus, "autonomy" becomes pivotal and the overriding character of the state.

Evans's (1995:58) argument that "without autonomy, the embeddedness will degenerate into a super-cartel, aimed, like all cartels, at protecting its members from changes" can be extrapolated further. One can say that where embeddedness cannot be achieved due to the absence of the necessary conditions, the relative autonomy of the state becomes the order of the day.

In this study, "relative autonomy of the state" connotes the autonomous role played by state executives in relation to the social classes of the society, particularly the prominent classes. The definition advanced by Skocpol (1985:9) approximates the situation I will describe as state-autonomy: "states conceived as organizations claiming control over territories and people may formulate and pursue goals that are not simply reflective of the demands or interests of social groups, classes, or society." The degree of state-autonomy can vary from single-issue policies that affect a small group to an overall political-economic project that affects the entire dominant/prominent class or classes. In this study, the relative autonomy of the state is conceived in the latter sense.

Framework of Analysis

Equally central to the arguments presented in this book are the concepts of intermediate classes, relative autonomy of the state, hegemony, and the leading premise that the formation and transformation of the state in peripheral societies needs to be understood within the framework of peripheral capitalism, in general, and colonial/post-colonial peripheral capitalism, in particular. Both historical and structural specificities have implications for the society and the social classes, and these specificities influence the capacity of the society and social classes. Here, the explanatory frameworks of Alavi (1973), Kalecki (1976), Thomas (1984), and Ahmad (1985), based upon empirical data gathered in developing countries, become extremely helpful in identifying the determinants of the state form in peripheral societies. Gramsci's (1971) notion of "hegemony" and "organic crisis" provides the tools to examine the crisis that contributes to the transformation process.

Formation of the State

The nature of the state in peripheral, especially post-colonial, societies is predicated by three factors: the genesis or the historical lineage of state structures, the composition of the classes of that society, and the state's relationship with the global economic system.

Genesis, Relative Autonomy, and the Centrality of the State

States in the capitalist periphery are imported entities, at least on two counts. First, the material basis upon which they rest is not a product of

16

indigenous evolution, and secondly, the structures of the state have been (largely) imported through colonial expansion.

There is no denying that capitalism serves as the material basis of states in peripheral societies and that the present form of capitalism has been implanted in the periphery due to Western capitalism's need to expand the geographical sphere and scale of its accumulation. Additionally, historical accounts show that the origins of the state in peripheral societies are either colonial, or, where they are not (for example, Thailand, China, Russia or Turkey), they are engaged in the conscious attempt to modernize based on a European model. Notwithstanding the fact that these states have their own local peculiarities, "they have been 'parachuted' by colonial rule and then taken over, lock, stock, and barrel, i.e. in their territorial claims, administration, and legal structures, by 'independence movements'" (Shanin 1982:315).

The origin of the state effects certain characteristics of the state, for example its potential autonomy. Degnbol-Martinussen has correctly noted "as an overall consequence of the way in which the colonial state was constituted, developed, and transformed into a post-colonial state, the contemporary states of the Third World probably feature a higher degree of relative autonomy vis-à-vis the internal structures and social forces than is typical of the states in the more industrialised countries of the North" (Degnbol-Martinussen n.d). The specific condition for autonomy is determined by the historical specificity and structural uniqueness of a given country. However, there are some general features of peripheral societies that foster its growth. The history of Pakistan, as analyzed by Alavi (1973, 1982), points to three sources of state autonomy in post-colonial societies: the absence of a powerful bourgeois class; the inheritance of the "overdeveloped state"; and the centrality of the state in the economy and society. Alavi argues that "at the time of independence the post-colonial society inherits that overdeveloped apparatus of state and its institutionalized practices through which the operations of indigenous social classes are regulated and controlled," and that the post-colonial state is "equipped with a powerful bureaucratic-military apparatus" (1973:147). Alavi considers the central role of the state in the economy as the "material base" of its autonomy. Alavi's principal argument is that the underdevelopment of

17

peripheral societies requires the state to be interventionist. As such, the state is given ample opportunity to appropriate economic surplus and to deploy these surpluses in bureaucratically directed activities, which provide the basis of an autonomous role for the executive. Petras (1982:416) and Thomas (1984:67-81) are in agreement with the sources of relative autonomy of the state. Petras contends that the main features of peripheral states include extensive and prolonged intervention in the economy, growing public sector activity, expanding and deepening of external ties, the creation of, and, in varying degrees, the elaboration of planning institutes and mechanisms, and the promotion of industrialization.

Thomas has argued that at least three sources contribute to, or serve as, the sources of the potential autonomy of the state. They are the nonequivalence of state power and the power of the ruling classes; the formation and rapid growth of the bureaucracy leading to the dominance of the executive within the state structure; and the absence of the tradition of "separation of power" among the judicial, executive, and parliamentary organs of the state. One can add two more sources of autonomy: its responsibility for the perpetuation of the capitalist mode of production, and the dependence on external resources or resources owned by the state (e.g., oil). Stallings (1985) argues, "In certain types of Third World countries, it may be possible for the state to obtain a significant amount of autonomy from the domestic ruling class by relying on foreign capital" (261). She insists that "in practice, one kind of foreign capital has been especially important—private bank loans" (261). In certain situations foreign resources coming from international financial institutions like the IMF and the World Bank provide ample opportunity for a state to act in opposition to the immediate interests of the economically dominant classes. Occasionally, peripheral countries are compelled to accept conditions attached to loans, aid, and grants that may adversely affect the economically dominant classes in the short-term. A state relying on external resources can and, indeed, does act as a relatively autonomous entity. The most obvious examples of this are *rentier states*—states that derive most or a substantial part of their revenues from the outside world and whose political system depends, to a large degree, on accruing external revenues that can be classified as rents (Schwarz 2004). The similar behavior patterns of rentier states, whether

18

they are located in the Middle East (e.g., Saudi Arabia, Iran) or in Africa (e.g., Nigeria, Gabon), demonstrate that these states enjoy similar kinds of autonomy vis-à-vis the social classes.

The centrality of the state in peripheral society, a key source of its autonomy, deserves special mention. The state is central not only in terms of its economic activity (measured by a share of GNP, employment, national investment, consumption, savings etc.) but beyond that to those functions that are essential to the economic process (such as determining and upholding the legal and statutory forms necessary for commodity exchange, stabilizing the growth of national product, determining the choice of development model etc.), and as an agency of hegemony/domination. It is nothing new to say that the capitalist state produces and reproduces capitalist social relations not only at the economic level but also at the political and ideological level. Gramsci (1971:258) reminded us that the capitalist state is the "organizer of [the] consent" in the bourgeois hegemonic system. But in the case of peripheral societies, classes are formed in a distinctly different way compared to advanced capitalist societies and the class formation processes, at times, prevent the emergence of a hegemonic bourgeoisie. Under these circumstances, the state is utilized by the ruling classes, whoever they may be, as the agency of hegemony/domination. And, through it, a new ideology (or value system), assumed to be superior to all others, is imposed. This accords the state apparatus a newer significance and situates it in a position of relative autonomy in relation to the ruling classes.

Thus, owing to their lineage, the state in peripheral societies in general and post-colonial societies in particular, emerges as highly centralized, interventionist, potentially autonomous, and an agency of hegemony and/or domination.

The State and Society

The second predicating factor is the configuration of the society where the state is located. Evans (1995:35), summarizing Robert Bates's study on Kenya, reminded us that the state should be viewed as "a historically contingent creation" whose properties depend on, among other things, "the character of the surrounding social structure." A significant characteristic of the social structure of the peripheral societies is their exceptional class composition. Peripheral societies experienced a massive discontinuity in the processes of indigenous class formation due to the intervention of capitalism from outside, primarily through colonization. In these societies, a dominant class in the classical capitalist sense of control over the means of production often does not exist to any significant extent (Shanin 1982:315). Also absent is the other fundamental class: the proletariat.

In the absence of powerful polar classes, Gramsci (1978:409) argues, "a broad spectrum of intermediate classes stretches between the proletariat and capitalism: classes which seek to carry on the policies of their own." In the peripheral societies that experienced direct colonial rule, a specific dimension is added to the class structure: the creation of a social stratum primarily dependent upon the state. By virtue of being employed in different state agencies, members of this group serve as intermediaries between the state and the (colonized) masses.

The classes Gramsci refers to as "intermediate classes" are completely different than those described by Marxists as "auxiliary classes." This is because the intermediate classes, unlike the auxiliary classes, tend to establish their dominance over state apparatuses, as well as other social classes including the proletariat and propertied classes. The structural significance of these classes is not derived from their location vis-à-vis the dominant mode of production, but mostly from their capacity to gain prominence in the political arena. It is indeed true that these classes can be economically dominant at a given point of time. But it is neither a necessary condition nor is it sufficient for them to emerge as the prominent class.

The potential for these classes to capture state power in the post-colonial situation and appear as the ruling class cannot be discounted; rather they should be taken seriously despite the fact that no single class has the ability to take over state power.[3] In such circumstances the classes form an alliance and entice support from other social classes. Kalecki (1976) firmly believes that in the absence of a well-developed industrial capitalist class allied with a powerful landlord class, the intermediate classes exercise state power to their advantage. He described such a regime as an "interme-

diate regime." In their exercise of state power, Kalecki posits, the intermediate classes develop an alliance with the wealthier sections of the
peasantry and take on an anti-feudal and anti-imperialist posture.

Thus, class formation processes produce a number of obvious characteristics of the social structure in a peripheral society: (1) though the
capitalist mode of production is the dominant mode of production, fundamental polar classes remain absent; (2) classes that may or may not be
economically dominant can and do appear as prominent classes; (3) the
intermediate classes tend to dominate other social classes including the
proletariat and propertied classes; and (4) intermediate classes can capture
state power.

The State and the Global Economic System

The relationship between the peripheral state and the capitalist global economy is far less complicated than it appears. Although capitalism in the
periphery is distinctly different from advanced capitalism, the material
bases of states in peripheral societies rest on capitalism. An interpenetration
and hybridization of non-capitalist forms of production, distribution and
exchange within the capitalist mode created new modes of production and
thus transformed social relations. The new mode of production, although
distinct from that of metropolitan capitalism, is capitalist in the ultimate
analysis. Of course, it also satisfies the basic structural conditions of the
capitalist mode of production (CMP):

> (1) "Free" labor: (a) free of feudal obligations, (b) dispossessed —
> separation of the producer from the means of production; (2)
> Economic "coercion" of the dispossessed producer; (3) Separation
> of economic (class) power from political (state) power; creation of
> bourgeois state and bourgeois law; (4) Generalized commodity
> production (production primarily for sale; labor power itself a
> commodity); (5) Extended reproduction of capital and rise in
> organic composition of capital. (Alavi 1982:179)

As opposed to the integrated form of generalized commodity
production present in metropolitan capitalism, peripheral capitalism expe-

21

riences a disarticulated form of generalized commodity production. The circuit remains internally incomplete. The realization of this condition occurs only by virtue of the links with the metropolis. The extended reproduction of capital, a crucial condition of the capitalist mode of production, is also fulfilled in a manner different from metropolitan capitalism. The surplus value generated from peripheral capitalist societies leads to the growth of productive power not in the peripheral societies but in the metropolis. Thus, the condition of extended reproduction of capital is met, but without allowing the forces of production of peripheral societies to grow at the pace prevalent in classical capitalism. Thus, the peripheral capitalist state is intrinsically integrated into the global capitalist economy by virtue of its structural nature. This relationship cannot be severed by political rhetoric or half-hearted policy measures.

Although these three structural factors, in combination, play a pivotal role in determining the nature of the state, they are influenced by conjectural developments, including the role of individuals and time. More importantly, none of these factors are fixed. The class composition of any society, for example, is the result of an on-going dynamic process and is bound to change over time. So, too, is the relationship between the different constituents of the state. Furthermore, the demands of the global economy vary according to time and necessity. As a matter of fact, all states undergo continual adaptation. The new demands, whether elicited from social classes or from the global economy, are accommodated through constant non-fundamental modifications. Therefore, at an abstract level, the nature of the state remains open to transformation at any time, and the possibility is always real. But we also observe, at times, a drastic change in the relations of power among the various constituents of the state and in the social role the state plays. This is what we describe as state transformation—change in the nature of the state. But the question is how does the nature of the state change?

Transformation of the State

The transformation of a state, it must be emphasized, is not a short-term phenomenon but a long-term process. However, spectacular events, for example military coups or popular uprisings, may expedite the process or occur at a critical juncture of the process. But as far as the transformation process is concerned, it occurs when two important factors coalesce. They are: political and economic crises undermining the fundamental undertaking of the state, and the emergence of a counter coalition to replace the ruling regime.

Political and Economic Crises

The crises that contribute to state transformation have their origins in the nature of the post-colonial state and in the class character of the ruling class. However, both of these, in the ultimate analysis, threaten the fundamental undertakings of the state and of the ruling class: the perpetuation of the dominant mode of production and the maintenance of social order necessary for social reproduction.

If one uses the four parameters advanced by Migdal (1988:4) in determining the strength of the state, that is "the capacities to *penetrate* society, *regulate* social relationships, *extract* resources, and *appropriate* or use resources in determined ways" (emphasis in original), one would conclude that the post-colonial state is a strong entity. The capacity of the state to regulate social relationships, for example, is immense. As a matter of fact, the peripheral state is an instrument of class creation. By virtue of its command over the internal and external resources, the state acquires enough strength to produce, transform, and even eliminate social classes (Thomas 1974:87; Farhi 1985:52; Bates 1989). Furthermore, as an interventionist state, it strives to restrict the social life of citizens by using draconian as well as petty means to assure its dominance. It also strives to exercise total control over all economic activities, using many different methods. In the political sphere, it is extremely intolerant of open public discourse and dissenting views. Despite this strong posture, the post-colonial peripheral state is also weak and subject to permanent crises. It is continually beset by political instability, regional disintegration, and the restricted effectiveness of government resources. The political instability of peripheral states is manifested through frequent changes in state forms, in the constitution, and in the interchangeability of political institutions and personnel. With particular interests being realized via the state, the growth of a state clientele and of corruption leads to its becoming the private preserve and instrument of ever-changing partial interests. This political instability often takes the form of a permanent political crisis (Ziemann and Lanzendorfer 1977).

The economic weakness of the peripheral state arises from the mode of its integration within the world capitalist system. The accumulation based on the realization of surplus value generated from raw materials and by the labor power of the periphery primarily accrues to the advanced industrial countries, while peripheral countries face a shortage of investment funds. The result is that they cannot produce what they need for themselves and, therefore, have to import both commodities and capital. This, in turn, means that price inflation is passed back to them whenever they buy essential foodstuffs, machinery, and oil. In order to purchase imports and pay other rising costs, the peripheral state must find funds in low levels of local accumulation. Subsequently, the peripheral state runs into a variant of the "fiscal crisis of the state." This forces the peripheral state to borrow from abroad—from governments, international agencies, and private banks. This eventually leads to a "debt trap." Additionally, the surplus that *can* be realized locally is used to maintain the dominant class and the state apparatuses. All of this adds up to a condition of permanent economic crisis. Thus, the states in most peripheral societies are often weak because of economic crises and yet strong in their capacity to penetrate society and regulate social relationships. Above all, they are in permanent crisis.

These two conflicting, yet perennial, characteristics of the state play a pivotal role in determining the methods of rule. When the intermediate classes appear as the ruling class in a peripheral society, their methods of rule differ dramatically from that of the bourgeoisie in an advanced capitalist society. The former rely more on the state apparatuses than the latter because the intermediate classes emerge as the ruling class not by virtue of their class-power, but rather because they succeeded in capturing state-power. In fact, capturing the state is the best, and perhaps the only, method of becoming the ruling class in peripheral societies. In colonial situations, it is very common that the intermediate classes form an alliance against the

24

colonial rulers. In their quest for state power, they evolve a counter-hegemonic ideology (most often, nationalism) and bring together other social classes. But the hegemony of the intermediate classes (that arises out of their nationalist project) is limited to the political and ideological leadership and lacks an adequate material basis. Thus, it remains incomplete and fragile, even as it succeeds in capturing state power.

The state possesses traits that play an influential role in determining the methods of rule. Here, one recognizes a paradoxical situation: the classes that apparently capture the state apparatuses are less powerful than the apparatuses themselves. Additionally, the latter have the potential to break free from the dictates of the former. What happens, then, is on the one hand cooperation between the ruling classes and the state apparatuses, while on the other hand there remains a continual confrontation between the regime and the bureaucracy, as one tries to control the other. However, in the long-run there is a progressive attenuation of the power of the ruling class because they rely on the state apparatuses to rule the masses and to augment the power of the bureaucracy in order to control resources. The expansion of the bureaucracy's control over resources takes place through the expansion of the state itself.

The gradual preeminence of the executive is also dependent upon the success or failure of the ruling class to maintain "authority" and contain the political and /or economic crises associated with peripheral societies. The crisis of authority of the ruling class in peripheral societies is directly tied to the rupture of hegemony of the intermediate classes. The rupture can be attributed to three reasons. The first and primary reason for the rupture is erosion in the fundamental basis of the ideological hegemony of the intermediate classes. Nationalism, or a variant of it, becomes the rallying point of the "nation" and suppresses other contradictions (e.g., class conflict, gender discrimination). But the new political realities of post-colonialism can undermine the relevance of an overarching "nationalist" ideology. The second factor is the schism within the ruling alliance. As noted before, the ruling class is an alliance of varied interests. As soon as state power and state resources become available to the members of the alliance, they plunge into internal conflict and contradiction. Members of the alliance begin to vie for power. Thirdly, the organizing consent of the subordinate masses (i.e., hegemony) is based on the ability of a social group to repre-sent the universal interests of the whole society. Representing universal interests cannot be achieved by ideological inculcation but by the realiza-tion of the interests of the subordinate masses "concretely" (Gramsci 1971:182). That is where the ruling class may begin to falter and a hege-monic crisis emerges.

As the ability of the ruling class to organize the consent of the masses weakens, the coercive elements inherent in a hegemonic system are gradually laid bare through the curtailment of fundamental human rights, legislation, the enactment of repressive laws, and, if necessary, through the introduction of a one-party system. The use of police-administrative restraints on freedom, and the administrative manipulation of the electoral and legal processes, and constitutionality in general, becomes common-place. These undermine the legitimacy and authority of the ruling classes. Because of its inability to obtain the consent of the broad masses, the ruling class fails in its major political undertaking: the perpetuation of the domi-nant mode of production. This, needless to say, invokes a subsequent economic crisis. This is the situation that Gramsci called an "organic crisis," a conflict between the represented and the representative, a rift between the popular masses and the ruling class.

A variant of the "fiscal crisis of the state" is rampant in these soci-eties and the state is always dependent upon metropolitan countries and international agencies for support. However, there is a tendency on the part of the ruling intermediate classes in peripheral societies to take a socialist posture. Though their policies do not challenge the larger framework of capital-labor relations and ultimately promote a mixed economy, they sometimes appear to be anti-capitalist. This endeavor is commonly referred to as a "non-capitalist path of development" (Ulanovosky 1969, 1974; Thomas 1974, 1978; Slovo 1974). It attempts to frustrate the development of a large fledgling bourgeoisie, but the conditions of capitalism remain in place and state policies favor the intermediate classes becoming a capitalist class. The socialist posture subjects the state to the pressure of global capi-talism and different varieties of sanctions, both overt and covert. This, in conjunction with the structural economic crises of peripheral states, serves as a source of continuous economic crisis. The pursuance of such policies also impedes the development of the society's productive forces, a necessary condition for the perpetuation of a capitalist economy.

The Counter Coalition

The centrality of the state, the gradual supremacy of the executives, and the rise of a repressive apparatus bring two forces, the bureaucracy and the military, to center stage, and make authoritarianism the dominant mode of articulating power. Democratic pretenses are then discarded and, usually, a one-party state results. If authoritarianism fails to provide a solution to the crises faced by the ruling class and fails to enhance the ability of the state to promote stable and expanded reproduction, or, in other words, to maintain the dominant mode of production, then it is likely that a reorganization of power relations among the constituents of the state will ensue. Thus, the need for a reorganization of "vast state bureaucracies," "organs of political order, i.e. political parties, trade union and other civil organizations," (Gramsci 1971:221) and the capitalist economy as a whole, create conditions conducive to state transformation.

But the transformation can only take place if a counterforce becomes powerful enough to remove the ruling classes. In peripheral capitalist societies, especially when ruled by the intermediate classes, neither the domestic environment nor the global economic logic permit the rise of a single class powerful enough to take on such a task. Therefore, more often than not, a coalition with the bureaucracy and/or military as its key member(s) emerges as an alternative to the ruling class, which seizes power. The counter coalition must also represent a definite social class and have an agenda for change in state policies.

Will these arguments stand? One need not take them at face value, nor should they be discarded at once. The validity of these arguments will be tested when the details of the Bangladesh case are laid out. However, a brief description will be helpful for familiarizing readers with the history of Bangladesh and will provide them with a sketch of the arguments presented in this book.

27

The Bangladesh Case

One can trace the roots of the Bangladeshi state back to the de-colonization of the Indian subcontinent in 1947 when the departing British colonial power partitioned the country into two nation states: India and Pakistan. Present-day Bangladesh became the eastern province of the newly formed Pakistan separated from the western part by about a thousand miles of Indian territory. The two provinces of this new state, from the outset, had almost nothing in common other than the fact that the majority of the population was Muslim. The social and economic structures of these two wings varied greatly, and culturally they were worlds apart. The differences between the two provinces came to the fore in the early 1950s over the issue of a national language. Despite constituting a numerical majority, Bengalis—the people of the eastern province—were excluded from the power structure dominated by the West Pakistanis, particularly the ethnic Punjabis. In the succeeding years, the disparity between the two wings of the country grew at an alarming rate owing to the transfer of resources from the east, large-scale appropriation of surpluses by the west, and meager developmental expenditure in the east.

The severe economic disparity and obvious political marginalization fomented discontent among the Bengalis. The policies of the Pakistani state also brought changes in the class structure of East Pakistan. In the rural areas, the social structure was differentiated into three classes: the non-cultivating intermediate class of *jotedars* and rich peasants at the apex; followed by self-sufficient peasants in the middle, and the poor peasants, *bargadars* (share-croppers), and landless laborers at the bottom of the hierarchy. In the urban areas, by the 1960s, a class of comprador bourgeoisie had emerged—very small in size but influential in terms of their newly earned wealth and connections with the colonial state. A working class and lumpen proletariat had also come into existence. But the most significant development was the emergence of an array of intermediate classes (i.e., petty traders, shopkeepers, and a salaried class serving the state and private enterprises such as junior officials and clerks, professionals, i.e., doctors and engineers, an intelligentsia involved in different educational and research institutions, and students coming from different strata of society) who were soon looking for a greater share in the surplus expropriated by the state from the poor peasantry and the massive external aid infused to perpetuate the capitalist system. The collaborationists, the disgruntled sections of the rising Bengali bourgeoisie, and the intermediate classes were searching for ways and means to establish control over the state apparatuses.

Throughout the 1960s, the leaders of the intermediate classes appeared to be the champions of the demands of the Bengali population and used the idioms and icons of "Bengali nationalism" to rally the people around the demand for regional autonomy. By the end of the decade, their efforts to create a counter-hegemonic ideology had succeeded and the most prominent political representative of the intermediate classes, the Awami League, had established its ideological hegemony. The general election of 1970, in which the Awami League won a popular mandate, provided them with constitutional legitimacy. The military-bureaucratic oligarchy and the elite political leadership of Pakistan, two of the principal beneficiaries of the exploitative relationship between the two provinces, not only declined to accept the popular mandate, but also waged a genocidal war against the Bengalis in March 1971. After a nine-month war, the Bengalis emerged victorious and the state of Bangladesh came into existence (see Chapter 1).

At the outset of independence, the emergent Bangladeshi state became an intermediate state in the sense that the state apparatus was captured by an alliance of intermediate classes led by the petty bourgeoisie. The economic policies pursued by the state were directed toward the benefit of the intermediate classes (see Chapter 2). But between 1972 and 1974, executives (primarily bureaucrats) established control over the ruling bloc and began to act somewhat autonomously from the prominent social classes. The struggle between these two contending sources of authority can be described as a conflict between the old state and the new regime. In the final analysis, it was the bureaucrats who succeeded in marginalizing the political regime. The growing bureaucratic control over the state began to shift the balance of power toward the executive. This trend was accompanied by a growing authoritarianism. That is to say the ruling alliance was not only becoming dependent upon the executive branches of the state but also on the coercive apparatus of the state. The drift toward authoritarianism took place in a very gradual manner as the intermediate classes failed to cope with the multiple sources of crises—rupture of hegemony, political opposition and internal feud, economic disarray, and crisis of authority (see Chapter 3). Faced with an array of crises, the ruling classes responded with efforts to obtain the consent of the masses by devising a new ideology and enforcing discipline through a strengthened repressive apparatus (see Chapter 4). Their responses also included manipulating the electoral process and the constitution, curtailing the freedom of the press, and introducing the one-party system. Meanwhile, there were discernable changes in terms of the state's relationship with the world economic system. Further integration with the world economic system as a dependent state made Bangladesh more susceptible to external pressure.

However, the final act of the transformation of the Bangladeshi state began when the interests of the new rich class, the bureaucracy, and the military converged and a counter coalition began to emerge in mid-1975. The state transformation took a clearer shape with the promulgation of martial law in 1975, especially with the emergence of General Ziaur Rahman at the helm of power. The state, employing Marx's (1974:149) words, vowed to "return to its ancient form, the unashamedly simple rule of military sabre and the clerical cowl." The political and economic projects of the new regime demonstrated the dramatic transformation of the Bangladeshi state (see Chapter 5). Although Ziaur Rahman died in an abortive coup in mid-1981, the process continued during the military regime of General H. M. Ershad between 1982 and 1990. The end of military rule in 1990 paved the way for a democratic beginning for the nation and, perhaps, created opportunities to return to the *raison d'etre* of the Bangladeshi state, but the elected civilian rulers of the country have been content with the state they have inherited. This is because over the previous twenty-one years, the leading political parties have also undergone changes both in terms of ideology and their patrons. The new rich class flourished under the patronage of the state, joined the ranks of the political forces, and has become the principal benefactor of the political parties.

The tale of the transformation of the Bangladeshi state is exciting in its own right but can the analysis provide us with conceptual tools to understand states in other post-colonial peripheral societies? The particularity of the Bangladeshi experience notwithstanding, it is my contention that the framework herein used for analyzing the formation and the transformation of the Bangladeshi state is equally valid for others; Tanazania is a case in point (see Chapter 6). The construction of nationhood under British colonial domination, the emergence of middle class prominence, the consolidation of their interests under the leadership of Tanganyika African National Union (TANU), the promulgation of the socialistic ideals in the Arusha declaration (1967), and the collapse of the intermediate state under the weight of crises and international pressure in the 1990s demonstrate a similar trajectory and can be analyzed with the proposed framework.

NOTES

1   Most of Gramsci's essays and notes are written between 1916 and 1935. But English translations were not available until *Selections from the Prison Notebooks* was published in 1971. For the purpose of this study four volumes of Gramsci's writings were consulted: *Selections from the Prison Notebooks, Selections from Political Writings (1910-1920), Selections from Political Writings (1921-1926),* and *Selections from Cultural Writings.*

2   Marx, in his *Contribution to the Critique of Political Economy* (Marx 1968:182) writes, "Legal relations as well as forms of the state are to be grasped neither from themselves nor from the so-called general development of the human mind, but rather have their roots in their material conditions of life... The sum total of these relations of production constitutes the economic structure of the society, the real foundation, on which rises a legal superstructure and to which correspond definite forms of social consciousness. The mode of production of material life conditions the social, political and intellectual life process in general."

3   The term "capture" refers to a phenomenon different from having influence over the state power. The capture implies that specific groups have total control over the policy process. It undermines a transparent and legitimate democratic policy process and reduces the access of rival interests to the state.

Chapter 1

The Intermediate Classes: From Margin to Center Stage of Politics

The end of direct colonial rule inevitably creates changes in class relations. On the one hand, it paves the way for the emergence of new classes and new forms of alliances between classes to perpetuate their vested interests. On the other hand, new forms of class conflict emerge between the dominant and subordinate classes, and within the leading classes themselves. Furthermore, "with the departure of erstwhile colonial rulers, leading classes of the indigenous society are elevated into the realm of rule and power and they search constantly for a viable mode to articulate power" (Uyangoda 1986:59). Pakistan was no exception to these general trends. In addition, some unusual characteristics of the newly emergent state and society necessitated a realignment of classes more sharply than is usually the case in post-colonial situations. It is of particular significance to note that the realignment of existing classes and their mode of articulation of this newly gained power determined the nature of the state in Pakistan. It also determined the relationship between the state and Pakistani society in general, and the socioeconomic structure of East Pakistan, as it existed at that time, in particular. As such, class formation processes in Bangladesh are incomprehensible without reference to the nature of the Pakistani state and the underlying causes of the latter's rise. Thus, this chapter begins with an analysis of the Pakistani state and its impact on social formations in Bangladesh. I will then proceed to examine the relationship between the state and the social classes of Bangladesh.

Prominence in a given economic and social arena by itself does not ensure a class the "leading" position in politics. Instead, the emergence of a social class or a group of classes as prominent political actors is dependent upon other factors such as their relationships to others. Additionally, at certain historical junctures, one or more classes can and do appear as the prominent actor(s) because of factors specific to a given social formation. In the third section of this chapter, I will trace the factors that prompted the growth of the intermediate classes led by the petty-bourgeoisie as the prominent political actors in Bangladesh politics. I will show that an array of factors abetted the rise of intermediate classes as the prominent group in politics. The prime cause of their rise was the conflict and collaboration of the middle classes with the colonial state, which cultivated the middle class as its political agent. Here, again, we must not lose sight of the fact that

33

although the mode of colonial subjugation, the nature of the colonial state, and state policies are important factors in determining the preeminence of the intermediate classes within the Bangladesh polity, they are insufficient for comprehending the total picture. In addition, it is important to see how the intermediate classes led by the petty-bourgeoisie, who themselves were subjected to the hegemony of the colonial state, established their "moral leadership" over the subordinate classes. This was achieved partly because of the weakness of other social classes, but principally because of the successful appropriation of the hegemonic ideology of Bengali nationalism. Thus, in the last section of the chapter, I will deal with the hegemony of the intermediate classes and their methods of achieving hegemony.

Nature of the Pakistani State

The regions that came to constitute Pakistan in 1947, in addition to their role as suppliers of raw materials to the British, were primarily the hinterlands of industries established in other parts of India, especially Bombay. East Bengal (later East Pakistan) supplied raw jute to the mills of Calcutta while West Pakistan supplied cotton to the textile mills of Bombay (Ahmed 1973:420). As such, when British colonialism formally ended, Pakistan received less than ten percent of the industrial base of the subcontinent (Jalal 1986:8). The contribution of industry to national income was less then one percent (Maniruzzaman 1982:48). Taken together, these statistics clearly indicate that at the time of its inception Pakistan had a very small bourgeoisie.

Furthermore, there was a sharp difference between the social and economic structure of the two wings of Pakistan. While the rural area of East Pakistan was dominated by various groups of intermediaries such as *zamindars* (landlords), *jotedars* (non-cultivating tenure holder), landowners, and various other rent-receiving sub-leasees— with the self-sufficient owner-cultivators in ascendancy—the situation in West Pakistan was entirely different.

The Propertied Classes in West Pakistan

The society and economy of West Pakistan was dominated by a firmly entrenched landed aristocracy. There had been a large concentration of landownership. In Sind, less than one percent of the population owned thirty percent of the total cultivated area. On average each owner possessed more than five hundred acres. In the North West Frontier Province (NWFP), 0.1 percent of the population, each owning more than five hundred acres, were in possession of nearly one-eighth of the total area. Even in the Punjab, a major beneficiary of agricultural development programs in colonial days, more than one-fifth of the cultivable land was owned by about one-half of one percent of the owners (GOP 1958:309). Taking Pakistan as a whole, about 0.1 percent of the total landowners, that is about six hundred people, owned land of five hundred acres or more (Khan 1964:50). According to an estimate of Alavi (1976:340), around five percent of all rural households in Pakistan (including absentee landowners) controlled about seventy percent of the land. It is in this context that the Pakistan National Board wrote "while taking stock of the conditions in the country, one is struck with their similarity to feudalism" (GOP 1958:309).

Consequently, the landlords dictated the politics of the country in both pre- and post-independence days. The extent of their preeminence can be understood from two sets of data. First, the composition of the different provincial assemblies of Pakistan constituted through the elections of 1951, 1953, and 1954; and secondly, the professional classification of the members of the Second Constituent Assembly of Pakistan. In the provincial elections in 1951 in Punjab, eighty percent of the members elected were landlords. In the NWFP Assembly, constituted through the elections of 1951, the landlord group held a majority. In the Sind elections of 1953, ninety percent of the members of the Assembly came from the landowning classes. In 1955, when the West Pakistan Assembly was set up, out of 310 members, 200 represented landed interests (Maniruzzaman 1982:45-46). The second Constituent Assembly of Pakistan comprised 80 members, 40 from each wing (i.e., East and West) of the country. Out of 40 members from West Pakistan 28 were landlords, 3 lawyers, 5 retired officials, and 4 involved in industry and commerce. In contrast, 20 members from East

Bengal were lawyers, 9 retired officials, 3 involved in industry and business, 8 came from other professions, and not a single member came from the landlord class (Ahmed 1963:115).

After partition, the preeminence of the landlords in Pakistan was matched by a peculiarity of Pakistani society; namely, the virtual absence of the bourgeois class. As I have noted previously, the areas that constituted Pakistan were practically hinterlands and thus lacked any industrialist class. It would, however, be a mistake to assume that there was a total absence of a Muslim bourgeois class. There was, indeed, a bourgeois class represented by families such as Bawanys and Fancys. But, the bourgeois class had two principal weaknesses. First, the wealthy Muslim bourgeoisie who extended their support to the Muslim League during the nationalist movement, and migrated to Pakistan after the partition, were conducting their businesses outside the region. For example, the Bawanys had their capital invested in Burma, while the Fancys invested in East Africa. Others, such as the Adamjees, Saigols, Habibs, Ispahanis and Rahimatools remained small entrepreneurs, mostly engaged in commercial activities outside the areas that came to constitute Pakistan. Secondly, the business families who hailed from Gujrat and Kathiawar, and belonged to minor sects of Islam, being mostly Memons, Bohras, Khoja Isnashari, or Khoja Ismailis, represented roughly 0.3 to 0.5 percent of the total population (Ahamed 1980:22; Ahmed 1973). As immigrants, as well as belonging to minority sects, the Muslim bourgeoisie were socially and politically weak. Yet, these communities formed the "initial nucleus of an entrepreneurial class" (Nations 1971:4).

Thus, during the formative stage of Pakistan, two indigenous, propertied classes were represented by the Muslim League, which led the political struggle of the Muslims in India. It was through the League that these two classes were elevated to the status of a ruling class, although they neither shared the same world-view nor did they have a mutually compatible confluence of class interests. Given that there was a preponderance of landed aristocrats in the Muslim League (out of 503 members of the Muslim League Council, 163 were landlords) and a leader (i.e., Muhammad Ali Jinnah) who attempted to articulate a bourgeois-populist ideology, it is obvious that neither succeeded in establishing total control over the party. In such circumstances, with the establishment of Pakistan, these two propertied classes came to form a class alliance or "ruling power bloc." The existence of two competitive classes in the power bloc necessitated a mediator between these classes.

State as the Mediator

Although the ruling party (i.e., Muslim League) appeared to be the mediator between these classes in the pre-partition period, it gradually lost ground in the post-colonial situation because the landlords held a relatively stronger position within the party and, hence, all legislative processes impeded the bourgeois hegemonic drive. The situation was further complicated because capitalism was the dominant mode of production and the state structure that Pakistan inherited was a capitalist state (with all the limitations of a peripheral capitalist state). Perpetuation of that capitalist mode of production was crucial for reproducing the conditions for the viability and continuity of the state itself. Necessitated by the structural needs of the state, in a situation where the ruling power bloc consisted of competing interests, the bureaucracy as an apparatus of the state mediated between the two, propertied classes. Thus, in the early days of Pakistan, the conflict between the propertied classes was not resolved through a struggle leading to subordination of one to the other. Rather, it was mediated through the state. In addition to this mediation, the state needed to fulfill another important function: to shape, produce, and ensure the viability of an industrial capitalist class; for it was in this class that the state attempted to anchor itself.

The logic of the capitalist expansion project initiated by the Pakistani state from its inception can be explained by the above-mentioned factors. The class upon which the state depended was so weak that it showed a reluctance to undertake risks with capital. The state intervened to shape the social class.[1] In this manner, the so-called "nucleus of [the] entrepreneurial class" became dependent upon the bureaucracy for patronage in the form of licenses and thus entered into a patron-client relationship.

Nevertheless, under direct state patronage, a capitalist class began to emerge. Their rise was so meteoric that in 1959, according to Papanek (1967:40-41), one community, namely the Halai Memon, "controlled one-quarter of investment in privately owned Muslim firms." Even as late as 1959, thirty-five percent of private and corporate firms in Pakistan were controlled by four trading communities: Memon, Bohra, Khoja, and Chinioti (Sayeed 1980:47).

The unusual origin of the industrial capitalist class gave a specific character to capitalist development in Pakistan which is best described by Gardezi and Rashid (1983) as "mercantilist." The doctrine of this burgeoning class was to buy cheap and sell dear. For this reason, from an early stage, Pakistan followed the Import Substitution Industrialization (ISI) policy. The Government clearly stated its position:

> Pakistan would...seek, in the first place, to manufacture in its own territories, the products of its raw materials, in particular jute, cotton, hides, and skin, etc. ...for which there is an assured market whether at home or abroad. At the same time, to meet the requirements of the home market, efforts will be made to develop consumer goods industries for which Pakistan at present (is) dependent on outside sources. (Gardezi and Rashid 1983)

From the above statement it is clear the state would do its best to increase raw materials, i.e., "squeeze" the primary producers. As the raw materials Pakistan could produce were primarily agricultural products, the underlying policy, essentially, was to exploit the peasants as much as possible to fuel the state's drive for autarchy. Additionally, it is obvious that the state would look for a protected and assured market within the country first. As an adjunct to this policy, the state adopted the method of providing incentives to entrepreneurs along with paternalistic guidance. These incentives include tax concessions, cheaper credits, and subsidies to the traders. The Economic Report of 1953-54 maintained, "Fiscal policy was designed to provide powerful incentives to private enterprise and investment in industry" (GOP 1953a).

The economic strategy of the state was evidently one of untrammeled growth without considering the consequences of such a policy. This sometimes gives the impression that the state gradually became an instrument of the propertied classes, especially the burgeoning capitalist class.

But a closer look into economic policies reveals that the state had never been an instrument of these propertied classes, and neither did these classes play an instrumental role in the formulation of policies pursued by the state. The government's policies regarding the Bonus Voucher Scheme, Open General License, Import list, and corporate taxation demonstrate the bureaucrats formulated the economic policies best suited to the interests of the state in order to gain leverage to control the propertied classes. For instance, the Bonus Voucher scheme "became an efficient tool of the state for redistributing economic benefits from one class to another" (Burki 1977:156) and was used against the Karachi-based industrialists. In a similar vein, the Open General License scheme was used to break the monopoly of the Karachi-based merchants. The import list formulated by the Ministry of Commerce in collaboration with the Chief Controller of Imports restricted importable items and, thus, determined who should be patronized. Corporate taxation had been set as high as fifty percent of corporate income in the knowledge that there would be large tax evasion and that periodically exemptions would have to be made. Nevertheless, all of these moves made the business community vulnerable to bureaucrats.

Thus, economic policies beneficial to the propertied classes were formulated by the bureaucrats not to serve the immediate interests of the propertied classes and pave the way for capitalist development, but to generate surpluses that could be appropriated by the state and later deployed in economic activities directed by the bureaucracy—a distinct feature of a relatively autonomous state.

Dominance of the Bureaucracy

At the time of partition, there were 1157 officers in the Indian Civil Service (ICS). Only 101 officers were Muslims and 95 opted for Pakistan, but the number grew rapidly after independence. Additionally, they began to place themselves in the upper echelons of the administration and to control political appointments. During 1958-1971, for example, there were 17 ministers for finance, industry, agriculture, and commerce; of whom 6 were civil servants, 3 army officers, 5 landlords, 2 industrialists, and 1 journalist. During the same period, there were 9 governors for the two wings of

Pakistan, of whom 4 were military bureaucrats, 3 were civilian bureaucrats, 1 was a lawyer, and 1 was a landlord (Ahmed 1980:40). In the area of economic development, the key policy making institutions were the National Economic Council, the Planning Commission, and the central corporations. All of these were dominated by bureaucrats (Braibanti 1966:444-447). In the sixties, there were 13 central public corporations. The Chairman or Managing Directors of all of them belonged to the higher echelons of the bureaucracy (Ahmed 1980:44-46).

Such a preeminence of bureaucrats in the apparatus of the state was largely a colonial legacy, which Alavi termed the overdevelopment of the superstructure. The legacy of bureaucratic preeminence went back to 1919 (i.e., Government of India Act 1919) and was entrenched by subsequent developments. The Government of India Act 1919 allowed Indians to hold the position of ministers in the provincial governments. This meant that senior civil servants, who were all British at that time, had to work under "native" Indians. However, because of protests from the civil servants, the relationship between the minister and the secretary was reversed making the Indian Minister a protégé of the British civil servants. The partition of 1947 did not change this administrative procedure and, thus, the political nominee remained subservient to the bureaucracy.

This was further exacerbated by the non-representative character of the first Constituent Assembly (CA) and the concentration of power in the office of Governor General. The members of the first CA had been elected before Pakistan was created. The "West Pakistan Muslim League nominated many members of the first CA of Pakistan who had no constituency of their own from where they could get elected" (Barua 1978:306). This made them vulnerable to pressure from the bureaucracy. On the other hand, power was concentrated in the office of the Governor General. It was he who picked the cabinet ministers and controlled the entire mechanism of government. Jinnah, the first Governor General, relied heavily on civil servants who had the administrative experience necessary for "proper" functioning of government. Further, not only did Muhammad Ali Jinnah, the founder of Pakistan, and Liaquat Ali Khan, the first Prime Minister, rely heavily on bureaucrats for day to day functions, they were also given important posts in the government. For example, the office of Finance Minister was given to the former bureaucrat Ghulam Muhammed (who became the Governor General in 1951) and Choudhury Muhammed Ali was given the post of Secretary General with powers to coordinate all activities of the government (in 1951 he became finance minister and in 1955 acceded to the post of Prime Minister).

It is, however, important to note that the dominance of bureaucrats was not confined to the policy-making upper level only. In addition, they were entrenched in local-level elected bodies in charge of the implementation of those policies. In the early 1960s, during the rule of General Ayub Khan (1958-1969), a four-tiered, local, self-government system was introduced. The lowest and most important tier was the Union Council, next the Thana Council, the District Council, and the Divisional Council respectively. The Union Council covered an area of eight to twelve square miles and represented a population of 8,000 to 12,000, where one councilor or Basic Democrat represented 800 to 1500 people, elected through universal adult franchise.[2] The Thana Council which covered eight to fifteen unions consisted of the Chairman of the Union Councils and an equal number of officials nominated by the government. Half of the District Council was elected by Union Council Chairmen, while the other half was composed of nominated government officials. The composition of the Divisional Council was identical: half elected and half nominated.

Like the civilian bureaucrats, the military bureaucrats established a firm grip over the state. The dominance of the military bureaucracy in the state apparatuses of Pakistan can be attributed to both internal and external factors. As Pakistan was situated in a strategically important area, which once served as the centerpiece of British imperial defense strategy of the subcontinent, early state-managers of Pakistan felt they could cash in on its strategic location to obtain a guarantee for their sovereignty against a perceived Indian threat. In their perception, Pakistan's potential contribution to the existing and future systems of Western defense would only be taken into consideration if Pakistan became increasingly involved in the international system. There was another impetus for more involvement in the international system: economic crises. Since it was quite clear to the state-managers of Pakistan that Britain was going to be an unlikely source of financial assistance, Pakistan was looking for allies with "power and pelf." Under such circumstances, the obvious choice was the United States. The United States, however, showed little interest at that point because of its narrowly defined interests in South Asia.[3]

The desperate attempt to secure the United States as an ally was dictated not only by the country's economic woes but also by the colonial tradition of the army. During British rule, the majority of Army recruits originated from the north-west region of British India (which would later come under the jurisdiction of Pakistan) particularly from the Punjab and NWFP. This army was used not only to defend the western borders against Russian advances, but also to crush the anti-colonial movement. The indoctrination of this imperial army successfully sensitized recruits against communism and any internal resistance (as the latter was viewed as an act of Russian infiltration). As such, the army's attitude to Pakistan's defense and foreign policy was pro-Western from its inception.

The Indo-phobia of the Army and the search for absolute authority by the bureaucrats finally began to yield results in May 1948 with the signing of a credit agreement with the United States. Empowered with this slight external support, the Pakistan army earned formal approval from the cabinet for a program of expansion and procurement of arms from external sources. Developments in international politics in subsequent years, along with the further isolation of the ruling party elite from the masses, finally completed the total "sell-out scheme" of the Pakistani rulers and ensured an abject dependency on the United States.

Following the Korean crisis in the beginning of the 1950s, the United States decided to take a calculated risk in South Asia and accelerated its plan to develop a West Asian defense strategy (Venkataramani 1982). Pakistan was willing to join the defense strategy and the United States military had "eyes on bases in Pakistan."[4] As a result, Pakistan was brought into the orbit of U.S. influence through the South East Asian Treaty Organization (SEATO) and the Central Treaty Organization (CENTO). Both the political leadership and the bureaucrats of Pakistan were very much in favor of the alignment.[5] With the consolidation of the bureaucracies, the state-managers of Pakistan "began in earnest to negotiate a military pact with the United States, offering military bases on Pakistan's territory for America to fight 'communist aggression'" (Gardezi and

Rashid 1983:8). These negotiations finally resulted in the "Mutual Defense Agreement" in 1954 followed by Pakistan's entry in SEATO (1954) and CENTO (1956). These treaties helped bring military assistance along with the economic assistance that had started to flow earlier and "expanded the size and capability of the armed forces, and its ability to handle both internal and external missions" (Wilcox 1965:147-48). The external mission meant having the police of the United States in the region; the internal mission was to maintain a repressive authoritarian state. The final show of this "internal mission" was staged in 1958 when the military usurped power after consultation with Washington (Khan 1967:59).

There was another important aspect of this bureaucratic dominance: the exclusivity of the bureaucrats in terms of their regional origin.

Exclusivity of the Bureaucrats

Available data reveal that the bureaucratic elite of Pakistan were an exclusive group in terms of their regional origin: almost all of them came from West Pakistan. Choudhury, who served in both the military regimes of Ayub Khan and Yahya Khan (1969-1972), explains:

> Except during [a] short thirteen-month interval...in 1956-7, the Bengalis had hardly any role in national affairs. Every vital decision, whether it related to political or defence [sic] or economic or diplomatic matters, was in the final analysis made by the ruling elite, composed of West Pakistani civil and military officers. (Choudhury 1972:6)

According to the *Report of the Pay and Services Commission* of 1959-60 (GOP 1969:66), at the time of partition there were only 2 ICS officers from East Pakistan, and up to 1950, only 17 new recruits entered the Civil Service of Pakistan out of a total of 175 such officers. The representation of Bengalis in higher policy-making positions of the bureaucracy, i.e., secretaries, and in official positions in different branches of the defense forces in 1956 was negligible. Of 741 high-ranking civil officials, only 51 were from East Pakistan. In the Army, 14 out of 908 officers, in the Navy 7 out of 600 officers, and in the Air Force 40 out of 680, came from East Pakistan (CAP 1956:1843-4).

Fifteen years after the independence of Pakistan, in 1962, not one of the 19 Secretaries were from East Pakistan. Only 7 of the 46 Joint Secretaries and 24 of the 124 Deputy Secretaries came from the eastern wing (Singhal 1972:199). Even as late as 1968, East Pakistan's representation in the civil service was only 36 percent. In the central services, the share of East Pakistan was about 27 percent in 1970; at the higher levels of administration it was even less: 13 percent. The share of Bengalis in Pakistan's civil service between 1950 and 1968, and East-West representation in Class I officers in some divisions in 1968 and 1969 was dismal. In 1968, for example, only 3 percent of officers in the Cabinet Division were Bengali. In 1969, the Planning ministry had the highest share of Bengalis: 28 percent.[6]

Similar to the situation in the civil bureaucracy, the overwhelming majority of military officers were West Pakistani in general, and Punjabis and Pathans in particular. In mid-1955, East Pakistan made up only 1.5 percent of army officers, while the corresponding percentage for the Navy and Air Force was 1.1 and 9.3 respectively (Jahan 1980:4). In 1964, the last year of the data available in this format, the share of East Pakistanis in the officer ranks rose to 5 percent in the Army, 10 percent in the Navy, and 16 percent in the Air Force.

The monopolistic grip of West Pakistani elites over politics, administration, and the civil and military bureaucracy was deliberately planned and executed by the ruling power bloc of Pakistan. It was through such exclusionary methods that they were able to institutionalize the system of inequality, uneven exchange, uneven development, and economic domination over East Pakistan. As I have noted previously, in the post-colonial situation in Pakistan, the classes elevated to the realm of rule and power did not ascend to that position through an ideological struggle that enabled them to emerge as "leading" classes (i.e., establish hegemony over the subordinate classes) before winning governmental power. Instead, it was governmental power that enabled them to appear as the "leading" classes. Thus, to the ruling bloc, the method through which they could express their domination was coercion, differentiation, and exclusion. This was commensurate with the ideology of the state apparatus inherited from the colonial state.

The Pakistani State and the Social Structure of Bangladesh

Despite the relative autonomy of the state and the dominance of the bureaucrats, the Pakistani state generally acted at the behest of all the propertied classes in order to preserve the social order in which their interests were embedded, namely, the institution of private property and the capitalist mode as dominant mode of production (Alavi 1973:148).

Capitalist development in any country, especially in peripheral societies, is bound to be uneven as it forces parts of the population into servitude. In Fagen's (1983:15) words, "the development of the more advantaged classes or sectors of a peripheral society occurs at the expense of the development and well being of the less advantaged classes or groups." In the case of Pakistan, this unevenness was far more distinct and was not only between the classes or sectors (*viz.* agriculture and industry), but also between the two regions of Pakistan—East and West. As a matter of fact, insofar as East Bengal is concerned, uneven development was extended as far as colonial exploitation. This, obviously, was "normal" because "the long-run consequences of [a] relationship between unequals (nations, classes, groups)—at least in circumstances where the capitalist mode of production prevails—are the multiplication and intensification of existing inequalities. This leads to widening gaps (both nationally and internationally), the fragmentation of communities, and decreased autonomy for the weak" (Fagen 1983:15). The state structure of Pakistan brought about the subordination of Bangladesh in such a manner that it replicated some of the important features of classical colonialism. These features included economic exploitation, political subordination, and that most extreme demonstration of imperialist attitudes: racial discrimination.

The extent of the economic exploitation of Bangladesh can be gleaned from the statistics regarding regional disparity. An array of data on revenue and development expenditure in East and West Pakistan—per capita revenue and development expenditure, per capita GDP of East and West Pakistan—documents the disparity between the two wings.

Regional Disparity

Data concerning revenue and development expenditure in East and West Pakistan from the fiscal year 1950-51 to the fiscal year 1969-70, clearly reveal that East Pakistan received a meager amount, not even half of that of West Pakistan (GOP 1970). During the fiscal years 1950-51 and 1954-55, East Pakistan received only a 20 percent share of total development expenditure. After much protestation, the amount was raised to 36 percent in the last fiscal year of united Pakistan. Though the share of East Pakistan in development expenditure was increasing in later years, the differences between these two wings were increasing at an alarming rate. For example, available statistics show that in 1960-61 West Pakistan's per capita income was 31 percent higher than that of East Pakistan. By the end of the decade, the gulf had widened to 61 percent (Singhal 1972:176). According to a Bengali economist, the disparity in per capita incomes between East and West Pakistan increased from 64 percent in 1959-60 to 95 percent in 1968-69 (Sobhan 1970).

Transfer of Resources

Through a surplus of international trade and a deficit in inter-wing trade, a sizeable amount of Bangladesh's foreign exchange was diverted to the West. Exports from East Pakistan earned the bulk of Pakistan's foreign exchange. At the same time, the major share of foreign imports was destined for West Pakistan. In terms of regional commodity trade East Pakistan had a continued deficit in its current account, which until 1957 was less than the surplus on its foreign trade account, thus indicating a net transfer of resources to West Pakistan (Stern 1971). Added to this was East Pakistan's share in foreign aid, which was mostly utilized in West Pakistan. Haq (1963:100) estimates that such transfers amounted to Rs. 210 million per year from 1950 to 1955 and perhaps Rs. 100 million a year from 1956 to 1960. The Advisory Panel of Economists showed that the net transfer amounted to Rs. 31,120 million at the rate of Rs. 1,556 million a year (GOP 1970:84-86). The net balance of payments of East Pakistan registered a surplus of Rs. 5,367.98 million during the period 1948-49 to 1960-61 and a deficit of Rs. 9,386.2 million during 1961-62 to 1968-69. West Pakistan, throughout the period, incurred a deficit amounting to Rs. 55,004 million. If the total foreign aid amounting to Rs. 35,140 million due to East Pakistan on a population basis was added to it, the net surplus amounted to Rs. 3,120 million, which was transferred to West Pakistan.

The economic policies of the Pakistan government were deliberately devised to expropriate the surplus from Bangladesh in general and from agriculture in particular as Bangladesh was predominantly an agrarian society. The expropriation of surplus was conducted in a planned manner to achieve two goals: first, to generate capital for West Pakistan, and second, to perpetuate the mode of production that best suited the interests of a colonial state, namely, the colonial mode of production characterized by deformed generalized commodity production and extended reproduction of capital.

Appropriation of the Surplus

Policies regarding jute production and marketing reveal how the surplus from agriculture was appropriated by West Pakistan. It also reflects the entire situation confronting the agrarian sector of Bangladesh under colonial domination by the Pakistani state. Jute became the principal commercial crop in East Bengal in the early decades of the century. When Pakistan came into being, the rich and middle peasants in Bengali monopolized jute production. In the 1950s, jute enjoyed a worldwide market, as synthetic fibers were not yet in common use. From the beginning, the Pakistani government established a total control over the production and marketing of jute and jute goods through various legal and institutional measures, such as the Jute Ordinance of 1949; Provincial Jute Dealers Registration Law of 1949; the Jute Act of 1956; Central Jute Act of 1956; establishment of the Jute Marketing Corporation in 1957; and the Jute Ordinance of 1962. Nearly 70 percent of Pakistan's foreign exchange was earned through the export of jute. According to one estimate, during the year 1948-49, Pakistan exported jute worth 1195.6 million Rupees, and, in 1963-64, 1065 million Rupees worth of Jute was exported (Shahidullah 1985:151). This huge amount of money, however, did not return to Bangladesh.

By centralizing the foreign exchange earned by agriculture to pay for imports, the government of Pakistan deprived the Bengali peasants of their legitimate share of foreign exchange. By carefully manipulating two aspects of international trade, the government of Pakistan set up its strategy of surplus appropriation from agriculture to provide the initial risk capital for industry. Nations (1971:7) explains: "The first was the power to determine the exchange rate of the domestic currency and the second to control imports into the country." Under the circumstances, "the strategic weapons of accumulation became the over valuation of the currency and strict control of imported products" (Nations 1971:7). The worst victims of this policy, obviously, were the Bengali peasants. The foreign exchange that the Bengali peasants earned from the sale of jute in foreign markets had to be surrendered to the central government in return for Pakistani currency at the official rate. The official rate of the Pakistani Rupee was fixed at least 50 percent above its market value vis-à-vis all other countries. Thus, the jute growers of East Pakistan lost approximately 50 percent of the buying price to the government. The foreign exchange earned was then passed on to the business clientele of the bureaucracy to pay for the necessary imports for which they had earlier been issued licenses. Thus, by reserving two important powers related to international trade, the government not only appropriated the surplus produced by Bengali peasants but also deprived the Bengali business communities of resources and opportunities. In issuing licenses, the Pakistani government always discriminated against the Bengali business communities in favor of their Punjabi counterparts.

Large-scale expropriation of surpluses, as in the case of jute, resulted in the stagnation of agriculture. In the absence of any investment equal to the amount realized as profits, agriculture in Bangladesh suffered from lack of growth. The Bengali rich and surplus farmers lost all incentive for productive investments in agriculture as they were squeezed through the extraction of the surplus. This also undermined their capacity to accumulate wealth by increasing their control over productive assets. In other words, this meant a return to the situation that existed during the British colonial era. Under British colonial domination, the expropriation of the agrarian surplus, without being followed by any significant investments for its development, restricted the development of rural capitalism (Patnaik

48

1972). In a manipulated, stagnant situation, as Patnaik (1972:146) argues, the "antediluvian" forms of capital—trading capital, money-lending capital, land purchasing capital—alone could flourish. The one form of capital which remains absent is capital in the sphere of agricultural production. Such a situation, essentially, thwarts any possibility of capitalist transformation of agriculture and the rise of a bourgeois class from within the rich and surplus farmers. The economic policies of the Pakistani state, in this way, blocked any possibility of capitalist development in Bangladesh and the rise of any bourgeois class.

Instead, it contributed to the utter impoverishment of the rural poor. On the one hand, stagnation in agricultural production contributed to their pauperization, while usury and land leasing contributed to their gradual alienation from the ownership of the means of production, on the other. The proletarianized peasantry was further exploited by the rural rich, as the latter found it profitable to carry out production with destitute landless or near landless peasants paying them the barest minimum in subsistence wages, most usually in kind.[7]

In order to strengthen the expropriation of surplus from agriculture, the state favored the non-cultivating, intermediate, tenurial holders, namely *jotedars*. The abolition of *zamindaris* in 1950 (i.e., promulgation of East Pakistan State Acquisition and Tenancy Act 1950), the introduction of Basic Democracy by Ayub Khan in the sixties, and the initiation of a Rural Works Program (RWP) sequentially consolidated this class of intermediate interests.

Intermediate Interests in Rural Areas

With the enactment of the East Pakistan State Acquisition and Tenancy Act of 1950, various groups of rent-receiving intermediaries in the rural areas disappeared and the government of the province acquired all rent-receiving interest in land. The Act recognized the former *ryots* (tenancy holders) as proprietors and gave them permanent, heritable, and transferable rights in land. A ceiling of 33.3 acres was imposed on the size of the holding of the individual family. According to the Act a "family" included " a cultivating ryot and all persons living in the same extended household, including a man, his wife, unmarried children, and any other person dependent upon

him and living in his household, excluding servants and hired laborers"
(Hussain 1976). The act provided for compensation to be paid for all lands
acquired by the state for redistribution. The rate of compensation varied
from ten times the net income of the estates with income below five
hundred Rupees to two times the net income for the largest income of one
hundred thousand Rupees and above per annum (GOP 1951:71). Though the
legislation appeared to be a drastic move against the feudal land tenure system,
essentially it was superficial, for it did not bring any radical change in existing
class relations except to legitimize the situation already in existence.

By 1950, the zamindari system in general was decaying and was
incompatible with the interests of the state. As early as in 1940, the Land
Revenue Commission (popularly known as the Floud Commission after the
name of its chairman Sir Francis Floud) suggested that the zamindari
system be abolished. After ensuring a substantial profit for themselves from
land, which also allowed them to meet their revenue obligations, the zamindars withdrew from the rural areas and settled in the towns and cities. The
responsibility of rent collection was left to the tenurial holders who
acquired these rights from the zamindars in return for fixed, cash rent. In
urban areas, the zamindars were able to ensure better education for their
children who went on to become members of the new urban middle classes.
In the absence of zamindars, the petty-landowners and the jotedars emerged
as direct employers of farm labor. Thus, under changed circumstances, the
intermediate tenurial holders, the jotedars, were now favored by the colonial state against the old zamindars (Alavi 1980:26). The newly emergent
Pakistani state followed suit. The East Pakistan State Acquisition and
Tenancy Act 1950 is a case in point. A large number of zamindars in
Bangladesh were Hindus and migrated to West Bengal after the partition.[8]
Taking advantage of the situation, the large Muslim jotedars expropriated
much of the land left behind by the Hindu zamindars. The East Pakistan
State Acquisition and Tenancy Act 1950, therefore, did not bring a dramatic
change in land ownership; instead, it simply legalized the expropriation.

Furthermore, two other points of this act warrant attention: the
limits of land on family holding, and the definition of the "cultivator." In
1951, when the average area per family of agriculturalists excluding the
rent-receivers was 3.91 acres, setting the limit at 33.3 acres on the individ-

ual family holdings was clearly in favor of the interests of the *jotedars*.[9] Secondly, the act retained the definition of the term "cultivator" as incorporated earlier in the Rent Act of 1859 and, thus, allowed the growth of non-cultivating interests in land. In other words, by failing to undermine the position of non-cultivating interests in land, the act, in fact, reinforced the position of the *jotedars* in the rural areas, yet it did not provide any legal protection to the *bargadars* (share-croppers). Instead, the act equated bargadars with agricultural laborers.

While the strategies of the Pakistani government helped rich peasants and *jotedars* consolidate their economic gains, subsequent policies helped the same classes gain political control over the rest of the peasantry. By gaining control over the local cooperatives and village governments, namely the Union Parishads and Basic Democracy, the rich peasants came to form a vital link in the chain of expropriation. Basic Democracy is a glaring example of the expansion of intermediate interests.

The 1962 constitution, promulgated by the military regime of Ayub Khan after the usurpation of power through a military coup d'etat in 1958, introduced "Basic Democracy." Under this new form of "controlled" or "guided" democracy, eighty thousand "Basic Democrats" formed the electorate for the Presidency, the National and Provincial Assemblies, as well as the channel through which developmental funds were distributed (i.e., Rural Works Program). The chief motive behind "Basic Democracy" was to enlist the support of the rural upper class through a distribution of favors among the rural elite and the establishment of channels of communication with them on the one hand, while disenfranchising the total population on the other. And, indeed, the regime succeeded in doing so. According to one survey, in 1962, only 10 percent of Bangladesh's farmers owned more than 7.5 acres of land, whereas more than 63 percent of Basic Democrats owned as much or more land (Sobhan 1968:168). After the 1964 elections, it was reported that 19 percent of Basic Democrats owned more than 25 acres of land (Jahan 1972:117). "As far as income is concerned," Westergaard reports, "about 15 percent of income earners had incomes above Rs. 3,000 against 46 percent of the Basic Democrats" (Westergaard 1985:52)

It is evident that with the patronization of the state, the rural rich were consolidating their positions in the rural area and, in fact, became

51

political agents of the colonial state and worked in close liaison with the bureaucracy and coercive apparatus of the state.[10] The situation was exacerbated as the rural rich were bestowed with some economic power. Basic Democrats were entrusted with the responsibility to handle the funds for the Rural Works Program.[11] This meant they could not only divert these funds according to their wishes and select projects beneficial to their interests, but they could also misappropriate funds as the government directly supported this blatant form of corruption by slackening supervisory and audit checks.

Hence, state policies for the agricultural and rural sector, in the main, helped the growth of a distinct middle class interest at the expense of the poor, as it was a necessary condition for the Pakistani state to increase the surplus. The impact of the economic policies of the state was not limited to the agrarian sector alone. Their influence was felt in the industrial sector as well.

Industrial (Under)Development and the Emerging Bourgeoisie

The state's expropriation of surplus made it almost impossible to accumulate and invest capital. The amount of private investment in Bangladesh reflects the situation. In 1949-50 private investment in Bangladesh was about Rs. 140 million, whereas in Pakistan it was Rs. 38 crore (380 million) (a crore is equal to 10 million). In 1954-55 the corresponding figure was Rs. 200 million and Rs. 550 million respectively. In 1959-60, the respective amount rose to Rs. 370 million and Rs. 770 million (Sengupta 1971:2319). Furthermore, most of the investments in Bangladesh came from Pakistani entrepreneurs. As a matter of fact, the bulk of the industries were held by Pakistan-based industrial capitalists. Available data relating to the manufacturing sector indicate that, excepting public sector assets, "Non-Bengali business houses controlled 47 percent of fixed assets and 72 percent of industrial assets" (Sobhan and Ahmad 1980:57). Notably, 45.1 percent of the total assets of privately controlled firms in Bangladesh were held by 43 families, only one of whom was a Bengali.[12] According to one estimate, the Bawanis, Amins, Ispahanis, and the Karims had their entire holdings in Bangladesh; 50.3 percent of Dawood's and 51 percent of Adamjee's total net assets were located in Bangladesh (Shahidullah 1985:154). In 1971,

Ahamed (1974) reckons about 66 percent of fixed assets in the jute manufacturing industry in Bangladesh were owned by the Pakistani bourgeoisie.

Thus, it is evident the economic policies pursued by the Pakistani state, on the one hand, blocked the capitalist transformation of agricultural sector; while, on the other hand, they frustrated any potential for industrial development in Bangladesh. This obviously helped the state appropriate a large part of the economic surplus and deploy it in bureaucratically directed economic activity. However, as far as the social structure of Bangladesh is concerned, it impeded the development of a bourgeois class.

In the non-agrarian sector, the state's economic policy, until the mid-1960s, left no room for a Bengali entrepreneurial class to flourish. In the face of massive discontent among the Bengali population and in response to the structural needs of the Pakistani bourgeoisie, a major change in policy was brought about by the middle of the 1960s: the government began to purposely encourage the growth of a Bengali super-rich class of industrialists and traders. Alavi (1973:169) distinguishes them as "contactors" and "contractors." The former transformed themselves into a parasitic class of people by living on the sale of permits and licenses to the non-Bengali entrepreneurs. These licenses and permits were obtained through their "contacts" with the bureaucrats and politicians. The latter group, on the other hand, starting with small construction companies, turned themselves into owners of industrial enterprises. Substantial support from the government in the form of loans from the Industrial Development Board and the East Pakistan Industrial Development Corporation (EPIDC) were advanced to help the growth. Actual public sector investments in East Pakistan doubled between 1960 and 1965 (Lewis 1970:146), leading to the emergence of a comprador bourgeoisie class, "who would have no doubts as to the source of their advancement and would thus promote and fund Ayub's political hegemony in East Pakistan" (Sobhan and Ahmad 1980:61-62).

The three financing agencies used for this purpose were the Industrial Development Bank of Pakistan (IDBP), Pakistan Industrial Credit and Investments (PICIC), and the East Pakistan Small Industries Corporation (EPSIC). The amounts of the loans were, on average, below 150,000 Rupees. However, along with them, the state sponsored a small segment of large Bengali capitalists. By the late 1960s, 36 Bengali-controlled enterprises were created in jute, 25 in textiles, and 1 in sugar. Additionally, at least 16 large firms were involved in jute exports, 12 in the inland water transport sector; 12 insurance companies and one Bengali-owned bank were also in operation. In the import business, 39 Bengalis were listed among those with import entitlements above Rs. one million. According to Sobhan and Ahmad (1980):

> The last two years of united Pakistan witnessed the apotheosis of the Bengali upper bourgeoisie. During the phase, the development allocations to the eastern region accelerated. In 1968-69 the East Wing received a record allocation of development funds of Rs. 2881 million, which was 55.45 percent of total public sector development of Pakistan. This trend was accompanied by a record net inflow of external resources into the regions of Rs. 1454 million and by accelerated financial allocations to the private sector in East Pakistan through the public financial institutions. Of the loans approved by PICIC and IDBP up to the end of 1971, 46.2 percent was approved between the period 1969 [and] 71. (Sobhan and Ahmad 1980:67-68)

Some other indices attest to how, in the late 1960s, a rich class began to emerge in Bangladesh. Changes in the average annual income per household of the upper strata of the society, for example, indicate such a trend. The average annual income of the upper 0.6 percent of households in Bangladesh increased by about 32 percent between the 1963-64 and 1966-67 fiscal years, as opposed to an average increase of about 10 percent for all households. The average annual income of households in Bangladesh in 1963-64 was Rs. 1740, and that of the top 0.6 percent households was Rs. 13,224 (Bergan 1967). In 1966-67, the average annual income per household rose to Rs. 1878 and that of the top 0.6 percent of households to Rs. 17,465 (Azfer 1971: Table III quoted in Abdullah 1972). Expenditure on urban housing for the elite increased nearly three times between 1964-65 and 1969-70 from Rs. 26.1 million to 73.0 million. By all standards, a comprador bourgeois class began to appear in Bangladesh in the last years of the 1960s. The policies of the Pakistani state also affected the urban middle classes and the working class.

Urban Middle Classes

Along with this emerging comprador bourgeoisie, an array of urban middle classes emerged during the same period. They were engaged in different sorts of professions ranging from petty trading to lower level official jobs, including even fraud and middlemenship centered in urban areas. The first generation of middle classes in Bangladesh were completely dependent on their education and skill, unlike their predecessors who had some kind of economic relations with the rural areas, emerged at this time.[13] This coincided with the expansion of educational institutions and large numbers of students coming in from the rural areas.[14] According to Gankovsky (1972:222), in 1971 there were about 500,000 small-scale merchants, as well as about 225,000 intelligentsia employed with low pay in different state institutions, private firms, and elementary schools.

Working Class

From the displaced rural landless peasants emerged a class of lumpen proletariat and a small industrial labor force. The lumpen proletariat developed primarily in the urban areas of Bangladesh, especially in Dhaka. This class was comprised of rickshaw pullers, street vendors, slum-dwellers, domestic servants, beggars, and so on.

A small working class developed during this period from similar origins. At the time of partition (i.e., 1947), the size of the modern industrial labor force was less than 50,000 and grew to about 300,000 by 1969 (BBS 1979:396). After 1965, the working class increased substantially. The growth in the number of workers employed in the cotton textile industries and jute industries, for example, reflects this trend. The number of workers in the jute sector rose from 78,077 in 1965 to 163,000 in 1970. Employees in cotton textiles increased to 59,500 from 35,989 (BBS 1975). On the eve of the independence of Bangladesh (i.e., 1970) the labor force employed in industry was estimated at around 976,000. Forty-one percent of the working class population (i.e., 403,000) was employed in modern industry.[15] The total work force in the major industrial centers of Dhaka/Narayanganj, Chittagong, and Khulna amounted to 287,000. An additional 101,000 were employed in tea gardens in Sylhet. Together, about 40 percent of the total industrial labor force was concentrated in these four areas. According to a 1970 survey by the Bureau of Statistics, at least 151,000 workers out of 863,578 workers employed in 304,481 small and household enterprises in rural areas of Bangladesh were wage laborers (BBS 1972).

Thus, the class structure of rural Bangladesh under Pakistani rule was sharply differentiated with the non-cultivating intermediate class of jotedars and rich peasants on the apex, followed by self-sufficient middle peasants. And, it was the poor peasants, bargadars, and landless laborers who were at the bottom of the hierarchy. In the urban areas, the social structure was far more complicated, including a class of nascent comprador bourgeoisie, very small in size but influential in terms of their newly earned wealth and connections with the colonial state. Between this burgeoning class, the working class, and the lumpen proletariat existed an array of intermediate classes including petty traders, shopkeepers, a salaried class serving the state and private enterprises as junior officials and clerks, professionals such as doctors and engineers, intelligentsia involved in different educational and research institutions, and students coming from different strata of the society, to name but a few. Over and above all of these groups was the most influential social force of the state, a relatively autonomous administrative entity manned by West Pakistanis, engaged in expropriating the economic surplus in a ruthless manner. Insofar as class relations are concerned, it is evident that the upper classes, both in rural and urban areas, were the beneficiaries of the economic policies of the colonial state and were links in the chain of surplus expropriation. The dominant contradiction, then, appeared as one between the Pakistani state, which was for all intents and purposes a colonial state, on the one hand, and the peasants (mostly landless), working class, and the lumpen proletariat on the other. This contradiction found its political expression under the leadership of the newly emerged intermediate, predominantly urban, classes.

Intermediate Classes as Prominent Political Actors

At the creation of Pakistan, the Muslim political leadership of Bengal was divided into various factions representing the upper Muslim landowning and commercial interests, the urban middle class elements, the rural Muslim landowning interests, and the relatively poor peasantry.

Each of these factions was expected to be dominant in the state apparatus of what was then East Pakistan. Each believed in their worst-case scenario, they would have to share power with others. However, the central leadership of the Muslim League deliberately chose the conservative, non-Bengali speaking faction representing the upper Muslim landowning and commercial interests and attempted to consign other factions to the political wilderness. This naturally created suspicion about the intentions of the central leadership. The discontent of other factions surfaced during a by-election of the provincial assembly held in April 1949. The disgruntled factions of the League nominated a young and almost unknown candidate against the official candidate of the Muslim League, a local zamindar, and defeated the official candidate by a large margin. The surprising result of the election demoralized the conservative faction of the League[16] and boosted the morale of their opponents. The election brought two of these disgruntled factions closer, one led by Hussain Shahid Suhrawardy, the former Chief Minister of undivided Bengal, and the other by Moulana Abdul Hamid Bhasani, a popular peasant leader, until finally, in June 1949, they formally launched a political party—the East Pakistan Awami Muslim League (EPAML), popularly known as the Awami League.[17] The initiation of a new political party was influenced by other important factors, such as government indifference in the face of severe famine conditions in the rural areas of East Pakistan and the central government's decision not to devalue the currency, which forced down the price of jute in East Pakistan.[18]

From the very beginning, the Awami League leadership favored the intermediate classes. The Vice Presidents of the party were lawyers from small towns and its General Secretary as well as Assistant Secretary were student leaders with "middle class backgrounds" (Jahan 1972:84-85). Of the 37 members of the Working Committee, 57 percent were lawyers, 14 percent businessmen, 1 percent landholders, 11 percent teachers, 3 percent labor leaders, and 3 percent religious leaders (Maniruzzaman 1980:20). In addition to the leadership, the newly formed party won support from the "middlemen." For example, in the northern districts, the landowning class in general and jotedars in particular, who once supported the Muslim

League, shifted their support to the EPAML (Sen 1986:81). The reason behind the support will be appreciated if we look into the policies of the party. In its twelve-point demand, EPAML called for the abolition of zamindaris, and, in order to prevent the monopolization of the jute trade by non-Bengali entrepreneurs, called for its nationalization.[19]

Though the peasants of Bangladesh were increasingly faced with the exploitation of the colonial state in the early 1950s, it was the intermediate classes who came forward to launch a movement against state policies. The question of a state language became the first issue of contention between the emerging Bengali middle classes and the colonial state.

From Language Movement to Electoral Victory

After 1948, the Pakistan Government deliberately excluded the Bengali language from all official usage, though Bengali was spoken by the majority population of the country (i.e., 54.6 percent). Muhammed Ali Jinnah, the founding leader of Pakistan, declared in 1948 that Urdu would be the only state language of Pakistan. The Bengali intelligentsia and students immediately opposed the idea but could not garner wider support for this stance until 1952, when the issue took a political form and people were mobilized. The language movement of 1952 was the first mass movement through which the middle class politicians established their hegemony over other classes.

The language question was a middle class issue. The Urdu-Bengali controversy had been prevalent in the Muslim society of Bengal for some time. Urdu was the language of the feudal alien elements and was esteemed by them as a symbol of their aristocracy. The Bengali, Muslim, educated middle classes were naturally in favor of wider use of the Bengali language. The introduction of Urdu as the state language was detrimental to the interests of the aspirant middle classes. They quite rightly thought that if Urdu was accepted as the only state language in Pakistan, they would be handicapped in competitive examinations for generations to come. For the poorly educated and mostly illiterate workers and peasantry, the issue had no immediate bearing. The movement was therefore launched by the students and people involved in cultural activities and was initially characterized by two limitations, one social (i.e., middle class) and one spatial (i.e., urban). But, given the economic hardship confronted by the peasants and workers due to state policies, especially the severe food crisis and remarkable decrease in the price of jute, they joined the movement and turned it into a mass upsurge against the Muslim League regime.

While the language movement contributed to the rise of the intermediate classes as a powerful political force, the provincial assembly election of 1954 consolidated their leadership over other classes. In the 1954 elections, the Awami League led by Bhasani and Suhrawardy, the Krishak Sramik Party (KSP) led by Fazlul Haq, along with some other political parties, including parties from the right and far left of the political continuum, formed an electoral alliance: the United Front.[20] What brought these disparate parties together was their opposition to the Muslim League regime and the realization of some demands beneficial to the people of East Pakistan. In the election, the UF routed the ruling Muslim League. Out of 237 Muslim seats, the UF secured 215 seats while the ML retained only 9 seats.[21] Such an astonishing election result vindicated the powerful presence of the middle classes in provincial politics. Furthermore, it was through this election that the Awami League established its claim over the leadership of the intermediate classes it represented. It was the only component-party of the Front to elect all 140 candidates nominated.

The election results alarmed the ruling Muslim League and terrified the military-bureaucratic oligarchy that had been running politics in Pakistan from behind closed doors since the death of Liaquat Ali Khan. By entering into an alliance with the United States in 1954, the military-bureaucratic oligarchy was about to obtain total control of the Pakistani state.[22] The election results posed a serious challenge to the military-bureaucratic oligarchy. The result also delivered a severe blow to the plans of this small coterie to hold power and run the country without any accountability. Faced with this situation, the military-bureaucratic oligarchy initiated various "palace intrigues." The ideological differences among the UF components helped the regime in succeeding; one section of the alliance was played against the other.

Military Rule in Pakistan

The ambition of one section of political leaders to gain the blessing of the central authority at the expense of others created a squabble inside the provincial parliament. In only four years, at least four coalition governments had come to power in the provinces. The scenario in the central government was almost identical. It was against this background that the military-bureaucratic oligarchy staged a *coup d'etat* in 1958 and overtly seized power. Following the promulgation of martial law, political activities were banned and remained so until 1962, when a parliament was elected by the Basic Democrats, and a new constitution enacted.

During the chaotic and uncertain political environment between 1954 and 1958, the Awami League faced a split. The left-of-center faction under the leadership of Bhasani quit the party and launched its own platform, the National Awami Party (NAP), in 1957. The rift can be attributed to the differences between Suhrawardy and Bhasani on two issues: the question of regional autonomy for the East and the pursuit of a neutral foreign policy. Suhrawardy, clearly deviating from party policy, sidelined the autonomy issue and championed Pakistan's alignment with the West through participation in SEATO and CENTO and the Military Assistance Agreement with the United States. The rift in the AL reflects the conflict between the urban educated middle classes, represented by the Suhrawardy-Sheikh Mujib faction, and peasants and the rural poor, represented by the Bhasani faction. The departure of Bhasani from the AL left the party leadership completely dominated by the intermediate classes. The NAP leadership was no different. Although, in terms of ideology and program, the party was oriented towards the poorer sections of the Bengali population, it was also led by middle class political leaders.

In 1962, when political activities resumed in Pakistan under the new constitution and a new parliament was elected, some remarkable changes in the social structure of Bangladesh had already taken place. Through the Basic Democracy (BD) system, an alliance between the rich peasants and *jotedars* and the state had already been formed. In the urban areas, a small segment of middle classes, mostly "contactors" and "contractors," emerged. Military rule, on the one hand, benefited a section of the middle classes of

Bangladesh, while it isolated a larger section from the state structure, on the other. To the aspirant political leaders of Bangladesh, military rule showed how meager their access was to state power; to merchants it was obvious that the non-Bengalis were taking advantage of the opportunities arising from their closer relations with the bureaucracy, while to the urban salaried class military rule represented clear domination by non-Bengalis. Thus, by 1964, at the time of the reorganization of political parties, the relationship between the intermediate classes and the colonial state reached a precarious position: one of both conflict and collaboration.

The collaboration of the intermediate classes with the Pakistani colonial state is clear as they functioned as its political agents. The social origin of the BD members mentioned in the previous section bears this out. Furthermore, there was a preponderance of middle class representatives in the Provincial as well as National Assemblies elected in 1962 and 1965. In the National Assembly, out of 78 members elected from East Pakistan, 31 were lawyers, 23 small businessmen and industrialists, and 12 landholders (Ahmed 1963:273). In the Provincial Assembly, of 130 members, 60 were small businessmen including contractors, 37 landholders, and 16 lawyers (Sen 1986:183).

However, there was conflict with the state. After political activities resumed in 1962, the question of regional autonomy came to the forefront of politics as never before. Apart from right-wing political parties, such as the Jaamat-i-Islami, and different factions of the Muslim League, all political parties of East Pakistan supported regional autonomy. The question of disparity between the two wings of Pakistan became inseparable from any political discourse.

Nonetheless, both collaborationists and disgruntled sections of the rising Bengali bourgeoisie and middle classes had one thing in common: they were looking for a greater share in the surplus expropriated by the state from the poor peasantry and the massive external aid/grant infused to perpetuate the capitalist system. Thus, both sections were in search of ways and means to establish control over the state apparatuses. This expectation found its political expression in the six-point demand advanced by the Awami League in 1966.

Six-Point Movement and the Middle Class as the Protagonist

The essence of the six-point demand was regional autonomy for the province under federal parliamentary government with total control over revenue earnings and foreign trade by the federating states. While the six-point demand led to the creation of a charter for the rising Bengali bourgeoisie and intermediate classes, it failed, initially, to appeal to the subordinate classes. It remained silent about the problems of sharecroppers, small peasants, *kulees* working in tea plantations, and industrial workers. However, by the late-1960s, the objective conditions for unrest among the poorer sections, such as decline in real wages of workers[23] and per capita income of peasants,[24] brought them closer to the Awami League and its six-point demand. It is, indeed, true the convergence was able to take place primarily because there was an absence of class consciousness among the working class and peasantry or, in other words, absence of a process that could transform the "class-in-itself" to a "class-for-itself." But, additionally, two significant factors contributed to the convergence of interests between the middle and working classes: the first was the failure of the left forces to present an alternative to the six-point program of the Awami League; and second was the success of the middle classes to appropriate the concerns of the poorer segments and incorporate them into demands of their own. Undoubtedly, the numerical preponderance of the middle classes in political leadership helped them too.

The Awami League's commendable success in appropriating the nationalist ideology and utilizing Bengali nationalism as a tool for establishing its hegemony over the subordinate classes of East Pakistan is critical to understanding the rise of the intermediate classes as prominent political actors. These factors, along with the Pakistani regime's suppression of the AL and its leaders, including Sheikh Mujib, turned the party into the legitimate constitutional representative of the intermediate classes of Bangladesh during the last days of Pakistan. I will reflect on the failure of the left and the numerical preponderance of the middle classes in political parties and address the issue of Bengali nationalism in a separate section.

In the face of the gradual rise of popularity of the six-point demand, the mass upsurge of 1966 in which the working class actively participated, and the structural factors I have described, the Ayub regime adopted a two-pronged policy developing a comprador bourgeois class in Bangladesh on one hand, and employing coercive measures against the Awami League on the other. The most glaring example of the coercive strategy was the *Agartala Conspiracy Case*, initiated against Sheikh Mujib and others for an alleged conspiracy to separate the East Wing by violent means, in collusion with India.[25] But soon the trial became the target of a mass movement opposing the Ayub regime and demanding autonomy for East Pakistan. This led to an upsurge in the popularity of the Awami League in general and Sheikh Mujib in particular making him the symbol of resistance to colonial exploitation. The mass upsurge of 1969, though initiated by the leftist student organizations and based upon the eleven-point demands— which included calls for the nationalization of banks, insurance companies, and all big business; reduction of the rates of taxes and revenues on peasants; fair wages and bonuses for workers; and quitting SEATO, CENTO, and Pakistan-U.S. military pacts—eventually led to a movement popularizing the Awami League. The mass upsurge in Bangladesh matched the mass agitation in West Pakistan and gradually turned into a violent anti-systemic upheaval. However, it was contained through removal of the Ayub regime and the promulgation of martial law bringing Yahya Khan in power. Nonetheless, by 1969, the intermediate classes led by the petty-bourgeoisie in Bangladesh had emerged as prominent actors in the political arena.

As I have noted earlier, the factors that facilitated this rise include a failure of leftist forces, the numerical preponderance of the middle classes in political leadership, and the Awami League's success in appropriating the nationalist ideology.

Since the inception of Pakistan, the Communist Party had been officially outlawed, but remained active. However, they failed to pursue a consistent line of action. As early as 1953, the Party was split on the question of whether party members should work inside a progressive, lawful, petty-bourgeois party or not. In the mid-1960s, the umbrella organization of the left, the NAP, also faced a rift as a consequence of the division in the international communist movement. The pro-Peking leftist organization experienced further disintegration when the Ayub regime established good relations with China. Maulana Bhasani, a staunch critic of the military-bureaucratic oligarchy and a supporter of regional autonomy, also extended his tacit support to the Ayub regime. The pro-Moscow groups favored a close relationship with the Awami League in realizing "national demands" as they considered the national contradiction to be the prime one. The radical, underground, leftist organizations overemphasized the class aspect of Pakistani colonial rule and overlooked the national question altogether. These weaknesses together made the leftist organizations a non-viable alternative and, thus, paved the way for political parties of intermediate interests to assume a preeminent position.

The numerical preponderance of the middle classes in political leadership can be gleaned from the study of the social origins of the leadership of different political parties, both right-wing and leftist. According to the study by Maniruzzaman (1973:241), in 1968, 28 percent of the members of the executive committee of Pro-Moscow NAP were lawyers, 23 percent professors and teachers, 15 percent small businessmen, 8 percent were engaged in journalism and literary professions, 5 percent were engaged in services to private firms, and 3 percent were doctors. As opposed to this, 20 percent came from the working classes (12 percent were peasant leaders and 8 percent trade unionists). The situation was markedly similar in the pro-Peking NAP committee; while 31 percent came from the working class (14 percent and 17 percent from trade unionist and peasant leaders respectively), it was dominated by intermediate classes (69 percent altogether, 33 percent lawyers, 14 percent from journalism and literature professions, and 10 percent from business). It is interesting to note that a preponderance of intermediate classes in leadership was not confined to the leftist parties. The leadership of Jaamaat-i-Islami, the most prominent Islamist party, also came from these classes. Maniruzzaman (1980:28), in another study, notes that according to the Jaamaat sources, in 1969-70, 56 percent of the leaders were college and school teachers; 24 percent were small businessmen; small government officers and service personnel from private firms constituted 8 percent each; however lawyers constituted only 4 percent. When we look into the composition of Awami League leadership in 1969-70, it is markedly different from the abovementioned political parties insofar as the class character is concerned. Lawyers constituted the largest segment of the party leadership, 57 percent. Businessmen had a 29 percent share while former school and college teachers constituted 6 percent of the leadership, equal to landholders. Only 3 percent came from a trade unionist background (Maniruzzaman 1980:28).

Nationalism as a Hegemonic Tool

From the mid-1960s, the idioms, icons, and symbols of nationalist ideology began to occupy more space in the political discourse of the Bangladesh polity. The concept of "two-economies" (i.e., meaning East Pakistan's economy should be considered separate from West Pakistan or the federal economy of Pakistan) propounded by the Bengali economists translated into the political discourse as a theory of "two nations"—Bengali and Pakistani. The underlying theme of the newly articulated concept of nation emphasized that the Bengali people had long maintained a separate identity through their distinctive culture, language, and lifestyle. And, it was held that the Pakistani ruling power bloc was up against these distinctive characteristics. The Bengali language and its place within the federal structure, as well as the language movement of 1952, had been portrayed by Bengali intellectuals as the prime example of the antagonistic attitudes of the ruling powers. The attempt to introduce the Arabic script and to ban Tagore's songs in the state-controlled media were other examples that reflected deliberate attempts of the state to crush the cultural heritage of the Bengali people and, thus, render them subordinate to the alien culture patronized by the state apparatus. The examples cited were in no way an exaggeration. Rather, they were quite reflective of the colonial attitudes of the ruling power bloc of Pakistan. However, it is important to note that the symbols and idioms of Bengali nationalism highlighted were precisely those that were part and parcel of the middle class culture of the Bengali population.

These were not new issues. In the early nineteenth century, the middle class, educated, urban population of Calcutta embarked on an ideological quest to seek their "legitimate share" from the colonial state. The political objective of the so-called "Bengal Renaissance" of the nineteenth century, led and eulogized by the *bhadrolok* (literally meaning gentlemen) community of middle classes, was to demand greater participation in the colonial administration. While this strand of nationalism sought to collaborate with the colonial state, building a sub-hegemonic structure under which other classes would be subordinated, the subordinate classes themselves created their own brand of nationalist ideology that altogether rejected colonial domination and resisted the colonial state and its functionaries on many occasions. The former strand of nationalism, considered to be the only nationalist movement by elite historians, had a number of limitations in terms of its social origins and the space within which it operated. First, it could not reach beyond the educated middle classes. Second, it willfully excluded the Muslim middle classes, for they were yet to be incorporated into the power bloc that performed the role of functionaries of the colonial state. Third, the entire movement was limited spatially within urban Calcutta. The latter strand of nationalism, reflected in the peasant uprisings of Bengal, was militant and deeply rooted in the class struggle of the subordinate classes. Given the social structure of the Eastern Bengal the latter was relatively more powerful than the former.

After the partition of 1947, the elite nationalist ideology lost ground, while the latter prevailed in a dormant form. Given the setback of the Communist Party in East Pakistan, the militant nationalist movement of the subaltern classes could not be transformed into a radical resistance against the newly emergent Pakistani state. However, sporadic resistance in different parts of East Pakistan continued. A severe food crisis in the early 1950s, and reductions in jute prices combined with the exploitation of jotedars, provided the impetus for the subaltern classes to confront the state. It was in this context that the language movement of 1952 erupted. As I have mentioned earlier, while the question of language was of little significance to the illiterate subaltern classes, they joined with the urban middle classes to exert pressure upon the colonial state. This was again possible because the ruling political party (i.e., Muslim League) emerged from within the landed class in Bangladesh. As such, resistance against the Muslim League rule and alien colonial rule were one and the same to the poor peasants of East Bengal.

The militant nationalist movement of the subaltern classes was defeated militarily by the Pakistani state in its very early days and, because no attempt was made by the ruling power bloc or the state apparatuses to incorporate them, the subaltern classes remained antagonistic to the state.

It was in this context that the Awami League advanced its six-point demand in 1966. As noted earlier, this was purely a petty-bourgeois political program. Yet two things brought the poorer segments of the society closer to the Awami League: first, the party's apparent opposition to the colonial state and, second, growing discontent among the poor.

In the very particular historical circumstances of the mid-1960s, when the intermediate classes in general and the Awami League in particular began to use the icons of Bengali nationalism to rally people of "all walks of life," the goal of the intermediate classes was to exert tightly controlled and well-orchestrated extra-legal pressure on the colonial state in order to open avenues of negotiations. Until then the intermediate classes had been kept on the periphery of power by the colonial rulers. As a result, the primary political objective of the intermediate classes, under the direct domination of the colonial state, was to create space for negotiation. In order to pressure the state to engage in such negotiations, the intermediate classes needed to counter the colonial state on an ideological plane. With this end in mind, the intermediate classes led by the petty-bourgeoisie set out to evolve a sub-hegemonic structure. The intermediate classes raised the question of Bengali nationalism at that historical conjuncture as an opposition to the dominant ideology of the Pakistani state. Here, the category of the nation was attractive to the intermediate classes because of its "predilection to suppress the class question" (Ahmad 1985:62), and its supra-class appearance. Indeed, a militant nationalist consciousness existed in dormant form, but never succeeded in becoming hegemonic. Ultimately, the ideas articulated and propagated by the intermediate classes, led by the petty-bourgeoisie, came to dominate nationalist discourse.

The Bengali nationalism in question emphasized "Sonar Bangla," a golden Bengal, a pre-colonial retreat of classlessness. The term "people of Bengal" was used as frequently as possible, as if the people of Bangladesh were an undifferentiated mass and all of them would equally benefit from the cancellation of the colonial state. Thus, another important aspect of underdevelopment—the exploitation of the subaltern classes by the petty-bourgeoisie—was completely subsumed within the discourse of Bengali nationalism. Under its rubric, the proponents, in the words of Kamal Hossain, an ideologue of the nationalist movement, "sought to forge a unity between the alienated urban elite groups and rural masses" (Hossain 1979:103). They transposed class conflict on to the inter-nation level identifying the whole of Bangladesh as "oppressed" and West Pakistan as an "oppressor" and "capitalist"; and, hence, the prime task was to eliminate the colonial presence that caused oppression and underdevelopment (Jahangir 1986). As I have pointed out before, the Bengali language and culture had been portrayed as the unifying symbols of the entire nation. The conflict between the Bengali political leadership from the inception of Pakistan was explained in terms of a conspiracy against the Bengali nation as a whole. The aspirations of different classes—subaltern, intermediate, and nascent bourgeoisie—were articulated in their own idiom and brought together in a common platform under the ideological hegemony of the petty bourgeoisie against colonial domination. The uprising of 1969 that ousted Ayub was the zenith of the ideological hegemony of the petty-bourgeoisie. The militant nationalist consciousness of the masses, especially of the rural subaltern classes, was incorporated within the politics of the intermediate classes on its own terms. Having firmly established the ideological hegemony of the petty-bourgeoisie through the mass upsurge of 1969, the Awami League now sought constitutional legitimacy for its leadership.

Constitutional Legitimacy of the Leadership

The general elections of 1970 were the first ever held in Pakistan with universal adult franchise. The elections provided constitutional legitimacy to the intermediate classes in general and the Awami League in particular to represent the majority population of Pakistan (i.e., Bengali);[26] the occupational background and annual income of the members of the National and provincial Assemblies elected from Awami League demonstrate this quite clearly (Table 1 and Table 2).

The election results, like those of 1954, posed a challenge to the Pakistani state and an impasse regarding the transfer of power to the elected representatives emerged. The election was projected by the Awami League as a referendum on their six-point program, which denied the center the right of taxation and transferred the authority of negotiating trade agreements with other countries from the central bureaucracy to the provincial

Table 1.
Occupational Background of the
Members of National and Provincial Assemblies, 1970
(Total Sample 268)

Occupation	Number	Percentage
Lawyers	79	29.47
Businessmen	72	26.86
Teachers	25	9.32
Doctors	20	7.46
Farmers	34	12.68
Large Landholders	12	4.47
Service	7	2.60
Others	19	7.07
Source: Jahan (1980:99).		

Table 2.
Annual Income of the
Members of National and Provincial Assemblies, 1970
(Total Sample 270)

Income (In Taka)	Number	Percentage
Less than Tk.20,000	138	51.11
Tk.20,000-30,000	65	24.07
Tk.30,000-50,000	43	15.92
Above Tk.50,000	24	8.88
Source: Jahan (1980:99).		

governments. Thus, the program, which essentially called for the removal of the mechanism for extracting the surplus from the hands of the bureaucracy, was unacceptable to the military-bureaucratic oligarchy. This is because without that mechanism, it was impossible to support "the coercive and administrative organizations (which) are the basis of the state power" (Skocpol 1979:30). Under such circumstances, a conflict between the Pakistani state and the intermediate classes of Bangladesh was inevitable. Protracted negotiations between the military-bureaucratic oligarchy and the representatives of the preeminent classes failed to bring about a compromise. This led to an armed conflict in 1971, which culminated in the establishment of independent Bangladesh.

NOTES

1   The extent of the state's role in the economy of Pakistan can be understood from the fact that, at the time, 40 percent of gross monetary investment had been public. These investments went either to create infrastructure required by industry or directly to industrial undertakings. In addition, these investments were made at a time when no private interest existed in the industrial sector (Papanek 1967).

2   Forty thousand Basic Democrats (commonly referred to as BD Members) were elected from what was then East Pakistan. They constituted the Electoral College for the national and provincial parliaments. I will discuss the role of Basic Democrats as well as the implication of this system on Bangladesh society later.

3   Pakistan, within a month of partition, made a request to the United States for economic assistance but attracted little attention. Later, in October 1947, a second and formal request to the United States for a two billion dollar loan was made. This time, Pakistan emphasized that the loan was necessary for its administrative and defense expenditure to forestall a Soviet threat. Pakistani representatives clearly indicated that Pakistan wanted to line up its defense policy with the United States and its domestic stability was dependent upon economic assistance; yet it failed to obtain any relief from the United States.

4   Harrison (1959:10) quoted a letter of Gen. Hayt Vandenbergh, the then Chief-of-Staff of the U.S. Air Force, written in September 1951, where Gen. Hayt wrote "we have our eyes on bases in Pakistan."

5   For example, in 1950 Liaquat Ali Khan, the first Prime Minister of Pakistan, brushed aside an invitation to the Soviet Union and went to Washington to plead for Pakistan's inclusion into any future West Asian defense strategy.

6   GOP, Establishment Division, Civil List of the Class I Officers Serving Under the Government of Pakistan, 1951 through 1969.

7   The rate of increase in pauperization and landlessness of the rural poor is reflected in the census of 1951 and 1961. In ten years, the number of landless agricultural laborers increased by 63 percent, while cultivators as a whole increased by 33 percent.

8   R. D. Lambert (1950:307-328) recorded that "out of 2237 large landowners in Bengal, only 358 of them were Muslims, who were concentrated in Chittagong and Dhaka Districts." He elsewhere (1959:52) noted, "eighty out of 89 estates with annual income of over Rs. 100,000 and 122 out of 137 estates earning between Rs. 50,000 and Rs. 100,000 annually were owned by Hindus."

9   Though the government claimed the act was made to redistribute land among the landless, the act failed to make enough land available for redistribution by setting the limit at too high a level. Initially, the government could acquire only 163,741 acres of land. Because the landlords were given an option as to which portion of land they were willing to surrender, it was quite possible that a significant amount of surrendered land was waste land. By 1959, total land acquired was 234,746 acres, out of which 159,537 acres or almost 60 percent was waste (Abdullah 1976:85).

10   In order to gain the support of the rural rich, the government raised the ceiling on private landholding to 125 acres in 1961 from the 33.3 acres set by the Act of 1950.

11   This program was initiated in 1962-63 primarily financed by United States Public Law (USPL) 480 counterpart funds, and, up to 1966-67, had spent Rs. 670.8 million in Bangladesh (GOP 1966:226). The USPL 480 is a U.S. government program for providing grant and concessional credit food aid to developing countries. This is the amended version of the Agricultural Trade Development and

Assistance Act of 1954. Public Law 480 is also known as the Food for Peace Program. The PL 480 food aid program is comprised of three titles. Each title has different objectives and provides agricultural assistance to countries at different levels of economic development. PL 480 programs, according to the U.S. government, exist in order to combat hunger and malnutrition; promote broad-based equitable and sustainable development, including agricultural development; expand international trade; develop and expand export markets for the agricultural commodities of the United States; and foster and encourage the development of private enterprise and democratic participation in developing countries.

12   White (1974) identifies the 43 families in Pakistan who controlled 72.8 percent of all assets of Pakistani-controlled firms operating in Pakistan in 1962, listed on the Stock Exchange. In 1963, these same families controlled 73.7 percent of such assets. In the manufacturing sector, their control was much higher—77.3 percent of assets. According to Sobhan and Ahmad (1980), even if the private firms not listed on the Stock Exchange are included, the control of these families, still remarkably high, constituted 58.2 percent of manufacturing assets. Furthermore, in the financial sector they commanded almost equal control. Insurance is a case in point. Fourteen companies from among the 43 families controlled 75.6 percent of all insurance assets held by Pakistani companies. Further, among these 43 families, 22 were at the apex who gradually took more control over the Pakistan economy.

13   The sheer growth of the urban population during the period 1951-61 reflects the trend of urban-based population. During this period, population growth in urban areas was 45.11 percent. In the previous decade, the corresponding figure was only 18.41 percent (Ahmad 1966).

14   There is no accurate figure for the actual proportion of students who came from rural backgrounds, but the *Report of the Commission on*

Student Problems and Welfare of the Ministry of Education written, in 1966, stated "Students are now drawn from all strata of society, but quite a number of them come from families in which they are perhaps the first to reach institutions of higher learning. Their background, outlook and behavior patterns are very different from those of earlier generations who belonged, for the most part, to the upper and middle strata of society" (pp.177).

15   Data relating to strength is derived from unpublished data of the Ministry of Labor, Government of Bangladesh.

16   It was after this by-election that the ruling faction decided not to hold any other by-election, though 34 seats were vacant.

17   Despite the word "Muslim" in its nomenclature, it was altogether a secular organization. Nonetheless, the word "Muslim" was dropped from the name of the party in 1953 (for a detailed history of the Awami League see Ghosh 1990).

18   Umar's (1970, 1975, 1979) illuminating studies on the language movement of 1952 provides a detailed history of political events from 1948.

19   The demand regarding the jute trade raised by the Awami League echoed the East Pakistan Jute Association's demand. The latter organization was pressing for equity among the traders of the East and West Pakistan.

20   After remaining politically inactive for a long time, Fazlul Haq, the former Chief Minister of undivided Bengal and a champion of the causes of rural peasantry, revived his party in 1953.

21   The strength of the UF was further increased when out of 72 non-Muslim members, 68 supported the UF and 8 out of 9 independent Muslim members joined the Front. One independent member joined

the League. Thus, the total number of UF members was raised to 223, while the corresponding number for the ML was 10.

22 The Announcement of the alliance treaty was quite significant to the elections. According to Spain (1954) and Hertzberg (1954), the announcement was made hastily on request from the Pakistan government, who thought that it would help the ruling Muslim League win the elections. Since the announcement was scheduled on February 21, the election was shifted from February 16 to March 8.

23 According to the survey conducted by Khan (1967), the real wages of a worker in all industries in East Pakistan sharply declined over the years. In 1954, the annual real wage was Rs. 794.50, but in 1962-63 the corresponding figure was Rs. 727.40.

24 Bose (1968) reckoned a decline in the per capita income of agricultural population in the 1960s. According to him, the amount was Rs. 228 in 1950s, while in 1962-63 the amount fell to Rs. 200.

25 The conspiracy was allegedly planned in the Indian town of Agartala near the border between India and East Pakistan. Whether there was any such attempt is still a mystery. During the mass upsurge of 1969, leaders of the opposition parties in East Pakistan denied these allegations calling them a premeditated move against the autonomists. However, after the independence of Bangladesh, a number of AL leaders and journalists acknowledged that there had been such an attempt.

26 In the elections of 1970, the Awami League won a landslide victory. It obtained 167 seats out of 169 seats allotted to East Pakistan in the National Assembly, 288 out of 300 seats in the provincial Assembly of East Pakistan, and gained 72.6 percent of the votes cast in East Pakistan. The victory, according to some analysts, was unanticipated even by the Awami League (Jahan 1980:53; Ayoob 1971:35).

Chapter 2

Formation of the Bangladeshi State

By 1970, an alliance of the intermediate classes emerged as the prominent political actor and established ideological hegemony over subaltern classes in East Pakistan. The endeavor of this alliance to take hold of state power led to an armed conflict in 1971 and eventually brought an end to colonial rule. The nine-month-long violent national liberation struggle ended on December 16, 1971 with the establishment of an independent state in Bengal. Although independence was achieved through armed struggle, some obviously conflicting conditions prevailed. The most significant of these was the existence of two contending sources of authority, the first being the state structures left behind by the Pakistani military-bureaucratic oligarchy, the second was rooted in the nationalist movement in general and the war of independence in particular.

Although a war was fought, a number of factors precluded the possibility of one source of authority being subordinated by the other. First, the liberation struggle was not initiated deliberately by its leadership to overthrow the colonial state structure or to bring about a radical change in the social order, but, rather, was imposed upon the people of Bangladesh by the military regime of Pakistan as they unleashed a reign of terror and genocide on March 25, 1971.[1] Second, the Bangladesh government-in-exile, in its first proclamation, accepted the continuance of the structures it inherited.[2] Third, the war was fought neither under a unified leadership nor under a single command of the political party that legitimately provided the political leadership and formed the government-in-exile (i.e., the Awami League). Fourth, the leadership of the Awami League was divided, even during the war itself, on vital issues such as who should be Prime Minister[3] and whether or not the government-in-exile should respond to the United States' initiative for a solution within the framework of the existing Pakistani state.[4] And, finally, the war was not long enough to bring about a clear polarization within the liberation forces and between the pro- and anti-liberation forces.

Nevertheless, the Awami League, by virtue of being the legitimately elected representatives of the erstwhile East Pakistani people through the elections of 1970, led the struggle, formed the government, and finally assumed power. The termination of colonial rule and assumption of power by the Awami League brought remarkable changes in the nature of the state

76

and an ongoing transformation after independence. At the outset of independence, the emergent Bangladeshi state was an intermediate state in the sense that the state apparatus was captured by the alliance of intermediate classes led by the petty bourgeoisie. The economic policies pursued by the state were directed toward the benefit of the intermediate classes. But gradually the nature of the state began to change. The executives (primarily bureaucrats) established control over the ruling bloc and hence began to act somewhat independent of the prominent social classes. The struggle between these two contending sources of authority can be described as a conflict between the old state and the new regime. In the final analysis, it was the bureaucrats who succeeded in marginalizing the political regime. Meanwhile, there were discernable changes in terms of the state's relationship with the world economic system. Further integration with the world economic system as a dependent state made Bangladesh more susceptible to external pressure.

In order to comprehend the changes over the period of three and a half years (i.e., January 1972-August 1975) one must look into five aspects of the Bangladeshi state: the constitutive elements of the emergent state, the class character of the power bloc and its economic agenda, the struggle between and among the components of the state, and the position of the state within the world economic system. I will address these issues in this chapter.

The Emergent Bangladeshi State

The emergent Bangladeshi state had three constitutive elements: the ruling party, the bureaucracy, and the military. The internal dynamics of these elements and the relationship between them were key factors in determining the nature of the state.

The Ruling Party

As the Awami League, from its inception, had attempted to represent a broad range of classes, cleavages within the organization always existed. Events prior to, and during, the liberation struggle accentuated divisions within the party and brought forth some new elements conducive to faction-alism. In 1972, there were at least four factions within the AL. First, the radical elements; second, the liberals; third, the conservatives; and, finally, those who fled to India but didn't actively participate in the war, often called the "free riders."

The radical elements within the party were, to some extent, new entrants, but they were remarkably powerful. They entered the Awami League in the mid to late1960s and were a product of the increasing radi-calization of the body politic. The mass upsurge of 1969 and the failure of leftist political parties to bring the youth under their umbrella made it possi-ble for the AL to attract these young radicals. Within a brief period, they acquired so much clout that they forced the leadership to incorporate a pledge to establish socialism in the election manifesto of 1970. This section of the party primarily drew its support from the student wing, the "Students League," and played a significant role in the landslide victory of the Awami League in the elections of 1970. When it became obvious the Pakistani military-bureaucratic oligarchy was unwilling to hand over power, the radi-cal elements of the AL began to put pressure on Sheikh Mujib in March 1971 to declare independence. They insisted that a war was imminent, although their idea of war was naive. The radicals viewed the struggle as a "people's war," one which would be a long drawn-out one. In a post-inde-pendence situation, these radical elements began to insist that massive restructuring under the leadership of Sheikh Mujib was necessary to estab-lish an egalitarian and just society.

The second strand, comprised of liberal elements of the AL, was more pragmatic. It was this section of the party that led the liberation war. The Prime Minister of the government-in-exile, Tajuddin Ahmed, belonged to this faction. In spite of pressure from both the radical and the conserva-tive sections, and severe resource constraints, the leaders of the liberal wing of the AL played a prominent role in coordinating the activities of the government-in-exile.

The third faction of the party, the conservatives, strove throughout the war to seize power from the liberals. A number of attempts were made to remove Tajuddin Ahmed from the position of PM. Interestingly, on several occasions this section worked closely with the radicals who also attempted to remove Tajuddin.

The fourth faction, often called the "free-riders," had fled the country to save their lives. But they allegedly used their affiliation with the Awami League to take advantage of their situation. After the war was over, they came home posing as heroes, warriors, and freedom fighters.

Infighting within the AL began as early as April, 1971.[5] On the very night that the Pakistan Army began the massacre, Sheikh Mujib was taken into custody and the top-ranking AL leaders fled Dhaka. Tajuddin Ahmed crossed the border into India in late March and sought help from the Indian authorities to continue the resistance against Pakistani forces. However, he had no information about other leaders. Tajuddin's aides insisted that he should shoulder the responsibility of the Prime Minister. Tajuddin, with great difficulty, assembled the leaders in Calcutta, the capital of the Indian state of West Bengal on April 9, and broadcast a speech over a clandestine radio network in which he proclaimed himself Prime Minister of the Government of Bangladesh. Khandaker Mustaque Ahmed, a senior leader, joined the other AL leaders the next day, but expressed discontent that Tajuddin had become PM. He argued that as the senior member of the team he should have taken the top job. He also expressed his desire to leave the country and go to Mecca for the rest of his life.

With the formal declaration of independence and the formation of a cabinet on April 17, the conflict subsided but did not end. The dissension resurfaced when the AL members of the National and Provincial Assemblies met in Shiliguri (Agaratala district of India) on July 5-6, 1971.

By then Sheikh Moni along with three other youth leaders, Tofail Ahmed, Abdur Razzak, and Serajul Alam Khan, had organized a separate armed group—the "Bangladesh Liberation Force" (BLF, later renamed *Mujib Bahini*). Significantly, this force was organized with the active help of an Indian counter-insurgency agency, the Research and Analysis Wing (RAW). An Indian Major General, Uban, was in charge of the training and supply of this group. The structure, leadership, training, and operation patterns of this force were deliberately concealed from the Bangladesh Government-in-exile. The BLF was operating on its own.

The Mustaque faction of the party, following an abortive attempt to conduct negotiations with the Pakistani regime, moved to oust Tajuddin Ahmed from power. On September 12, forty elected representatives of the

Southern administrative zone belonging to the Mustaque and Sheikh Moni groups, met and adopted a resolution calling on the AL high command to force Tajuddin's resignation from both the General Secretary position of the party and cabinet membership. In September, another faction led by two prominent AL leaders, Kamruzzaman and Yusuf Ali, attempted to increase their influence over the freedom fighters in the northern part of the country. They even contacted some pro-China, leftist political parties operating out of Calcutta.

It would be a mistake to assume that one can draw easy connections between the members of these groups. These groups were neither well organized nor monolithic. But insofar as the struggle for power within the party was concerned, the members of these groups fought against each other.

Thus, at independence, though that there was euphoria over the victory, the ruling party was sufficiently factionalized that it was little more than a conglomeration of groups jockeying for power. There was no charismatic leader and no rallying point except power. The first significant decisions of the government after reaching Dhaka were the removal of Khandaker Mustaque Ahmed from the post of Foreign Minister, for his alleged involvement with the United States, and the induction of five new members into the cabinet on December 27, 1971. Although the induction was made to lessen the conflict, it did not lead to any significant changes. On the other hand, Mustaque's removal from the Foreign Minister position further accentuated the schisms. Anthony Mascarenhas (1986:7) described the situation after independence and before the arrival of Sheikh Mujib[6] as follows: "if he (Mujib) did not get to Dacca very quickly there was grave danger of the new government falling apart and risk of civil strife. The war was over. The in-fighting, the jostling for power in the Awami League had begun." The intrigue subsided when Mujib reached Dhaka and became the PM. But it would resurface on many future occasions.

The Bureaucracy

As with the ruling party, factionalism beleaguered the bureaucracy.[7] In the early days of independence (i.e., December 1971-December 1972), the higher public service officials could be divided into three categories: (1)

officials who went into hiding inside Bangladesh, (2) those who joined the exiled government, and (3) those who were attending to their duties and willingly or unwillingly, cooperating with the military regime.[8] In addition, there was another source of factionalism evident: those who had served the central government of Pakistan (i.e., CSP) and those who were under the provincial government (i.e., EPCS). These groups engaged in a bitter feud regarding their positions in the emerging state apparatus. The factionalism was enhanced by the decision of the government to put all those who had worked in *Mujibnagar* at the forefront, brushing aside the established rules and procedures.

Despite internal divisions and some intimidation from party members, the bureaucracy was firmly entrenched as there were clear indications that the ruling party had no plan to dismantle the bureaucratic structure. Instead, they would rely on them to a great extent. The first indication was the Laws Continuance Enforcement Order. The government-in-exile, instead of attempting to build a parallel administration, made no moves to replace the existing structure. As a matter of fact, the government completely relied on the "civil administration" for the restoration of law and order. In a cabinet meeting held on November 22, 1971, the issue of "civil administration set up in liberated Bangladesh" was discussed. The cabinet opined, "A large purge of the Government employees may create an administrative vacuum" and formed a subcommittee of the secretaries "to examine the serious facets of the problem of setting up civil administration" (Hasan 1986:327-330). The subcommittee was comprised of the Secretaries of Defense, Home, Cabinet, Finance, and General Administration (GPRB 1971). Furthermore, on December 16, after the liberation of Bangladesh, a memo from the Establishment Secretary was sent to the Deputy Commissioners of the different districts to take control of the civilian administration. The memo also stated, "The magistracy and the police have to be put back in their proper position as the lawful authority for maintenance of law and order" (GPRB 1971b).

A number of factors contributed to the government's reliance on the existing civil administration for restoring law and order. First, there was no single command of the freedom fighters that could be mobilized for this purpose, because in addition to those freedom fighters trained by the government-in-exile, there were a number of groups operating autonomously from within the country. Second, as mentioned earlier, no alternative structure had been put in place to take over. Third, the ruling party was neither a monolithic organization, nor was it ready to shoulder the total responsibility.

The Military

At independence, the military faced a precarious situation. There were cleavages within the military establishment and they had been deprived of their due share in the glory of liberation. The division within the military was along various lines. The primary division was, of course, along the line of involvement in the liberation war. According to Azad (1972), the Bangladesh armed forces were comprised of five types of erstwhile Pakistan Army personnel:

> (1) Those who actively participated in the liberation war by joining the Mukti Bahini officially, (2) those who helped organize the resistance movement in their homes and villages, (3) those who left the Pak Army and did not participate further, (4) those who were arrested and remained in Army custody until liberation, and (5) those who served the occupation army. (Azad 1972:1)

The members of the military were also divided ideologically. The fundamental point of contention was whether or not the military should be reorganized according to the existing colonial structure. While the larger section was in favor of maintaining the status quo, a small segment was trying to push for a thorough restructuring and organization of a "people's army." Additionally, rivalries and jealousies among the top-ranking leaders that had originated during the liberation war started to surface.

The conventional army did not get its proper share of the glory because of the common perception that it was only the non-professional guerrillas drawn from all walks of life who had made independence possible. This perception was rooted in the long-standing alienation of the military from the common people and the military's attitude toward political movements preceding the war. In fact, it became public knowledge that most of the Bengali military personnel were least interested about the political developments taking place before the military assault of the Pakistan Army.[9]

Although the Army was reluctant to become embroiled in politics, face the threat of being disarmed, or become targets of the Pakistani Army, military units stationed in different parts of the country along with the paramilitary forces (especially the EPR) mounted the first resistance against the military operation. They were numerically insignificant compared to the Pakistani Army,[10] but until April 10, 1971 these forces fought practically without direction or leadership from the leading political parties. This had both positive and negative consequences. It is true, had there been no resistance from them, the course of the liberation war may have taken a different turn. But, on the other hand, it gave military officials a feeling that the war could be fought without political leadership *per se* or at least that military leadership should supersede political leadership. This feeling was expressed when the military leaders first met with the leaders of the government-in-exile on July 10-15. Ziaur Rahman and seven other commanders proposed to set up a "war council" led by military officials to coordinate the war. The proposal was opposed by a section of military officials and rejected by the government (Hasan 1986:54).

Rivalries and jealousies among prominent military personnel began to surface as early as April. At the first meeting of the resistance forces after the war began on March 25, Colonel Osmani was appointed Commander-in-Chief.[11] Major Ziaur Rahman declared himself the Commander-in-Chief in his address broadcast from the clandestine radio on March 27 and expected that this meeting would validate that announcement. But both Major Khaled Musharraf and Major Shafiullah repudiated his action (Sayeed 1989:157).[12] Personal rivalries resurfaced among this trio in July, 1971. Col. Osmani decided to raise a brigade comprised of three battalions (1 East Bengal, 3 East Bengal, and 8 East Bengal). Major Ziaur Rahman was appointed as the head of the brigade, which was named "Z" force in his honor. Soon after the decision was made, Khaled and Shafiullah pressured the central command for two more brigades named in their honor. Despite the lack of trained manpower (especially officers) and ammunition, within two months two further brigades had been raised: "K" force and "S" force (Hasan 1986:61; Sayeed 1989:158).

The ideological differences over how the Bangladesh army should be organized in the post-independence period were a continuation of the differences raised during the war over how it should be conducted. Colonel Osmani was initially in favor of raising a regular force and conducting a conventional war. He was never enthusiastic about guerilla warfare.[13] Ziaur Rahman, in contrast, was more interested in dividing the regular army battalions into small companies and conducting commando-style activities along with the guerrillas. Both of them, however, were chiefly concerned with equipping the regular army. Shafiullah and Khaled preferred a coordination of activities between the guerrillas and the conventional forces, with the latter in command. What was common among them was their interest in raising the army to a preeminent position in the war. In October, when the sector commanders met in Calcutta, Lieutenant Colonel Abu Taher and Lieutenant Colonel Ziauddin, both of whom joined the war effort after fleeing from Pakistan, raised serious objections to this line of thinking. They suggested that instead of increasing the number of regular forces, they should strengthen the guerrilla brigades involving both regular army and peasants to fight a long-term war. They strongly opposed the dependence on Indian forces for the supply of arms and ammunition. They recommended that the forces' Head Quarters be moved to a position inside Bangladesh. Most significant was their plan for the future Bangladesh Army. They maintained that if guerrilla brigades could be raised, they would act as the core of the production-oriented army in independent Bangladesh. Ziaur Rahman also supported this idea (Islam 1983:103).

The rapid developments of early December leading to full-scale war and direct Indian involvement in the liberation of Bangladesh were so overwhelming that these conflicts within the Bangladesh army could not be resolved. Thus when Bangladesh became independent these differences would re-emerge as a point of contention.

It was not surprising, therefore, that the emergent Bangladeshi state in 1972 was in shambles. All three components of the state had been damaged by infighting. The liberation war neither built a consensus nor had any single component succeed in subordinating the others. Nevertheless, the ruling party had an edge because of its legitimate claim on constitutional power. One further point should be noted: the ideological differences within and among these components had not yet come to light. It did not take much time, however, for them to surface. As soon as the ruling party began to articulate and, subsequently, implement the economic and political agenda of the intermediate classes—whom they were representing—the differences among them and between them began to appear. Nevertheless, at the early stage it was the ruling party that succeeded in implementing the economic and political agenda of the intermediate classes, which turned Bangladesh into an intermediate state.

Class Character of the Power-Bloc

In the capitalist periphery, as I have mentioned previously, the relationship between the state and social classes is mediated by a power bloc, which is comprised of the political leadership and members of the higher echelons of the state apparatus. Hence, both help determine the nature of the state. Although it is possible to have heterogeneity within the bloc itself, this was not the case in Bangladesh. With the assumption of state power, the political representative of the intermediate classes (i.e., the ruling Awami League) rushed to establish total control of its constituent classes over the power-bloc.

The Awami League nominees in the elections of 1970 and the leadership of the party were predominantly from the intermediate classes. The first full-fledged cabinet of ministers formed in 1972 indicates the preeminence of this class. In the 23-member cabinet, 13 were lawyers, 4 businessmen, 3 (including Mujib) professional politicians, a college professor, a landholder, and a former military official (i.e., the C-in-C of *Mukti Bahini*) (*Bangladesh Observer* 1972:12).

The elections of 1973 brought a few new faces to the regime, but the old guard of the party remained largely in place (66 percent of the former Constituent Assembly members were re-elected and only one new member was added to the cabinet). The class character of the regime remained substantially unchanged. One study shows "the majority of the MPs belonged to the urban middle class professions, such as law, business, teaching, and medicine" (Jahan 1980:148). Twenty-seven percent of the MPs were lawyers, 24 percent were businessmen, 3 percent were large landowners, 15 percent were rich and middle farmers, 10 percent were teachers and 5 percent were doctors. More than 56 percent of the MPs enjoyed an annual income of between Taka 20,000 and Taka 50,000. Thirty percent of the MPs owned more than 25 acres of land and 10 percent owned more than 40 acres. If we take into account that 75 percent of the farmers of the country at that time owned less than 3 acres of land while the same proportion of MPs owned more than 6.5 acres of land, their social position becomes clear.

At the local level administration, the picture was the same. The leadership of the Union Parishad, elected in 1973, came predominantly from the rich and middle-income peasants. Data drawn from Solaiman and Alam's (1977) study on the UP leadership of the Comilla area, located in the eastern part of the country, reveals that 63.6 percent of local leaders owned 2 to 7 acres of land, while 18 percent owned more than 7 acres. Wahab's (1980) study of Rangpur, a district in the north, shows that 50 percent of the UP leaders owned more than 9 acres of land. The remaining 50 percent owned 2-9 acres of land. None of the UP leaders came from the ranks of landless or poor peasants.

The ascent to political leadership by the intermediate classes was matched by the rise of middle class professionals in different parts of the state. The Planning Commission and the public enterprises are the best examples. The Planning Commission in Pakistan was an exclusive preserve of the bureaucrats. This not only put them in a privileged position in terms of enjoying the benefits, but also (and perhaps more importantly) gave them unlimited power to chart the course of the economy. In contrast, the Bangladesh Planning Commission, established in 1972, was headed by academic economists and manned by professionals drawn from various sectors of the economy but only a few members from the traditional civil service and bureaucracy. The Planning Commission was composed of an ex-officio Chairman (the PM), and four members—a deputy chairman and three others—all of whom (with the exception of the Chairman) held positions in universities or other academic bodies. Four academically brilliant young economists, "who had very little direct experience in government administration" (Islam 1978:xi), virtually ran the planning commission. Excepting Rehman Sobhan, who had a tripos from Cambridge University, all had Ph.Ds—Nurul Islam, Deputy Chairman; Mosharraf Hossain; and Anisur Rahman. Additionally, almost all of the positions, including chief, deputy chief, and assistant chief, in the ten divisions of the commission "were offered to university teachers and fresh university graduates who were either loyal to the Awami League or supported the liberation movement" (Islam 1978:62).

With massive nationalization in 1972 there emerged a large public sector and public enterprises became an important instrument of the state in economic planning and development. A large section of the higher echelon of management of these public enterprises was composed of middle class professionals. According to the account of Sobhan and Ahmad (1980:535), of 76 chief executives appointed during the period January 1972-August 1975, 44 belonged to the professional class as opposed to 25 from government services. The rest were military officers.

Economic Agenda of the Power-Bloc

A kind of "de-bourgeoisification"[14] existed at the heart of the economic policies implemented by the new regime between 1972 and 1975. These policies attempted to expand the role of the state. Although the Planning Commission maintained that in order to avoid "serious and sudden dislocation in the economic system" (Islam 1977:31), drastic institutional and economic changes should be averted and, hence, a continuation of a "mixed economy" as a transitional stage in the evolution of a socialist society should be sustained, they proposed a number of institutional changes that accorded the state a preeminent position in the economy. The *First Five Year Plan* (FFYP) document reflected the basic underpinnings of the economic policies of the regime:

> The removal of the capitalist system of income distribution, the private ownership of the means of production and of the pre-capitalist mercantile or feudal forms of production relations is a necessary pre-condition to social transformation... Reforms to such an end are

needed to be worked out in phases. In landownership, cooperatives among small and landless farmers; in large, heavy and basic industries ascendancy of the public sector; in trade, both domestic and international as well as in housing, transport and distribution, state and cooperatives will largely rule leaving small enterprises and retail trade in private hands. In such a society, where the function of the state is usually more than in a welfare state, the public sector performance will be expanded. (GPRB 1973:2)

The principal feature of the economic policy envisaged in the Planning Commission document showed the regime's desire to heighten the role of the state as never before. Implementation of these policies primarily began in the industrial sector even before they were delineated publicly, initially through taking control of properties abandoned by Pakistani entrepreneurs and then through the nationalization of other industrial units. The policy move was not restricted to a single sector. An analysis of the investment and agricultural policies of the government elucidates how a deliberate attempt was made to elevate the state to a central position.

Nationalization

Securing a predominant position for the state in the economy began as early as January 1972 through the government's actions toward industrial enterprises, which later served as the genesis of the nationalization program. Primarily because a large number of properties (including industrial enterprises) belonged to Pakistani entrepreneurs who had left the country, abandoning their properties,[15] the government promulgated a law on January 3, 1972 (*Acting President's Order No. 1*, 1972), enabling it to take control of the properties and organize their management. While the APO 1 of 1972 vested the right of control and management in the government, the Bangladesh Abandoned Property (Control, Management, and Disposal) Order 1972 (i.e., PO 16 of 1972) promulgated on February 28, 1972, transferred the abandoned properties to the government.

Simultaneously, the Planning Commission outlined a policy for massive nationalization. In early February, the Commission submitted a paper to the Cabinet on policy options and recommendations for the nation-alization of industries (Bangladesh Planning Commission 1972). It was recommended by the Commission that all enterprises in jute, textile, and sugar industries with fixed assets of over Taka 1.5 million be nationalized. An inter-ministerial committee to examine the recommendations was created.[16] Accordingly, the PM, in a policy statement on March 26 1972, announced that all large industries and financial institutions with assets over Taka 1.5 million were henceforth nationalized and would be managed by the state. It was also announced that compensation would be paid for the nationalized enterprises owned by Bangladeshi citizens.

This announcement changed the nature of the Bangladesh economy overnight. According to Sobhan and Ahmad "on the 27th of March, 1972 Bangladesh was faced with a situation where under law public ownership and control over the economy had increased from 10% of GDP to 16%. In the sphere of industries public ownership of fixed assets increased from 34% to 92% of modern industry and the number of enterprises under public management from 53 to 392" (Sobhan and Ahmad 1980:142).

A total of 254 large industrial units (jute, textile, sugar, iron and steel, engineering and shipbuilding, fertilizer, pharmaceutical and chemi-cal, oil, gas and mineral, paper and paper products, and forest industries combined) were nationalized. Additionally, 12 commercial banks with 1,175 branches all over the country and 12 insurance companies were brought into the public sector. About eighty percent of trade was now concentrated in the hands of public sector trading corporations.

Following nationalization, the economic picture reflected the state's central position: ten corporations had been set up to manage the national-ized industries; many commercial banks were organized into six nationalized banks; the insurance business was brought under the purview of two insurance companies; in order to meet the special needs of different sectors, such as agriculture, housing, and industry, four specialized finan-cial institutions had been set up; and a trading corporation was established for controlling import business. Finally, three corporations were set up to steer the jute business. All of these together transformed the state into the largest economic enterprise by far. It also became the nation's largest employer. This made the state the central actor in the economic arena,

Table 3.
Large-Scale Industrial Ownership in Bangladesh
Before and After Nationalization

	Number of units	Value of fixed assets million TK	Percent of fixed assets
Total Industries	3051	6137.5	100
Before Nationalization			
EPIDC	53	2097.0	34
Private Pakistani	725	2885.7	47
Private Bengali	20	118.8	18
Private Foreign	20	36.0	1
After Nationalization			
Nationalized of which	392	5637.5	92
Former EPIDC	53	2097.0	34
Private Pakistani	263	2629.7	43
Private Foreign	1		
Private Bengali	75	910.8	15
Private Bengali	2178	208.0	3
Abandoned: to be sol d	462	256.0	4
With foreign participation	13	36.0	1
Total Private	2653	500.0	8
Source: Sobhan and Ahmad (1980:192).			

turned it into a reservoir of opportunities, and, in the long term, benefited the intermediate classes in a number of ways.

Before going into the details of the consequences of nationalization, we need to briefly review the rationales for the massive nationalization program. There are two lines of explanation—pragmatist and ideological.[17] According to the former, it was circumstantial necessity that compelled the regime to follow a policy of nationalization. First, the large number of enterprises (including banks and insurance companies) abandoned by Pakistani owners needed to be restored. Second, the entrepreneurial class of Bangladesh was relatively small and ill-equipped in both capital and management skills and, hence, could not be entrusted with the responsibility. As such, the government had very little choice but to take control of the abandoned units. A government document narrated the situation in following manner:

> As an immediate and direct result of the liberation war, the predatory Pakistani industrialists had "abandoned" their industries in

Bangladesh but only taking with them everything they could, including in some cases, the provident fund money of the employees. They left behind only such plant and machinery which they could not remove and also left behind huge liabilities. In this situation, the government was faced with the immediate task of restoring the existing industries. This meant the assumption by the Government of the enormous responsibility of replacing the entrepreneurs and managers for efficient and effective management in the public sector. (GPRB 1972b:1)

Although there is no doubt that this situation played a vital role in the formulation and implementation of nationalization policies, it was not the driving force behind the sweeping measures. If such had been the case, the industrial units owned by Bangladeshi nationals would have been spared. In the jute and textile industries, for example, the proportion of total assets owned by Bangladeshi nationals was 34 percent and 53 percent respectively.

The ideological explanation for nationalization contends that the AL regime was committed to the cause of socialism, which motivated them to nationalize industries. This explanation is extremely problematic, because the beneficiary of nationalization was mostly the intermediate classes, not the working class. Secondly, the policy of nationalization alone cannot create a socialist society, especially where agriculture constituted the core of the economy. Analysis of the agrarian policy of the regime reveals that the landowning classes were favored, rather than the landless peasants who constituted the majority of the population. Moreover, the nationalization policy of the government left foreign interests completely untouched.[18] It is, however, true that the government adopted a socialist posture and made this driving force behind the nationalization policies. In order to broaden the base of the party and contain the radical elements both within and outside the party, the AL made electoral pledges in 1970 that the banking and insurance sectors would be nationalized. They also promised that if they were voted to power, they would work to eliminate exploitation and establish a just and egalitarian society. Following the liberation struggle, these commitments were interpreted as a promise for a socialist transformation of the society. The industrial policy became the test case for the fulfill-ment of electoral pledges and nationalization became the "first step" toward a socialist transformation of the society.[19] In addition to the rhetoric of the AL leaders, a number of government documents emphasized similar points. The preamble to the industrial investment policy states the following:

> The Government in moving forward to deal with this problem (abandoned properties) recognised that this situation presented a historic opportunity to lay the foundations of socialism in the indus-trial sector of the economy. Socialism being one of the fundamental precepts of State policy, the government decided that when it had to assume responsibility for the bulk of the industrial sector, this should be affected within the total perspective which would identify the areas which should immediately be nationalized and taken into public sector (GPRB 1972a:1).

It was also stated in the same document that the present phase was one "of consolidation of nationalization, of stabilization of new institutions and of development of a socialist consciousness among management and workers."

The justifications for the nationalization of industries in 1972, therefore, were based on circumstantial necessity and the regime's desire to prove its socialist credentials. Now, the most significant question: who benefited from the nationalization policy? Close examination reveals that the urban intermediate classes reaped the benefits of nationalization in the same way that they benefited from other economic policies and, indeed, from the workings of the economic system as a whole. Some of the bene-fits gained by the intermediate classes from the nationalization policy in particular mentioned below will bear out the claim. The immediate, yet significant benefits included enhanced job opportunities, appropriation of the potential surplus of nationalized industries, and personal enrichment through control of state enterprises.

The expansion of state activities necessitated an increase in the number of state-personnel. Nationalization contributed directly to the creation of job opportunities for the urban intermediate classes. From the outset, large numbers of management staff, including administrators, were appointed to the nationalized enterprises. These new appointees largely came from the party connection, being either members or acquaintances of party leaders. White-collar jobs increased substantially in subsequent years. A study of 39 public enterprises reveals two interesting facts in this regard. Firstly, between 1972 and 1975, a total of 1,169 officers were recruited. Of these new appointees, only 50 had management training and 86 had technical training specific to their job (Sobhan and Ahmad 1980:545). Secondly, 25 percent of the total employees were promoted from the unskilled to the skilled clerical level, 56 percent were promoted from the clerical to officer level, and of these, at least 30 percent did not have the required qualifications for the posts (Sobhan and Ahmad 1980:544). The class origin of those involved in the management of the nationalized enterprises is revealed in a study on the social origins of business executives of Bangladesh (Habibullah 1976). The study shows that only 4.54 percent of business executives had a rural and agricultural background, while the remaining 95 percent of upper class executives of the nationalized industries came from urban areas. The study further reveals that they were the relations of people employed in high positions in government and semi-government organizations (34.85 percent) and self-owned business firms (15.15 percent) (Habibullah 1976:206).

The expansion of employment opportunities was not limited to the nationalized enterprises. Given the heightened role of the state, it grew in many different ways. In fact, employment in public services witnessed a dramatic expansion. At the time of liberation, there were 450,000 employees of all grades in the public services, of whom only 320 were officers at the level of joint secretary or above. By 1973, total employment in the public services had increased to over 650,000 with officers in the higher grade increasing to 660 (IBRD 1984:109).

The potential surplus of nationalized enterprises became a source of rapid private accumulation for the intermediate classes. Two methods were used for appropriating the surplus: direct sale of the distribution licenses gained through political connections with the regime, and/or siphoning off the margin gained from the difference between the ex-factory price and the market clearing price. Interestingly, although the industries were nationalized, the distribution of products remained in the hands of the private sector. The government retained the authority to issue distribution licenses to private citizens. On paper the licenses were issued to genuine businessmen, but in practice a large group of people associated with the ruling party obtained distribution licenses pretending to be businessmen. The output of the nationalized industries was sold to these private distributors at a price that was well below the market clearing price. The margin between the market price and the ex-factory price was substantial and the difference was appropriated by the private distributors. In most cases, these fake business-men sold distribution licenses to legitimate traders at a price close to the market clearing price. This practice essentially created a number of inter-mediaries between the factory and the market and helped increase the price of the product besides increasing the wealth of the intermediaries.

The senior managers and the bureaucrats in the ministries and corporations responsible for managing the nationalized enterprises obtained numerous benefits in cash and kind, legally and illegally. The "legal" ones were primarily the benefits obtained in kind: transport, personal services, supplies, and other consumables. The illegal ones ranged from bribes (from suppliers, which were later passed on to the consumers in the form of higher prices) to under-invoicing and over-invoicing. All of these, on the one hand, increased the burden on the consumers while, on the other hand, they siphoned off the potential surplus.

The former owners of industrial units, on many instances, were appointed managers of the nationalized units. This gave them a rare oppor-tunity to control the productive enterprises without ownership (i.e., without the obligation to service the debt). The control itself was a source of economic power and was used for personal aggrandizement. Given that there was little discipline—financial or industrial—and that it was unclear to whom the new managers were accountable, it was an unprecedented opportunity for these new "managers" to embezzle. The situation was made worse because detailed inventories of equipment were not performed before appointing the new managers. Thus, some managers were able to liquidate machinery. Moreover, it was these managers who were authorized to appoint marketing and sales agents, which helped the process of personal gain. Maximization of personal profit within a short span of time very often became the ultimate goal of these new managers.

The implications of the nationalization policies pursued by the post-independent regime clearly show the state was accorded a pre-eminent position in the economic and social arena. In addition to its heightened command over resources, the state became the chief source of patronage. The other feature that stands out is the class character of the beneficiaries of the nationalization policy. It was the interests of the urban intermediate classes that were promoted. It must be recalled that this was not incongruent with other policies pursued by the state, but rather an example of one consistently pursued. Some more examples are in order.

Investment Policy

The salient features of the investment policy declared in the beginning of 1973 included a ceiling on private investment, a moratorium on nationalization, and severe restrictions on new foreign investment (GPRB 1973). According to the policy, private enterprises were limited to units with fixed assets not exceeding Taka 2.5 million, which could grow up to Taka 3.5 million through reinvested profits. Regarding possible nationalization, the policy stated "there will be a moratorium on nationalization for ten years from the date of publication of this policy for old units up to Taka 25 lakhs (i.e., Taka 2.5 million) and from the date of going into production for new units set up during the First Five-Year Plan."[20] Foreign investments were permitted only in collaboration with the Government, whose share in the equity capital would be 51 percent. Foreign collaboration in the private sector was confined to licenses and patents only.[21]

Essentially, the investment policy was a continuation of the nationalization policy of the regime, which did not, however, cover all sectors of the economy. As a result, a supplementary policy was required to set the direction for the remainder. We have seen that the nationalization policy limited the consolidation and expansion of a bourgeois class.[22] A policy to foreclose all avenues of development for a big industrial bourgeoisie in Bangladesh was prompted by the social class that was haunted by the memories of the economic and political power of the big bourgeoisie in Pakistan. Having achieved that goal through nationalization, the intermediate classes moved to the second phase: ensuring state patronage for their expansion. The investment policy was formulated to that end.[23] It is clear the imposition of a ceiling and restrictions on foreign investments favored small and medium-size enterprises. Those engaged in trading, such as small-scale industries (transportation, construction etc.), benefited from this policy immensely.

Here, some gaps in the policy should be elucidated. Firstly, the policy neither prohibited the setting up of several units with the maximum limit of assets (i.e., Taka 2.5 million), nor did it make any attempt to prevent disaggregating a unit with assets over Taka 2.5 million. Secondly, the policy did not indicate what an enterprise should do with its surplus beyond the limit of reinvestment. Both of these questions were discussed at length in cabinet subcommittee meetings and Planning Commission meetings. Yet, no clear-cut answers were given because the policy-makers were not sure how much the small enterprises would be able to grow.

Nevertheless, the investment policy gave a boost to the traders and businessmen and sent a discouraging signal to those involved in industrial enterprises. The government intended to disinvest 462 small and medium-sized industrial units to private entrepreneurs and to help create an industrial base, but evidently there was hardly any interest from the inter-mediate class. Instead, the intermediate classes looked for quick-yielding opportunities in trading, dealership, and businesses like transport and construction. Access to the government was exploited to reap benefits, legally and illegally.

The extent of private ownership and the rapid proliferation of new entrants in these fields can be understood more clearly after analyzing a few facts. In the road transport sector, only 15 percent of passenger services were under public corporations, 85 percent were controlled by private owners. In the inland water transport sector, almost 50 percent remained in private hands. During the year 1972-73, "56.56 percent of cash imports were in fact handled by private commercial importers" (Sobhan and Ahmad 1980:195). Patronage in the form of issuing licenses, permits, and dealer-ships to the party-members was so widespread that fake businessmen outnumbered real businessmen. According to the Commerce minister, of the 25,000 licenses (for import business) issued by the government between January 1972 and April 1973 15,000 went to fake companies (Dainik

Bangla 1973:1). It is alleged that these fake companies either sold those licenses to other traders and made a huge margin or engaged in smuggling items imported under the licenses.

In addition, the government not only issued licenses to these new traders, but also provided other facilities that helped them amass large sums of money in a short time. One method employed was to exempt import duties on essential goods like food grains, fertilizers, seeds of all types, metallic ores, and infant foods, and establish a low rate of import duties on an intermediate range of essential goods such as coarse fabrics, pharmaceuticals, industrial raw materials, machinery, and machine parts. Although these goods were taxed at low rates, the market price of these goods was high due to large scarcity margins. According to an account of the Planning Commission, the scarcity margin on essential goods like sugar was 100-150 percent, on milk foods was 150 percent and on coconut oil was 200 percent (Bangladesh Planning Commission 1974a). The fortunate recipients of the import licenses appropriated this huge margin.

Owing to rampant corruption, widespread state patronage, and the smuggling of jute and other exportables to India, much wealth had accumulated in the hands of a section of the intermediate classes—so much wealth that by the end of 1973 strong pressure began to mount for a revision of the investment policy. The pressure primarily came from within the party and from the ministry of industries.[24] It was argued that a low ceiling of investment had a discouraging effect on private investment and, hence, large sums were being diverted into unproductive channels. Another argument was that an upward revision of the ceiling would provide a legitimate outlet for unlawfully earned wealth, commonly described as "black" money, to be invested in industrial sector. In addition, over the years equipment prices in the international market had increased while the value of the Taka had dropped significantly. Thus, the ceiling in effect was lower than was initially set and without an upward revision the government's goal of encouraging small and medium-size enterprises could not be achieved.

The pressure for an upward revision of the ceiling also came from external sources such as donor agencies, which were in favor of a larger role for private enterprises in the economy, and insisted that the ceiling was inhibiting entrepreneurship. The World Bank recommended raising the ceiling to Taka 10 million or removing it altogether (IBRD 1974:312). Foreign investors also began to press for collaborative opportunities with private investors.

Pressured by internal and external sources, the government finally revised the investment policy drastically in July 1974 with immediate effect (GPRB 1974). The central features of the revised investment policy were the following: 1) the ceiling for private investment was raised to Taka 30 million; 2) private foreign investors were allowed to enter into partnerships with domestic private investors, mainly, but not exclusively, in projects where "technical know-how is not locally available, technology involved is very complicated, capital outlay is high and to industries based on local raw materials or wholly export-oriented industries" (GPRB 1974:4); 3) the moratorium on nationalization was extended from ten to fifteen years and fair and equitable compensation was guaranteed in the event of subsequent nationalization; and 4) eighteen sectors were reserved for the public sector leaving the rest open for private investment, in the field of industry proper, eleven industries remained exclusively in the public sector.

The revised investment policy, as we have noted, was needed to accommodate the emerging, newly rich class, which appropriated the potential surplus from the public sector and accumulated wealth through a number of illegal means under the patronage of the ruling party.

Agrarian Policies

While the nationalization and investment policies of the regime favored the urban intermediate classes, agrarian policies served the interests of their rural counterparts. In the agrarian sector, the government legislation served the rich and upper class peasants and increasingly intervened in the agricultural sector through different public corporations including the newly established Bangladesh Agricultural Development Corporation (BADC).

The most influential laws affecting the agrarian interests during the period under review were the limitation on landholdings at 33.3 acres and the abolition of land revenue on landholdings of up to 8.3 acres. The government issued the Bangladesh Landholding (Limitation) Order of 1972 (Presidential Order 98 of 1972) at the beginning of that year. The order lowered the upper limit of landholdings from 125 to 33.3 acres. Although the regime identified this measure as "land reform," it is interesting to note that the "new" limit set by the government was not new at all. The East Bengal State Acquisition Act of 1950 had imposed this ceiling, but ten years later, during the Ayub era, the upper limit was raised to 375 acres through a proclamation (East Pakistan Ordinance no 15 of 1961). Thus, the new limit on landholdings was essentially a return to the legislation of 1950. In a country like Bangladesh, where anyone owning up to 7.5 acres of land was considered a rich or surplus farmer and only 4.5 percent of the land was in units 25 acres or larger in 1968, it is clear who benefited from such "reform" measures.[25]

Nearly three-fourths of the members of parliament owned more than 10 acres of land. Thus, it was no surprise that both the proposal of the Planning Commission to set the upper limit at 8 acres and the demand of opposition political parties to set the limit at 10 acres were rejected altogether by parliament. Initially, the Landholding Limitation Order departed from the Tenancy Act of 1950 in defining the "family." The definition of family was broadened to prevent people evading the ceiling through transfer of ownership. But, in the face of pressure from the powerful landed interests, the government revised the definition twice within 45 days bringing it back to its former position, which defined family as only a husband and wife (*The Bangladesh Gazette* 1972; *The Bangladesh Gazette* 1972a). Thus, other members of the household including unmarried sons and daughters were considered as separate family.[26]

The second influential measure of the government concerns the system of land revenue and agricultural income tax. The State Acquisition and Tenancy Order (Third Amendment), 1972 (Presidential Order No. 96 of 1972), was promulgated in early 1972. The law exempted landholdings of 8.3 acres or less from payment of land revenue.[27] This brought relief to small peasants. However, the major beneficiary was the middle peasantry because this measure essentially exempted them from paying any income taxes.

In addition to the explicit favoritism manifested in these legal measures, there was a deliberate silence about two crucial and interrelated issues of agriculture: absentee landlords and the tenant's right to land. A govern-

99

ment report of 1981 reveals the extent of absentee landlordism, its relationship with tenant rights, and why these issues remained un-addressed:

> It is estimated that 3.63 lakh acres of land which is 1.74 percent of the total owned land are held by 1.45 lakh absentee families. The lands they own are let out on barga [share cropping]. About 52 percent of the absentee owners are service holders. 30 percent belongs to business and the remaining 18 percent belongs to other occupations. (GPRB 1981:107)

Blair's (1978) study of rural development and bureaucracy also points out that a large number of the members of the civil and military bureaucracy, members of parliament, and the members of political parties either belonged to this section or had close contacts with them.

It is, therefore, clear from the foregoing discussion that the laws related to agrarian issues passed by the regime during the period of 1972-1975 unambiguously promoted the interests of the rural intermediate classes and guaranteed resources and patronage through the heightened role of the state.

The state became involved in agriculture primarily through two means: control and distribution of agricultural inputs such as seeds, fertilizers, etc., and the provision of credit to producers. The government exercised a virtual monopoly over the distribution of agricultural inputs, principally through the Bangladesh Agricultural Development Corporation (BADC), which was responsible for the purchase (mainly in the international market) and distribution of minor irrigation equipment, spare parts, fertilizers, and pesticides. These agricultural inputs were highly subsidized by the government and, hence, could not be marketed privately. Additionally, the government provided agricultural credit through a number of specialized banks. The state practically arrogated the roles of merchant (as the government began to buy rice and jute at fixed prices under its internal procurement policy), moneylender (as the nationalized banks became a significant source of credit), and equipment dealer (as the BADC became the only source of agricultural equipment).

The extent of subsidies on agriculture is evident as one considers that in 1973/74 fertilizers were sold at less than half the cost of procurement or distribution[28] and in 1975/76 the total cost of fertilizer subsidy was as high as Taka 800 million. The annual amount of subsidies to the irrigation program for tubewells and low-lift pumps in 1974/75 amounted to over Taka 710 million (Bangladesh Planning Commission 1975:45-6). The rate of subsidies on other agricultural inputs, according to Islam (1977:201), included about 50 percent for improved seeds and about 100 percent for insecticides and extension services. The subsidies indicate how deeply the state had become involved in the distribution of agricultural supplies. It is important for the purpose of our study, however, to identify the beneficiaries of this subsidy.

The procedures for fertilizer distribution necessitated a middleman between the users and the BADC. The BADC was responsible for procurement, transportation, and storage up to the *thana* (local administrative unit) level, from where licensed dealers (either individuals or cooperatives) could purchase and sell at stipulated prices.[29] Apart from the procedural bias toward the rich and upper peasants that enabled them to maintain control over this basic supply, it gave them ample opportunity to manipulate the market and appropriate the scarcity premium, which was sometimes as high as 100 percent (Rahman 1973). The "small farmer" cooperative program evolved at Comilla during the second decade of Pakistani rule was replicated on the national level under the Integrated Rural Development Program (IRDP)[30] after independence and became the primary vehicle to disburse agricultural inputs and rural credit. Given the importance of this institution, the rural intermediate classes took control of its structures and manipulated it in their favor. A number of studies have shown how large farmers took over the IRDP program from the very beginning and continue to play a leading role. Examples of such studies include those by SIDA/ILO (1974), Abdullah, Hossain, and Nations (1976), Hamid and Rahman (1977), Blair (1978), Jones (1979), Khan (1979), Schendel (1981), and Rahman (1986), to name a few.

Hamid and Rahman (1977) concluded after their evaluation of two IRDP projects in northern Bangladesh that the benefits of the cooperatives largely went into the pockets of large farmers. They write, that "while in Natore and Gaibandha about 30% of cooperative farmers fell under the category of big farmers (having more than five acres of cultivable land of their own), all the executive committee members are surplus farmers" (Hamid and Rahman 1977:2). The picture was the same in the southern part of Bangladesh. Majumdar's (1978) study of a village in southern Bengal shows that 83 percent of the members of the managing committee of a cooperative owned land of 2 acres or more.

Abdullah et al.'s (1976) study of four villages reveals that the members of the IRDP cooperatives owned an average of 4.2 acres of land (whereas non-member households in these villages owned 2.8 acres) and the functionaries (chairmen, managers, model farmers) owned 6.16 acres, on average. As early as 1974, a report by the Planning Commission on the IRDP cooperatives arrived at a similar conclusion: the entire structure seems to become dominated by "...the rural elites...in conspiracy with the urban rich" (Bangladesh Planning Commission 1974).

Another source of agricultural credit was the specialized banks. The system of granting loans on the basis of land security kept the tenants and sharecroppers out of the jurisdiction of banks and placed small farmers at a disadvantage in securing loans. One account of the loans granted to the farmers by the Agricultural Bank shows that 70 percent were provided to farmers with more than 3 acres and about 30 percent went to those with 12.5 acres or more (IBRD 1974a:Appendix II).

The discussion of selected economic policies of the regime presented above shows that urban and rural intermediate classes were the principal beneficiaries of the industrial and agrarian policies of the government. In other words, the intermediate classes of Bangladesh utilized the state as their prized possession. This feature of the Bangladesh economy is very similar to other post-colonial situations where intermediate classes capture state power. This is why Mahmood Mamdani's generalizations about petit-bourgeoisie politics rings true in Bangladesh:

> Given that it is located within the state (state bureaucracy) and outside of it (Kulaks, traders), the petit-bourgeoisie has two alternative methods of accumulation open to it: either use the state to create public property which the petit-bourgeoisie would control indirectly through its control over the state, or use the state to expand private property which the petit-bourgeoisie would control directly through

102

ownership. The former necessitates an ideology that justifies the use of state economic action, of nationalizations. This ideology is socialism stripped of its emphasis on class struggle, robbed of its political (class) content, and put forth as an economic ideology. (Mamdani 1976:313)

In Bangladesh, although a policy of nationalization was pursued and socialism was declared one of the high ideals of the state, private ownership was not precluded.[31] As such, it was not necessary for the intermediate classes to envisage the creation of public property as an alternative to that of private property; rather, they saw them as complementary. Hence, they used the state to create private and public property to accentuate the processes of accumulation. Although the extent and pace of accumulation in the early days of independence resembles a somewhat "primitive accumulation of capital," closer scrutiny reveals that during the period under review the intermediate classes in Bangladesh amassed not capital, but wealth. It was not the productive accumulation of an industrialist but the unproductive riches of a merchant. These riches were not destined to be transformed into means of production, thereby expanding the productive base of the economy; they merely lubricated the export-import economy, at most permitting the creation of small-scale consumer good enterprises, thus encouraging the habit of consuming luxury goods. Quite clearly, this was not the emergence of a bourgeoisie for capitalist development; it was plunder by the intermediate classes in search of a sumptuous life-style.

An extensive use of the state, indeed, benefited them in the short-term, for without employing its authority these classes would not have had the opportunity to grow so fast and the rules of competition for accumulation would not have permitted them to acquire so much wealth. But this had a serious and far-reaching repercussion: the enlargement of the distributive power of the bureaucracy over society. With increasing power at its disposal, the bureaucracy gradually assumed a preeminent position within the power-bloc. That is why, as we will see in the next section, the hard rhetoric and reform measures directed against the bureaucracy in the early days of independence lost steam, and eventually the political apparatus was itself subsumed by the bureaucracy.

The Old State and the New Regime

Following independence, the attitude and actions of the new regime toward the bureaucracy were quite ambivalent. On the one hand, the regime opted for the perpetuation of the existing structure of the state and augmented its role in an unprecedented manner. Hence, conditions for an expansion of the power of bureaucracy enabling it to establish control over all social classes were implemented. On the other hand, rhetoric against the bureaucracy was increased and some constitutional and reform measures to bring the administration under political control were launched. The structural imperatives, nevertheless, subdued the rhetoric and defeated these new measures within a very short time and thus bureaucrats regained their preeminent position. The other factor that facilitated the rise of the bureaucracy was the growing dependence of the state on external assistance in the form of aid. The decline in its relative importance and its subsequent ascent can be described as the crucifixion and resurrection of the bureaucracy.

Extensive control over the policy-making machinery by the bureaucracy, and their "happy marriage" with military regimes during Pakistani colonial domination (1947-1971), made the bureaucracy a much hated word in the political lexicon of Bangladesh. Though a large number of disgruntled Bengali bureaucrats sympathized with the Awami League and personally remained on good terms with Sheikh Mujibur Rahman in the 1960s, the Awami League in its election manifesto of 1970 pledged a radical restructuring of the administrative machinery and to replace the elitist Central Service of Pakistan (CSP) with specialized professional cadres (Awami League 1970).

In the early post-independence period, the crucifixion of the bureaucracy began. Political leaders, including the PM himself, continued the denunciation of bureaucrats in parliamentary debates and public meetings, as well as in meetings with officials. In line with their election pledge and verbal assaults, the AL proceeded to "reorganize the entire system of administration" in order to establish a machinery that could effectively meet the "urgent task of national construction." And, "to give effect to the reorganization of the entire administration," The government introduced a law: The Government of Bangladesh (Service) Order 1972 (i.e., the President's Order No. 9 of 1972).

Contrary to their earlier pronouncements (for example, the Laws Continuance Enforcement Order promulgated by the government-in-exile on April 10, 1971), the order maintained that no person had any claim to employment in the service or any other claim whatsoever against the Government on the basis of having been employed at any time in the service of Pakistan. This order also provided that if, in the opinion of the Government, employees of the state or of any corporation were not required in the interest of the Republic, the Government could remove such persons "without assigning any reason notwithstanding anything contrary contained in any law or in the terms and conditions of the service." The law provided that no legal action could be brought against the Government arising out of or in respect of an act made under the Order.

The President's Order No. 9 was followed by another Order in June 1972, The Government of Bangladesh (Service Screening) Order, 1972 (President's Order No. 67 of 1972).[32] This law established administrative machinery whereby corporations, nationalized enterprises, local authorities, and government-aided institutions would be free from corrupt persons, collaborators, officials, and other employees wedded to the ideology of Pakistan; the law aimed at effectively carrying out the urgent task of national reconstruction. The law was evidently self-contained and excluded the force of any other law, rules, or terms and conditions relating to service which would otherwise give an employee certain protection. The established principles relating to the removal, dismissal, or disciplinary punishment, particularly with regard to government employees, were abolished. The latter law (i.e., P.O. 67), however, provided a procedure (i.e., setting up two Screening Boards) for punishment, including a right to be heard.[33]

These ad-hoc laws challenging the authority of the bureaucracy were followed by concrete and long-standing measures including the appointment of a Planning Commission without bureaucrats in prominent positions, the creation of constitutional provisions that took away their job protection, and the appointment of an Administrative and Services Reorganization Committee (ASRC) headed by the Vice-Chancellor of Dhaka University.

The Planning Commission, as I have mentioned earlier, was headed by academic economists and manned by professionals drawn from various sectors of the economy but only a few from the traditional civil service and bureaucracy. The only key position that was held by a bureaucrat was that of Secretary. The position, however, lost its previous importance, because the commission members maintained close contact with, and enjoyed the confidence of, the Prime Minister. The attitude of the Planning Commission members was quite hostile to the bureaucracy and vice versa. The Planning Commission, in this respect, became the battleground of the old state and the new regime, represented by the bureaucrats and the professionals, respectively. As such, the experience of the Commission is indicative of the eventual winner in the battle. Further details of this experience are presented later in this section and will show that the bureaucrats succeeded in overpowering the professionals.

The constitution, enacted in 1972, not only incorporated the Presidential Orders promulgated as ad-hoc laws (see the Fourth Schedule of the Constitution), but also made a serious break with the past and denied the constitutional protection civil servants had enjoyed under the 1956 and 1962 constitutions of Pakistan.[34] The Bangladesh Constitution stipulated that civil servants "shall hold office during the pleasure of the President" (GPRB 1972b, Article 134) and that "the decision thereon of the authority empowered to dismiss or remove such person or to reduce him in rank shall be final" (GPRB 1972b, Article 135(3)). The principles regulating recruitment and conditions of services, which were incorporated in the 1956 and 1962 constitutions, were also omitted.

The Administrative and Services Reorganization Committee (ASRC) recommended a single, classless grading structure covering all services in ten grades and maintained that the inherited structures of the services were neither adequate nor appropriate for fulfilling the needs of the government (GPRB 1973a:10). It also stipulated that civil servants should be attuned to the hopes and aspirations of the people, and should demonstrate a "firm dedication to democracy and socialism" (GPRB 1973a:10). The main recommendation of the committee was the abolition of the elite cadre: there would be no reservations of posts for any cadre and there would be adequate opportunities for talented persons to quickly rise

106

to the top from any level of the service. Essentially, these recommendations were contrary to existing practice and were aimed at undercutting the power of the bureaucracy, especially the administrative cadres.

While the new regime clearly favored a reduction of bureaucratic power, it met with significant resistance. Bureaucrats either attempted to prevent the regime from implementing policies that would curtail their power and privileges, or they forced changes in the institutional structures where the policies were generated. The first instance of such resistance occurred within two months of independence. On February 1, 1972, the same day the Prime Minister addressed officials at the Bangladesh Secretariat and severely criticized the bureaucrats, 53 senior civil servants were removed on the grounds that civil awards had been conferred on them by the Pakistani military regime during the period of the liberation war (Bangladesh Observer 1972a). But the PM's office faced serious pressure from the other bureaucrats. The principal argument advanced in support of these civil servants was that their removal would demoralize their colleagues and that the reconstruction effort of the Government would be adversely affected. The Government took back some of the officials the next day and all except two were reinstated by the end of the month.[35] The reports of both the ASRC and NPC were "accepted" by the Government. But, in the face of overwhelming pressure from the bureaucracy, no attempt could be made to implement the recommendations. The reports were shelved.

The composition and structure of the Planning Commission in and of itself was disturbing for the established civil bureaucracy. The bureaucrats felt that they had been ostracized by the regime. Hence, from the very beginning there existed a lack of effective cooperation between the Commission and the civil service. As soon as the Planning Commission undertook the task of framing the First Five Year Plan, they ran into further difficulties with the bureaucracy. The administrative elites viewed the Planning Commission as a "supra-bureaucracy" and looked upon them with serious suspicion. The attitude of the Commission expressed in the First Five Year Plan accentuated the conflict. The Commission did not conceal its disdain toward the bureaucracy and maintained that "they [the bureaucrats] can be neither innovators nor catalytic agents for a social change" (GPRB

107

1973a:4). The Commission contended that the latter, by virtue of their training, work habits, and methods, were on the side of the status quo and established traditions. Such harsh criticisms of the bureaucracy fueled their fury and made them more hostile to the Commission, whom they viewed as "outsiders."

The regime's antagonistic attitude toward the bureaucracy was not limited to the civil bureaucracy, but was also directed toward the military bureaucrats. The defense allocation of 1972 and 1973 show that the military under Sheikh Mujibur Rahman did not receive the largesse it was accorded in India and Pakistan. In 1972, the total amount of military expenditure was $29 million. The corresponding figure for 1973 is $15 million. In terms of its share in national wealth (i.e., GNP), defense expenditure constituted 0.9 percent and 0.6 percent, respectively. In terms of its share in total government expenditure, it was 9 percent in 1972/73 and 7 percent in 1973/74.[36] In conjunction with a decreased military budget, the regime practically stopped new recruitment and removed a large number of senior officers. At the beginning of 1975, the whole defense administration amounted to less than 60,000 men (Blair 1978:80). The suppressed discontent of the military personnel is reflected in a statement made in 1973 by Col. Ziaur Rahman. Ziaur Rahman, while commenting on the role of the army in the liberation struggle and their position in post-independence Bangladesh, said "in other countries soldiers have been glorified [even] when they did not fight for a sacred cause as ours did in 1971. But I seek no glorification for our soldiers" (*Weekly Wave* 1973).

The statement, by implication, indicated that the army men were not awarded appropriate treatment befitting their sacrifice and services. At the same time, the government established a parallel paramilitary force named Jatiya Rakkhi Bahini (JRB, National Defense Force). The Bahini—20,000 well-trained and well-equipped soldiers—irked the conventional armed forces and was viewed by the latter as an "alternative army" (see Chapter 3). The plan to increase the strength of the JRB from 20,000 to 130,000 by the year 1980, as opposed to the gradual reduction of the army, and the allocation of a large portion of the defense budget to the JRB, became sources of indignation for the military bureaucrats. To organize a force apparently as powerful as their own beyond the control of the military command was a suspicious move in the eyes of the military bureaucrats, and this was compounded by negligence toward the conventional military. This attempted marginalization of the conventional army did not last long but this initial gesture of the regime illustrates its attitude toward the existing military bureaucrats. The determination to undermine the power of the existing bureaucrats—both civil and military—was the basis of these specific moves.

By 1973, the civil bureaucrats began to pressure the regime in many different ways. In the case of economic planning, not only were they blocking the implementation of policies envisioned by the planners, but they also reopened issues in Cabinet meetings to repeat their point of view whenever they felt neglected by the Planning Commission. The political leadership was caught in the middle, for without the cooperation of the bureaucracy they could not implement policies, while without the intellectuals in the planning machinery, the rhetoric of a "new golden Bengal" would have no concrete policy backing. However, this was an apparent rather than a real dilemma for the regime, because the structural imperatives left unaltered were working in favor of the bureaucrats. Therefore, whether the regime was willing or not, the bureaucrats were bound to reappear in their privileged positions. And, this is precisely what happened by late 1973 in the Planning Commission: "one of the most senior civil servants—a generalist-administrator, who had experience over many years of working in development ministries associated to agriculture—was appointed as a member of the Planning Commission" (Islam 1977:59). The appointment was the culmination of a process wherein considerable pressure was put on the Prime Minister to change the composition of the leadership of the Planning Commission. The new appointee replaced Anisur Rahman, who resigned in November 1973. In the following month, another member of the commission, Mosharraf Hossain, also resigned, tilting the balance of the leadership toward the bureaucrats. The two remaining members, Rehman Sobhan and Nurul Islam, left the Commission on August 11, 1974, and January 11, 1975, respectively.

With the aggravation of economic and political crises in 1973 and thereafter (discussed in chapter 3), the shift toward reliance on the civil bureaucracy and the military accelerated. In the public corporations, a large number of professionals were replaced by bureaucrats. From the middle of 1974, Sheikh Mujib began to rely more on the bureaucrats for advice and implementation of policies. The proclamation of the emergency in December 1974 marked the final shift toward the abdication of political civilian authority. The regime's increasing dependence on bureaucrats and the bureaucratic system of governance continued in subsequent years. The final days of the regime in 1975 can be described as the zenith of the ongoing expansion of executive power and the emasculation of the Parliament. On January 25, 1975, the Constitution was amended to provide for a presidential form of government and a one-party system. The single party authorized to operate in Bangladesh under the amended constitution, the Bangladesh Krishak Sramik Awami League (BAKSAL), was constituted under the leadership of Sheikh Mujib in June 1975. The 115-member Central Committee of the party included 21 senior bureaucrats. Of them, 9 were former CSP officers, 1 a police officer, 4 were top military officers, and 7 were senior members of other services (*Bangladesh Observer* 1975). Though the proponents of the BAKSAL system claim that it gave preeminence to political elements, there is evidence that it instead strengthened the power of the bureaucrats. As a matter of fact, a BAKSAL leader and parliament member complained that the bureaucrats had become "active again" after the introduction of the BAKSAL. "These sycophants," he complained, "are trying to make Bangabandhu (friend of Bengal) an Ayub Khan (military dictator of Pakistan)" (Bangladesh Jatiya Sangsad 1975:168).

The formation of the BAKSAL was followed by a restructuring of the civil administration wherein the existing 19 districts were reorganized into 61 districts and 61 District-Governors were appointed. Of these new Governors, 14 came from the bureaucracy, 9 of them were former CSP officers, 1 was a military officer, and 4 were senior members from other services (GOB 1975:2181-2189). In order to enhance the power of the civil and military bureaucrats, the government declared that along with political representatives, representatives of the army, navy, air force, BDR, and government employees would be included in the local-level (district level) administration (GOB 1975).

The growing bureaucratic preeminence in the later years of the Mujib regime was matched with an increase in expenditure on administration. In 1972/73, Taka 1321 million was spent (2.61 percent of GDP), while in 1974/75 the amount rose to Taka 2462 million, i.e., 4.86 percent of GDP (Bangladesh Planning Commission 1980:31).

The rise of the bureaucrats to their previous powerful positions was predicated by another important factor—growing dependence on external assistance. As we will see in the next section, the Bangladeshi state, forced by internal and external pressures, gradually became dependent upon foreign aid during the period under review. The government had to rely on the civil bureaucrats for aid negotiations, which brought the bureaucrats to the center stage of economic planning and entrenched their power to allocate resources. Their control over, and access to, capital available for "development" essentially made them more powerful than the political regime. Additionally, the injection of external aid ensured the necessary finances for the state machinery and relieved state functionaries from having to depend on indigenous social classes and their political representatives.

The Bangladeshi State and the Global Economic System

Prior to 1971, the external linkages of the region called Bangladesh were always mediated by the Pakistani state. During 1947-1971, its primary role was to supply raw materials to, and serve as the captive market of, Pakistan. Thus, although, Bangladesh was producing cash crops like jute and tea, which had a large international market, its linkage with that international market was indirect and insignificant in terms of its contribution to the domestic economy. Foreign investments were almost non-existent. These conditions, however, do not imply that the country was completely isolated from the global economic system. Instead, its relationship was different from that of other countries, which also experienced an inordinate presence of external capital. The situation in Bangladesh was significantly different because of the presence of two conflicting sets of structural imperatives. First, the post-colonial Bangladeshi state entered into a dependency relationship with core countries because a large resource gap existed, both internally and externally, and because of the class composition of the ruling bloc. Second, the pronounced ideals of the new regime created an obstruction.

111

As I have shown in the previous chapter, colonial style domination by the Pakistani state established and reproduced a social structure that contributed to widespread poverty and underdevelopment in the country. In such circumstances, a huge resource gap was bound to exist, which compelled the peripheral state to depend on external sources for basic needs such as food. As a matter of fact, this condition was prevalent even before independence. In 1959/60, for example, 5.9 percent of the food available in Bangladesh was imported from international markets. Over the years, dependency increased at a progressive rate. In 1969/70, 12.7 percent of available food was imported from external sources. In 1959/60, the share of external resources in GDP was 0.7 percent; for 1969/70 the corresponding figure was 4.2 percent (IBRD 1974). Colonial domination, for understandable reasons, stultified the economy and very little capacity for internal resource generation existed. Thus, when Bangladesh emerged as an independent state, it was "necessary" to turn to external sources, especially for aid.

A reason behind the dependence on external resources was the class composition of the ruling bloc. The intermediate classes gained political prominence and captured the state, aspiring to secure a large share of state resources. The class structure, therefore, was characterized by a high degree of instability inhibiting the potential for capital accumulation. In order to stabilize the situation for capitalist expansion, it was necessary for the core countries to boost the power of the bourgeoisie and the apparatus of the state through a complex network of "aid" operations. Thus, there were enough reasons for Bangladesh, at the onset of its liberation, to be a member of the capitalist global economic system as an aid-dependent, peripheral state.

In contrast to these factors, the pronounced ideals of the ruling alliance posed an obstacle in moving toward integration with the global capitalist system. The alliance of the intermediate classes of Bangladesh, which came to power in 1971, claimed to be socialist.[37] Notwithstanding that this was a populist strategy to win broad support, the attempt to establish greater control over the investment of, and surplus generated by, capital posed an apparent threat to overseas capital and foreign political interests. In such circumstances, foreign interests usually attempt to destabilize or disrupt the economy instead of helping out the regime.

112

Therefore, it is evident that at the outset of independence there were two sets of structural features of the Bangladesh economy acting against each other in order to determine its future relationship with the global capitalist system. The conflict was, however, resolved within a very short time in favor of the forces predicating a closer relationship with the world capitalist system. A number of factors, including the dominance of non-productive, rent-seeking intermediate classes in the polity and the regime; the vested interests of the bureaucracy; and the pressure from core countries to bring Bangladesh into the orbit of dependency aided the process. The processes began with the relief efforts of Western countries as the massive destruction caused by the nine-month war was cited as the justification for asking for help from the international community. In addition to its destructiveness, the war severed the relationship with the former West Pakistan. And, before the conflict, 32 percent of Bangladesh's exports and 35 percent of its imports were exchanged with West Pakistan (IBRD 1974).

War ravaged the country and caused a loss of about $938 million (United Nations 1972:11-14) (for details of damages see Table 4). Subsequently, the country was virtually inundated with relief materials and aid poured in at an unprecedented rate in the very first year of its existence.

In addition to the massive relief operation carried on by the United Nations Relief Operations in Bangladesh (UNROB) until December 31, 1973, there were a number of countries that came forward to help the country avert a famine and begin reconstruction. For example, the United States, which had supported and aided the Pakistani regime in 1971, committed $287 million of reconstruction and relief aid in the first year (Franda 1982:29).

Bangladesh's dependency, however, did not come to an end after the major reconstruction works were completed. Instead, dependency began to grow steadily over the years. In the first six months after independence, a total of $612 million was committed to Bangladesh followed by a commitment of another $886 million in 1972/73 (Sobhan 1982:7).[38] During the first two years, according to government sources, a total of $1,377 million as grants and credits was injected into the country (Bangladesh Observer 1974:1).

113

Table 4.
Estimated War Damages to the Bangladesh Economy
(In million Taka unless specified)

Sector/Assets	Extent of Damage	% of GDP of 1972/73
Agricultural		
Output (mostly food)	2400	5.29
Capital Stock	127	0.28
Fishery	100	0.22
Forestry	33	0.07
Livestock	96	0.21
Industry/Public Sector		
Jute	70	0.15
Cotton Textile	32	0.07
Sugar, foods and allied products	31	0.06
Iron and steel, engineering & Ship building	25	0.05
Paper Board and Forest	23	0.05
Chemical, fertilizer, pharmaceutical, mineral oil and gas	27	0.06
Others	16	0.03
Total Public Sector	224	0.49
Private Sector	68	0.15
Total Industry	292	0.64
Housing	1600	3.53
Communication and Transport	1040	2.29
Others	3912	8.63
Total Damage	9600	21.19
Source: Government of Bangladesh.		

The extensive aid infused into the domestic economy gradually established unbridled control of the donor community over Bangladesh's economy. The dimension of aid dependency can be appreciated from two sets of statistics. The first set concerns the share of aid in GDP and role of aid in financing the gap in trade, investment, and development financing. The second set concerns the pervasiveness of the impact of aid on the Bangladesh economy and society. In 1972/73, aid constituted 9.5 percent of the GDP, financed 75.85 percent of total imports, and amounted to 126.09

Table 5.
The Dimension of Aid Dependence, 1972-1975

	1972/73	1973/74	1974/75
GDP	45,112	50,569	52,282
Aid Disbursed	4289.9	2451.7	4459
Aid as % of GDP	9.5	4.8	8.5
Aid as % of imports	75.85	50.79	69.75
Domestic Savings as % of GDP	1.5	1.5	0.9
Aid as % of investment	126.09	65.57	78.45
Disbursed Aid as % of Development Budget	107.77	120.39	203.38

Notes:
1. GDP at Market Prices of 1972/73 in millions of Taka.
2. Aid Figures in millions of Taka computed at 1972/73 prices using the import index of the World Bank.
3. Imports in market prices of 1972/73. Re al value of imports taken from World Bank data.
4. World Bank estimate.

percent of investments. As for the development budget, it was entirely dependent on external aid. Aid even financed part of the revenue budget. In 1973/74, the share of aid in GDP was 4.8 percent, 50.79 percent of imports, 65.57 percent of investments, and 120.39 percent of the development budget. The corresponding figures for 1974/75 were, 8.5 percent, 69.75 percent, 78.45 percent, and 203.38 percent, respectively (Table 5).

The impact of aid on the Bangladesh economy and society is demonstrated by the following statistics from 1973/74: food aid contributed 10.6 percent of food consumed and commodity aid financed 47.9 percent of raw materials and intermediate goods consumed in the economy. In 1974/75, the share of food aid in total food consumption was 13.7 percent, and commodity aid financed 92.0 percent of import of raw materials and intermediate goods (Table 6). As a matter of fact, all imports of intermediate goods were financed by commodity aid. Among the raw materials, petroleum products were purchased with cash and thus not dependent on aid money.

These statistics reveal that the country became completely dependent upon foreign aid in order to feed its people, to keep the economy

Table 6.
The Contribution of Aid to
the Bangladesh Economy, 1972-1975

A. **The % share of disbursed project aid to development expenditure in the Annual Development Plan in various sector**	1973/74	1974/75
1. Agriculture	3.04	8.75
2. Rural Development	1.56	19.32
3. Water & Flood Control	22.87	15.38
4. Industries	25.81	43.17
5. Power, Scientific Research & Natural Resources	26.42	30.31
6. Transport	38.98	10.61
7. Communications	13.38	21.01
8. Physical Planning and Housing	11.63	0.00
9. Education	7.27	0.00
10. Health	16.94	32.18
11. Population Planning	82.89	64.58
12. Social Welfare	3.79	38.62
13. Manpower and Employment	0.00	27.32
14. Cyclone Reconstruction	7.97	54.46
Total	21.36	24.25
B. **The % share of disbursed food aid to total food availability**	10.6	13.7
C. **The % share of disbursed commodity aid to import of intermediate goods**	47.9	92.0

Source: Sobhan (1982:26).

running, and to implement any development projects. It is nothing new to say that the degree of aid exposure inevitably influences the degree of leverage available to donors and "the influence of donors is inevitably much greater, and the leverage that can be exerted correspondingly more intense, when a country is considered to be unable to function without aid" (Faaland 1981:100). In such circumstances, aid conditionalities are used as a weapon

116

to impose policy changes on the government of the recipient country; Bangladesh was no exception. With the growing dependency on aid, Bangladesh succumbed to pressure from the donors. Two separate events in 1973 and 1974—acceptance of pre-independence debt liabilities by Bangladesh and the agreement to form an aid-consortium—illustrate how aid was used as a coercive instrument. In both cases, Bangladesh was forced to accept aid conditionalities under the threat of withdrawal of development assistance. These, however, constitute only a small segment of the whole story. In both cases, the donors only threatened to withdraw their assistance in the event of failure to comply with their demands. In reality, they did not go that far. In 1973-74, the United States, however, used food aid as an explicit political instrument to teach Bangladesh a good lesson for its "disloyalty." The U.S. decision to suspend its food aid to Bangladesh contributed to the worst famine in Bangladesh in twenty-five years taking the lives of about 100,000 people. The cause of the famine was not only the suspension of the U.S. food aid, which reduced the availability of food, but also problems of distribution, due primarily to the government's decision to provide subsidized food to a politically important section of the population while the poor starved. The events leading to the famine do, however, show the extent of external control over the lives of Bangladeshi population and the survival of the Bangladeshi state.

Acceptance of Pre-independence Debt Liabilities

At the outset of independence, Bangladesh officially took the position that it was in no way responsible for external debts incurred by the Pakistan Government during its period of colonial rule over Bangladesh. The fundamental rationale for the position was (1) Pakistan had not recognized Bangladesh and claimed that Bangladesh was as yet legally a part of Pakistan and, thus, should repay the debt it had incurred for what they were calling "East Pakistan"; (2) external aid liabilities incurred by Pakistan for projects in Bangladesh had been compensated by internal resource transfers from the East to West Pakistan on the export account and heavy imbalance in imports and accumulation of assets in favor of West Pakistan; (3) it would force Pakistan to recognize Bangladesh and negotiate divisions of liabilities and assets between Bangladesh and Pakistan.

The World Bank, on behalf of the donor countries, deplored Bangladesh's position and insisted that Bangladesh accept all the debts incurred for the projects in Bangladesh completed prior to independence as well the on-going projects at the time of independence. Although Pakistan was responsible for the debt and, under the laws of a number of donor countries, could be penalized by cessation of all further external assistance, the Bank persuaded the donors that Bangladesh would agree to accept a share of the debt. The latent tension between the Bank and Bangladesh surfaced in the meeting of the donor countries and Bangladesh held at Dhaka in March 1973 (almost seven months after Bangladesh became the member of the Bank). Bangladesh made it clear that it would rather go without pledges of assistance than accept conditions. Yet, all delegations persisted in announcing conditional pledges, one of which was the acceptance of pre-independence debt liabilities by Bangladesh. The World Bank took a back seat at the meeting, but played a key role behind the scenes in mobilizing leading donors to use the meeting to collectively pressure Bangladesh to accept debt liabilities. Having failed to quell the resistance of the Bangladesh representatives in the meeting, the Bank arranged a meeting with the Prime Minister through its former connections in the bureaucracy. The PM himself also refused to accept any such condition for future development assistance.

By mid-1973, Bangladesh conceded to the pressure and accepted liability for the on-going projects. In order to sign new loans for twenty-three on-going projects, Bangladesh accepted liabilities totaling $151 million for expenditure already incurred on the projects (GPRB 1981a). This, however, was not satisfactory to the World Bank. The pressure continued. With further aid in the subsequent year, Bangladesh had very little strength to resist the pressure. Following recognition by Pakistan in early 1974, Bangladesh found a diplomatic way to retreat. Hence, in 1974, Bangladesh accepted liabilities for $483 million against completed projects visibly located in Bangladesh (GPRB 1981a). The extraordinary act of self-assertion by the country and its leaders fell apart in the face of pressure from the donor countries.

Formation of the Bangladesh Aid Consortium

Early in 1972, it had been proposed by Western donors that an aid consortium for Bangladesh should be organized with the World Bank as coordinator. The arguments in favor of the consortium were (1) the donors should be given a shared perspective of the country's problems and should then effectively seek to find solutions to these problems; (2) a common review of aid operations would prevent duplication of efforts and encourage countries to concentrate on those activities to which they were best suited; and (3) the presence of the consortium and a regular meeting of the forum would stimulate donors to contribute and to maintain their commitments. Undoubtedly, these arguments were valid. But, Bangladesh had seen how Pakistan in the past had become a prisoner of the aid consortium as the donors met annually and found ample reasons to apply pressure for policy changes. Furthermore, it was quite obvious to Bangladesh that the formation of a consortium dominated by Western donors would isolate the nation from its war-time allies such as the USSR. Bangladesh did not want to identify itself with Western donors.

The proposal was advanced sometime in 1972. Bangladesh, pressed by its immediate need, did not reject the idea altogether, but indicated quite clearly that it would prefer bilateral negotiations with the donors. Bangladesh, however, proposed a meeting of the donors in Dhaka. After some initial objections from the World Bank, IMF, and some other donors, the meeting took place in March 1973. Attended by nineteen countries and agencies, this two-day meeting brought the donors and planners of Bangladesh together, but achieved little due to the inflexible attitude of those concerned. Bangladesh maintained its position of not constituting a formal aid consortium, though "it seemed to Bangladesh to be a moot point as to whether more aid, on better terms and in more convenient forms, would be forthcoming if a traditional type consortium were to set up than if it were decided to continue to do without it" (Faaland 1981:111). In subsequent months, the debt issue became the focal point of the discussion between the donor countries and Bangladesh. But, the donors kept up the pressure for an aid consortium.

It was at this stage that the economic report of the World Bank on Bangladesh was published. The draft of the report used what can be described as denigrating language. Moreover, it made sweeping generalizations about the administration and political leadership.[39] In the context of this report, Bangladesh's fear and intransigence about a consortium with the Bank in its leadership increased significantly: "The experience of the Report gave fuel to the fire of suspicion that in any enterprise dominated by the World Bank there would be pressures amounting to little less than attempts to determine the country's economic policies from the outside" (Faaland 1981:117).

But, in the face of economic crises (discussed in Chapter 3)[40] and donor pressure, this intransigent attitude could not endure for a long time. In 1974, deterioration in the domestic economic situation, an unprecedented flood, and a decline in Bangladesh's external purchasing power drained much of the country's vitality. As a result, it became more vulnerable to external pressure. Finally, in July 1974, the government ceded to the pressure of the donors and requested the World Bank to constitute an aid consortium. Faaland (1981) explains that, in addition, "the IMF was approached and asked to give short-term assistance and to send a mission to Bangladesh for consultations. At the same time, major Western donors were also contacted individually and a request for an early meeting of a consortium [was] conveyed to them" (Faaland 1981:118). On request from Bangladesh, two meetings of the consortium were scheduled, one on an emergency basis in August, and another regular meeting in October. The emergency meeting enabled Bangladesh to receive first and second tranches of $37.5 million each from the IMF to counter its immediate problems. At the same time, some major changes in domestic economic policies became obvious. For example, in July 1974, the investment policy (enacted in January 1973) was modified to raise the ceiling on private investments from Taka 2.5 millon to Taka 30 million and relax the restrictions on foreign capital investments.

Following the emergency meeting of the consortium, Bangladesh was "advised" by the Fund to devalue its currency before the general meeting in October. Since Bangladesh refrained from doing so, the country did not receive substantial commitments of assistance. In March 1975, a mission of the Fund visited Bangladesh and an agreement was reached to devalue the exchange rate by 58 percent. The donors underscored the necessity for further changes in economic policy and as a sign of compliance Bangladesh demonetized 100 Taka bills in April 1975, just two months before the consortium meeting.

Food Aid and Famine

Following independence the government of Bangladesh, much to the annoyance of the donors, attempted to pursue a non-aligned foreign policy and work in solidarity with other Third World countries. In 1973, Bangladesh lined up with the Third World countries in international forums in support of a new international economic order despite an oil price hike by OPEC, which caused serious dislocation to its economy. Owing to the grievous consequences of the sudden escalation in oil prices, Western countries, especially the U.S. administration, considered exploiting the dependence of the poorer LDCs such as Bangladesh on U.S. food aid to exercise leverage on OPEC to reduce oil prices.[41] The strategy was, to put it in simple terms, that the poor nations affected by the hike in oil prices would request OPEC members to reduce the price. Bangladesh took the hint. But the government of Bangladesh showed reluctance to join the Western strategy and thus annoyed the United States further. Unfortunately, this was a difficult time for Bangladesh in terms of its reserves of food and foreign exchange.

In the summer of 1973, as Bangladesh was preparing its food budget for 1973/74 (i.e., July 1973 through June 1974), it was estimated that the country would face a food gap of 2.2 million tons even in a "best case" scenario. Bangladesh informed the U.S. government and requested a supply of 300,000 tons of food grains by the end of the year under PL 480, Title I. The United States paid little attention to that request. In desperation, the Bangladesh government requested the USSR to divert 200,000 tons of grains under shipment from its cash purchases in the United States and Canada. The delivery was completed between July and October 1973. It was agreed that Bangladesh would repay the Russian wheat loans out of shipments of PL 480 wheat, which Bangladesh was due to receive toward the end of the year. Bangladesh accordingly requested the United States to agree to this arrangement. No immediate response came from the U.S. sources. In the face of the dubious silence of the U.S. government about making a commitment of new aid or shipping committed aid, Bangladesh went ahead to buy grain on the open market. Meanwhile the price of grain in the open market had increased substantially (from $115 per ton to $199 per ton). This further depleted the meager foreign reserves of Bangladesh. By the beginning of the second quarter of 1974, total foreign reserves had been reduced to $60 million. The amount, in fact, was less than outstanding claims on bills for imports. Essentially, this meant the country went bankrupt. U.S. commercial grain exporters promptly canceled two shipments of grain to Bangladesh in the summer of 1974.

The crisis was further aggravated as the monsoon season began in June 1974. Massive flooding caused serious damage to the crops and a large number of people faced immediate unemployment. With only 56,000 tons of grain in stock, an imminent monsoon, and a derelict foreign reserve, the Bangladesh government came to know in late May that the U.S. government was imposing a food embargo on the country because of its trade relationship with Cuba. Bangladesh was told that the agreement signed with Cuba to sell 4 million jute bags (worth less than $5 million) was prejudicial to the further commitment of PL 480 food aid.[42] Bangladesh repeatedly requested a presidential waiver on humanitarian grounds, but in vain.[43]

Finally, Bangladesh succumbed to the pressure and gave an assurance on July 10 1974 that its trade relationship with Cuba would be severed. The assurance was not enough to make the United States happy. Until the last shipment left Bangladesh in October 1974, the U.S. government remained silent about signing a new commitment. A new agreement was signed on October 4 and the first shipment under the new commitment reached Bangladesh in December, eighteen months after the initial request was made. In the intervening period a severe famine took thousands of lives.[44]

The description of the events leading to Bangladesh's acceptance of pre-independence debt liabilities, conceding to the donor's demand of an aid consortium, and the devastating famine of 1974 reveal that the relationship between the post-colonial Bangladeshi state and the world economic system changed substantially during the period under review (i.e., 1972-75). The regime, encouraged by its nationalistic sentiment and strengthened by its intermediate character, attempted to distance itself from donors' principles and, in some cases, attempted to muster a resistance against the latter's wishes. But, owing to economic crises, primarily because of its inability to generate domestic resources, the Bangladesh regime gradually capitulated to the pressure of the donors and entered into a dependency relationship with the metropolitan countries. By 1975, the Bangladeshi state essentially became a dependent state in terms of its relationship with the world economic system.

NOTES

1   In his speech on April 17, the Prime Minister of the government-in-exile, Tajuddin Ahmed, recognized the fact saying, "we did not want this war" (Chowdhury 1982).

2   On April 10, 1971, the day the Proclamation of Independence was adopted, the government-in-exile issued the Laws Continuance Enforcement Order. According to the Order, all the government officials—civil, military, judicial, and diplomatic—who were willing to take an oath of allegiance to Bangladesh would continue in their office and the terms and conditions of service so long enjoyed by them.

3   For details see Hasan (1986) and Islam (1985). Hasan (1986:146-47) reports that a faction led by Sheikh Fazlul Hoq Moni, nephew of Sheikh Mujibur Rahman and a youth leader, attempted to assassinate Tajuddin Ahmed sometime in October 1971.

4   In late July 1971, the United States attempted to contact the Bangladesh government-in-exile through George Griffin of the U.S. consulate at Calcutta to bring an end to the conflict. A section of AL

leaders under the leadership of Khandaker Mustaque Ahmad, foreign minister of the government, favored such negotiations and established contact, which was later foiled by the pro-independence leaders (for details see Hasan 1986:94-102; Chowdhury 1989:155-170; Kissinger 1979:869-73). It is worth noting that Ahmad became President after the assassination of Sheikh Mujib in 1975.

5   The following description of the conflict within the AL during the liberation struggle is drawn from two sources, Hasan (1986) and Islam (1985). It is worth noting that both Hasan and Islam worked closely with the government-in-exile. Islam, an Awami Leaguer, was the person with whom Tajuddin Ahmed crossed the border. Later, Islam was appointed as the principal aide of the PM of the government-in-exile. Hasan, a close friend of Tajuddin Ahmed, joined him on May 5 and later became the principal emissary of the government in dealing with the Indian counterpart.

6   Sheikh Mujib, incarcerated in a Pakistani prison during the entire war, was released on January 8, 1972 and flew to London the same day. On January 10, he reached Dhaka via Delhi.

7   In order to deal with the state of the bureaucracy in early 1972, we should describe, in brief, its structure during the Pakistan period. In Pakistan, Government services were classified under different categories: Class I, II, III, and IV. According to prestige and privileges, there were gazetted and non-gazetted officers. All the top administrative positions were filled by the Central Superior Servants who were selected by the Central Public Service Commission of the Government of Pakistan. The Central Superior Service was divided into several branches: 1) Civil Service; 2) Foreign Service; 3) Police Service; 4) Taxation Service; 5) Audit and Account Service; 6) Postal Service; 7) Controller of Exports and Imports. Among all these services, the officers belonging to the civil service occupied the most important administrative and executive positions. With

enormous power in their hands they virtually controlled the entire administration. In addition, there was another provincial service known as EPCS (East Pakistan Civil Service) whose members occupied the subordinate and less important positions in the provincial administration.

8   A fourth group emerged in 1973—officials who were stranded in Pakistan during the war. They were repatriated in August and, subsequently, the issue of the stranded Bengali bureaucrats became prominent.

9   Colonel Osmani (Retired), the Commander-in-Chief of the Freedom Fighters, stated the fact quite candidly: "Bengali personnel in the Army might well have stayed neutral had the Pakistani authorities confined their crack-down to selected Bengali politicians. It was the overkill, the systematic 'elitocide' campaign to exterminate the professionals, intellectuals, and army officers, which caused them to revolt" (Singh 1971:22). It is also reported by Patil (1972) that at the request of Sheikh Mujib, Colonel Osmani sent a secret communication to Bengali commanders on March 19, 1971, regarding the political crisis. But, one of the three points Osmani made to them was that they should not get "embroiled in politics." Actually, this was the mood prevalent among the Bengali military personnel. Major Ziaur Rahman, who happened to be the highest ranking military officer to lend his voice to the proclamation of independence on March 27, 1971 over a clandestine radio station in Chittagong, is another example. In early March, he commented on the political situation: "these are political problems and politicians' headaches. We as soldiers have nothing to do. You must keep away" (Islam 1983). As late as March 24, Ziaur Rahman dissuaded his colleagues from making any move against the Pakistani Army stating that there was nothing to worry about (Islam 1983:67). Ziaur Rahman, nonetheless, became a symbol of patriotism in the army because of his involvement with the proclamation of independence. Events

surrounding the proclamation of independence by Major Ziaur Rahman from Chittagong on March 27, 1971, however, remain controversial to date. Ziaur Rahman's followers claim that it is Ziaur Rahman who first declared independence over the radio on March 27. But the organizers of that clandestine radio station assert that the President of the local unit of the AL, Abdul Hannan, proclaimed independence on the afternoon of March 26 after receiving a message from Sheikh Mujibur Rahman. It is assumed that Ziaur did not hear that announcement. He initially declared himself the Acting President and C-in-C of the Bangladesh Liberation Forces. However, he later made another statement wherein he affirmed that he was making the announcement on behalf of the "supreme leader" Sheikh Mujibur Rahman. The AL leaders claimed that Mujibur Rahman sent a message through East Pakistan Rifles' (EPR) wireless in the early hours of March 26 declaring independence. Mujibur Rahman, in his message, called upon the people to resist the Pakistani forces.

10   The total number of members of the Bengal Regiment stationed in East Pakistan in March 1971 was about 3,000. The East Pakistan Rifles, who played the key role in the resistance, had 10,000 members. The latter bore the brunt of the first attack by the Pakistan Army and lost a large number of their members within the first two days (Muhith 1978).

11   The meeting was attended by a number of army officers including Colonel Osmani, Lieutenant Colonel Abdur Rab, Lieutenant Colonel Salehuddin Muhammed Reza, Major Kazi Nuruzzaman, Major Ziaur Rahman, Major Khaled Mosharraf, Major Shafiullah, Major Nurul Islam, Major Shafaat Jamil, and Major Mainul Hossain Chowdhury.

12   A war strategy was devised in this meeting. Bangladesh was divided into 4 sectors: Chittagong, Comilla, Sylhet, and Kushtia. Major

Ziaur Rahman, Major Khaled Mosharraf, Major Shafiullah, and Major Osman Chowdhury were appointed sector commanders respectively. In the July meeting, the territory was reorganized into 11 sectors.

13   For details see the OPS Plan drawn up by Osmani in September 1971, quoted in Hasan (1986:269-275).

14   The term "de-bourgeoisification" is intended to mean the condition wherein the regime thwarted the flourishing of the indigenous bourgeoisie.

15   Private Pakistani citizens left 725 industrial enterprises with assets worth Taka 2885.7 million. These companies controlled 47 percent of Bangladesh's modern industrial assets and 71 percent of its private industry. They relinquished six of the leading commercial banks which controlled 70 percent of the deposits of the entire banking system in the region and also the insurance companies that constituted 90 percent of the assets of insurance business.

16   The committee consisted of the ministers for Industries, Finance, Commerce, Law, and the Deputy Chairman and Member (Industries) of the Planning Commission. The decision to nationalize all industries was not unanimous. The Commerce Minister opposed the recommendation. He argued for the nationalization of only abandoned industries.

17   These two lines of arguments are not mutually exclusive and analysts do not cancel out one in favor of the other. Sobhan and Ahmad (1980), Islam (1977), and Akash (1987), for example, maintain that both circumstantial necessity and the ideological commitment of the AL were factors in the nationalization program. Akash (1987), however, emphasized the ideological aspects, while Khan and Hossain (1989) find nothing in the history of the Awami League to suggest that the party was implementing socialism and

127

that nationalization was a step toward that end. A radical interpretation, advanced by Umar (1980), suggests that nationalization was a sinister move of the AL to discredit socialism and pave the way for the development of a comprador bourgeoisie.

18   By 1972, there were 20 private industrial enterprises owned by foreign companies: 16 of them were pharmaceutical companies, while four others include the Bangladesh Tobacco Company, Lever Brothers, Bangladesh Oxygen, and Pakistan Fibers. There were two branches of foreign-owned banks (which accounted for 8.41 percent of deposits at the time of nationalization) and 33 tea-estates were owned by the British. None of these were nationalized. As a matter of fact, Bengali private enterprise in the tea industry, though quite significant, was also spared from nationalization. According to Bangladesh Tea Board estimates, after March 1972, about 27.25 percent of the acreage of tea-estates was under the control of Bangladesh nationals. They accounted for about 19.4 percent of the output.

19   The context of the electoral pledge for nationalization of heavy and/or basic industries by the Awami League in 1970 was completely different from that which they encountered in post-liberation Bangladesh. Heavy industries such as iron and steel, fertilizers, heavy chemicals, paper, were already under public ownership before the emergence of Bangladesh. The jute, textile, and sugar industries in pre-independent Bangladesh were owned and controlled by Pakistani industrialists and, thus, Bengalis had very little control over these sectors, though the raw materials were coming from Bangladesh. As such, it was perceived that nationalization of these sectors would provide the Bengalis with an opportunity to share the profit and give the growers their due share. The situation drastically changed with liberation, yet the electoral pledges before liberation was carried over into post-liberation Bangladesh.

20   There was, however, another provision that empowered the government to nationalize any unit any time in case of mismanagement or under-utilization.

21   All acts of foreign collaboration, according to the policy, were to be approved by a committee called the Investment Board. The Board was chaired by the minister of industries.

22   Sobhan and Ahmad, members of the Planning Commission, eloquently described the intention of the nationalization policy: "The nationalisation decisions of March 26, 1972 were intended to extend the role of the state sector and thereby limit the possibility of the upper bourgeoisie of Bangladesh from consolidating and expanding their position in the social hierarchy of Bangladesh" (Sobhan and Ahmad 1980:191).

23   Nurul Islam, another member of the Planning Commission, wrote, "the basic rationale behind the ceiling was that private industrialists were not to be allowed to grow into big capitalists through the expansion of the existing enterprises either by reinvestment of profits or by means of external financing" (Islam 1977:220).

24   From the very beginning, the ministry of industries was opposed to the idea of imposing a ceiling on private enterprises and was interested in reviving the private sector. In the second half of 1972, the ministry took published an industrial investment schedule. But the Industry Division of the Planning Commission foiled the move and presented a policy paper to the cabinet outlining the investment policy. They again made a move in late 1973 in favor of private enterprise and became the representatives of a revision of investment policies. The minister of industries suggested removing the ceiling altogether in a cabinet meeting held on March 3, 1974 (The minutes of the Cabinet meeting, March 3, 1974). According to Islam, "in the rank and file of the ruling party and amongst its lead-

ers...there was no unanimity and no firm commitment to the extension of public ownership or the ultimate goal of socialism. On the one hand, the conservative elements in the party consisting of trading classes, the aspiring industrialists and the ex-owners of the nationalized enterprises were all pressing for a revision of the policy. On the other hand, the radical wing of the party, consisting of the militant factions of the students and trade unions, were pulling in the direction of a further extension of public ownership. The Prime Minister stood in the middle of the contending forces" (Islam 1979:247).

25   The government maintained that one of the reasons for the reform was to recover land and distribute it among landless laborers. This was one of the pre-election pledges of the ruling party. However, since the limit was set too high, the government failed to acquire additional land for distributing among the landless. According to Siddiqui's (1981:68) estimate, the maximum amount of recoverable land would have been 0.4 million acres. By the end of 1973, the government announced that only 900 acres had been redistributed as a result of the reform (Blair 1978:70-71). The government accounts of 1976 show that they have succeeded in identifying 58,409 acres of land that could be brought under government control. Until then only 31,250 acres of land were actually acquired by the government (Siddiqui 1981:68). Whereas it was estimated by Zaman (1975:108) that an eight acre limit, suggested by a number of opposition political parties at that time, would have enabled the government to recover 2.63 million acres of land.

26   After that, the government did not attempt any changes to laws regarding land ownership. The Land Revenue Committee headed by M. A. Taher, appointed in 1972, recommended that there be no interference with the existing laws of inheritance (GPRB 1972:20). Another Land Revenue Committee headed by K.M.M. Mosharraf Hossain appointed in July 1974 which finalized its report in April

1975 concurred with the earlier recommendation (GPRB 1975).

27   Previously, agricultural income tax collection was postponed for two years from 1973/74 on the grounds that agricultural production suffered from dislocation during and immediately after the liberation war. While land revenue was abolished, a number of taxes or fees such as development and relief tax, education tax, and local tax were levied.

28   In 1973/74, the cost of Urea fertilizer per maund (about 80 pounds), for example, was Taka 40.77 and the sale price was Taka 30.00. The cost of TSP fertilizer was Taka 56.16 and the sale price was Taka 20.00 and the MP fertilizer was sold at the rate of Taka 15.00 while the cost was Taka 42.56. In the following year, the sale price increased marginally whereas the cost increased substantially. The cost of Urea was Taka 58.00, sale price Taka 40.00; TSP cost—Taka 115.00, sale—Taka 30.00; MP cost—Taka 70.00, sale price—Taka 20.00 (Bangladesh Planning Commission 1975:52-54).

29   The steps involved in obtaining a license were time-consuming and cumbersome. A person intending to acquire a license was required to apply to the Thana Inspector of the BADC with the documentation including a certificate from the Union Parishad Chairman as well as a trade certificate. On the basis of the Thana Inspector's recommendations, the application would be placed before the Agricultural Development Committee (ADC) headed by the Thana Circle Officer (Development). After attaining the committee's approval, it was to be forwarded to the sub-divisional level Manager of BADC who was the final issuing authority. Without having good connections with the authorities involved, and ample time to spend for this purpose it was impossible to obtain a license. Both of these factors hampered the success of primary producers.

30   The essential structure of this program consists of: a) the primary cooperatives (KSS) located within the villages and organized by the farmers themselves; b) the primary cooperatives which are federated at the Thana level (TCCA). TCCA coordinates the credit procurement form the apex and distributes it among the village cooperatives. In 1972 the number TCCAs was 33 and the number of KSSs was 5630. The number of cooperatives increased dramatically over the years. In 1973, the numbers were 87 and 10,171; in 1974, 152 and 14,690, and in 1975, 161 and 17,691 for TCCAs and KSSs respectively.

31   The Bangladesh Constitution of 1972 permitted three forms of ownership: state ownership, cooperative ownership, private ownership (*The Constitution of Bangladesh*, Articles 10, 13, 14, 15, 19 and 20).

32   The law was later amended under The Government of Bangladesh (Service Screening) (Amendment) Order of 1972, President's Order No. 92 of 1972.

33   Superficially, it seemed that these orders were promulgated to reorganize the administration. One could also say that given the extraordinary situation after the war, such moves were justified as temporary arrangements. But, significantly, there was no reorganization in sight, while the law took its own course. A large number of cases containing allegations of corruption were handled by the screening boards and a sizeable number of employees were punished under the law on charges of corruption. Whether or not all of them were just is difficult to determine. But, it is indeed true that these laws, particularly P.O. No. 9, were used against the political opponents of the regime and to resolve petty conflicts among government employees. An example of such use is the removal of 24 bus conductors of the Bangladesh Road Transport Corporation, the state controlled corporation for public transport. The most significant impact of these laws was not the *actual* removal or

punishment, but the *fear* of being removed from services and the social humiliation associated with such removal.

34   See Articles 179-183 of the Constitution of the Islamic Republic of Pakistan, 1956 and Articles 174-179 of the Constitution of the Islamic Republic of Pakistan, 1962.

35   Failure to remove top-level bureaucrats, however, did not stop the regime from their anti-bureaucracy posture, only that lower cadres of the government service became the victims. Maniruzzaman (1982:140, fn. 14) reports that from July to November 1974, about 300 of them were removed.

36   Computed from *World Military Expenditures and Arms Transfers. 1969-1978* (US Arms Control and Disarmament Agency, 1980). According to another account, defense expenditures in 1973 ($U.S. at 1980 prices) was 55.8 million (0.5 percent of GDP) and in 1974, 65.5 million (0.6 percent of GDP) (Kukreja 1991:135).

37   Similar situations can be found in Africa and Latin America. For a general discussion on this trend see Mafeje (1977).

38   Compared to 1969/70, the peak of aid disbursement in the region after 1947, the amount was astounding. In 1969/70, $320 million was disbursed in the then-East Pakistan (IBRD 1974).

39   Two sentences from the draft report of the Bank, commonly referred to as the "Green Cover Report," illustrate the Bank's attitude: "New men had access to political power for the first time with little conception of how to use it for purposes other than self-aggrandizement...The example is set at the political level where scarcely a foreign exchange transaction takes place, either on import or export, without some funds being deposited in the foreign bank account of a politician, businessman or well-connected private individual."

40   The economic crises of 1974 are due to both domestic and external factors. In 1973, the Bangladesh economy faced a major shock because of price hikes in oil and food grains in the international market. Bangladesh's import cost went up dramatically. The import price index rose 53 percent in 1973/74 and 115 percent in two years by 1973/75. While export prices improved by 33 percent in 1974/75, there was a sharp deterioration in the terms of trade, which deteriorated by 32.1 percent.

41   This was not an exceptional situation. According to Hopkins (1977), the United States used food as political weapon to enlist India's support in Vietnam, to squeeze textile trade restraints from the Koreans, and to punish Jamaicans for raising prices. If one considers the broad policy of food aid, these events are very much consistent with that.

42   The PL 480, as amended in 1966, disqualified any country that exported (sold or furnished commodities) to Cuba or North Vietnam, or allowed vessels under its registry to call at the ports of these countries, from receiving assistance under this act. The law permitted only limited exceptions to its stipulated provisions, but a presidential waiver might be made in respect of sales of non-strategic agricultural commodities and non-strategic raw materials for agriculture or medical supplies, provided the waiver was in the national interest of the United States.

43   Egypt, however, was granted such a waiver at the very same time. Although Egypt was trading with Cuba and exporting raw cotton, the United States signed an agreement with Egypt where Egypt would purchase 4000 tons of tobacco from the United States under PL 480 Title 1 on June 7, 1974. Another agreement was signed on September 12, 1974, allowing Egypt to buy 100,000 tons of wheat under PL 480 (Morgan 1974).

44   A number of authors have discussed the relationship between the U.S. food embargo and the famine of 1974 in Bangladesh. McHenry and Bird (1977) first revealed that the U.S. government deliberately withheld food while a severe famine was taking its toll. Rehman Sobhan, who happened to be a member of the Planning Commission at that time, wrote an illuminating article based on unpublished minutes of relevant meetings between representatives of the governments of the U.S. and Bangladesh and internal memos of the Government of Bangladesh and provided a detailed account of the events (Sobhan 1980). Molla (1990) also focuses on the issue. All three authors emphasize the role of the U.S. embargo, though they recognize that the distribution system of the government had a role in this disaster. Choudhry (1986) and Ben Crow (1987) feel that it is the domestic policies of the government and structural bias toward the urban rich that should be blamed instead.

Chapter 3

The Crises Unfold

At the moment of triumph over an oppressive colonial power, the granting of authority to liberators is very broadly based and essentially unquestioned—one might even say unexamined. But, it does not take much time or much of a change in circumstances to erode this authority. Often, the erosion of authority occurs quite easily because of the problems inherent in the structure of post-colonial societies. Additionally, the conjunctural factors, which vary according to the historical background and concrete circumstances of a given society, serve as the sources of crises that lead to an attenuation of power of the ruling class. This largely favors the civilian bureaucracy but, at times, can favor of the coercive apparatus. The speed at which this process unfolds, and the degree of its development, will depend on the nature and magnitude of these crises as well as the capabilities of the ruling classes to deal with them.

In this chapter, I will discuss the crises faced by the ruling alliance in post-colonial Bangladesh. The crises were both political and economic. They include the rupture of ideological hegemony established during the anti-colonial struggle, the crisis of governability, the feuds and cleavages within the ruling party, the political opposition they faced from contending political forces, and the failings of economic policies to generate the surpluses necessary to maintain the dominant mode of production.

Rupture of Hegemony

The principal tool of the intermediate classes for establishing ideological hegemony over other social classes during the Pakistani colonial era was Bengali nationalism—a shared identity as Bengalis, as opposed to a Pakistani identity. The development of this oneness cutting across barriers of interests and social backgrounds, or in other words, the growth of a common sense of identity, was not automatic. The rise of nationalism, in Bangladesh as elsewhere, was accomplished through a process of selection, standardization, and transmission of specific symbols from a vast pool (Cohn 1967). As I have shown in Chapter 1, the objective conditions prevalent in society made it possible for a given class to manipulate the symbols to their advantage. Success was not only dependent upon the capabilities of the given class to manipulate the symbols and objective conditions, but it

137

was also dependent upon the failure of the other contending social classes to do so. Nevertheless, the willingness of the subjects of this hegemonic order to identify with particular symbols and share a common identity was contingent upon whether or not the common identity held positive prospects for their own well-being. Thus, the hegemony of the intermediate classes during the colonial period was a fractured compromise among the social classes opposed to colonial exploitation. The discourse of Bengali nationalism subsumed all other discourses, including that of class exploitation, and a "unity" among the social classes was achieved through consensus. Unity, identity, and consensus were based on the objective conditions of colonial rule and were mapped out against the colonial rulers.

But the passing of colonial rule, especially the war of liberation, changed the objective conditions altogether. The "enemy" against whom nationalism was pitted disappeared. Post-colonial society required the fashioning of a new social order. The emergent arrangements threatened the very basis of social hierarchy created during colonial rule. This created a tension that inevitably undermined the so-called national cohesion. Unity was replaced with class conflict. This conflict occurred not only between the ruling class and the subaltern classes, but also involved conflict among members of the ruling class. Thus, the relevance of nationalism as the hegemonic ideology was lost and the hegemony of the intermediate classes was ruptured. The increased popularity of an alternative ideology proved as much.

The Awami League declared that the objective of the regime was to establish an exploitation-free, just society and, hence, socialism was included in the constitution as one of the ideals of the state. But their concept of socialism was challenged by the radical elements of the party as well as by small leftist parties. At independence, the radical fraction of the AL, mostly students and youth, contended that the liberation struggle was an unfinished revolution and called for the establishment of "scientific socialism" under the leadership of Sheikh Mujibur Rahman.[1]

But, disenchanted with Sheikh Mujib and the party, the radical members of the AL left in April 1972. The student leaders who played a significant role in the liberation struggle initiated the split and their lead was soon followed by the peasants' wing (May, 1972) and the workers' wing (June, 1972). Finally, these splinter groups launched their own party—the Jatiyo Samajtantrik Dal (JSD, National Socialist Party) in October 1972. Within a brief period of time, the JSD not only captured the attention of the public but also became so popular that its leaders were compared with Sheikh Mujib who was still called *Bangabandhu* (the friend of Bengal). Significantly, these leaders not only broke away from the ruling party but also took a position that was ideologically opposed to that of the ruling class. They insisted that the socialist transformation of society could be achieved only through a revolution of the proletariat class. Furthermore, they maintained that the (nascent) bourgeoisie of Bangladesh had captured state power and were perpetuating the exploitative social structure; they also maintained that a revolutionary uprising of the proletariat was the only way to make independence meaningful to the oppressed classes. In spite of incoherence and inconsistencies in their ideological positions, they demonstrated that the principal contradiction in independent Bangladesh was between social classes and that one's identity stemmed from one's class affiliation.

Around the same time, another clandestine radical left political group, the *Sorbohara Party* (SP, Proletariat Party), under the leadership of Siraj Sikdar, gained considerable support in rural areas. The SP, in one of their pamphlets, characterized the AL regime as a puppet of the Soviet social imperialists and Indian expansionists. The *Sorbohara Party* engaged in armed conflict with the police and other paramilitary forces and began to annihilate the "enemies of the revolution"—the rich farmers. On most matters, these two new parties were pursuing different paths. But their rise clearly indicated that the ruling classes' hegemony over the subaltern classes was ruptured. The ruling classes did not fully dictate or control the political discourse. As opposed to the "consensual politics" of the ruling classes, the politics of "class conflict" gradually occupied center stage.[2] The rupture of the hegemony of the ruling classes was accentuated by the internal feud within the ruling party.

Internal Feuds

The cleavages prevalent within the ruling Awami League were intensified after independence. Although the presence and charisma of Sheikh Mujib succeeded in containing open conflict among these groups, it could not resolve the differences. The departure of the most radical faction of the party in May-June 1972 did not bring an end to factionalism within. Instead, ideological conflict, as well as acute personal rivalries, factional struggles, and regionalism plagued the party. Members of different ideological convictions began to push for implementation of their policies. They could not reach a consensus. Their differences regarding the introduction of socialism provide an example of the ideological divergences prevalent in the party.

In accordance with the spirit of the liberation struggle, the Awami League regime declared the high ideals of nationalism, socialism, democracy, and secularism would constitute the fundamental principles of the constitution. But there was no consensus among different sections of the party regarding these fundamental principles and how they would be implemented.

The differences between various factions began to surface in June 1971, during the height of the war. The government-in-exile appointed a research cell to prepare a position paper on the problems necessarily confronting the government after independence. The cell was wrecked by these differences and thus failed to make any substantial contribution. The final document was a statement with conflicting propositions. The section that deals with the political situation after independence aptly reflects the divergence: "AL was committed to constitutional politics. It was committed to socialism to the extent which would be achieved only through reforms and legislation, keeping the overall economic system a capitalistic one" (Ahmed 1984:273). Thus, one can validly ask "how can a country achieve socialism while keeping *the overall system* a capitalist one?" No one in the ruling party knew the answer.

The differences that produced such a self-contradictory document resurfaced in independent Bangladesh. The left-of-center faction led by Tajuddin Ahmed was in favor of introducing a socialist strategy of economic transformation, while the right-of-center faction led by Khandaker Mushtaq opposed such measures. Nurul Islam, then a member of the Planning Commission, acknowledged the existence of such conflicts within the regime:

The lack of consensus as to the nature of the socialist economy which Bangladesh should establish in the transitional phase as well as in the long run was not thus a matter of differences between the ruling party and the opposition parties; there existed differences of opinion between the factions of the ruling party and among the members of Parliament as well as of the cabinet. (Islam 1977:27-28)

It was not only the ideological differences that divided the party into different factions, but also the acute personal rivalry and jockeying for power. The younger leaders of the party, Sheikh Fazlul Hoq Moni (a nephew of Sheikh Mujib and the President of the party youth front), Tofail Ahmed (Political Secretary of the Prime Minister), Abdur Razzak (Organizing Secretary of the AL), and Abdul Mannan (General Secretary of the party labor front), led contending groups and became involved themselves in confrontation. They established firm control over three front organizations of the party—student, youth and labor—and created different private forces. In 1973, the contending groups threatened to launch *Suddhi Avijan* (a purification campaign) primarily to eliminate the other factions. At one point in the conflict, Sheikh Moni declared that his organization had no connection with the AL and was loyal only to Sheikh Mujib (Moni 1973:5). In the parliamentary elections of 1973, at least 40 AL members defied the party and contested the elections as independent candidates (*Morning News* 1973:1).

In the face of growing factionalism, the party council had to be postponed several times. The possibility of an open split was averted by retaining Sheikh Mujib as President and surrendering the powers of the council to select office bearers to the president. This measure lacked legitimacy, even in the eyes of the party followers because the party constitution barred any person from simultaneously holding the position of party President and the Leader of the House.

What made the situation worse was the rampant corruption of AL leaders. In late 1972, a number of AL members, including 43 Members of the Constituent Assembly, were expelled from the party (*Dainik Bangla* 1973a:1). But this measure was negligible considering the extent of the involvement of the AL leaders in corruption. Many were receiving patronage and support from the high-ranking party officials and thus were beyond control.

While the cohesion of the party was declining, opposition to the regime was growing.

Political Opposition

The first open political challenge to the ruling party came from a dissident faction who later formed the JSD in October 1972. Other leftist forces also began to gain support from the public and by the end of the year a seven-party electoral alliance (All Party Action Committee, APAC) was formed under the leadership of Moulana Bhasani, a populist octogenarian leader and the President of the National Awami Party, to contest the upcoming parliamentary elections (*Dainik Bangla* 1972).

On January 1, 1973, two student supporters of the National Awami Party (NAP, led by Muzaffar Ahmed, a pro-Moscow leftist political party and a close ally of the ruling AL) were shot and killed by police during a procession against the Vietnam War and U.S. aggression. Initially, the NAP and the Communist Party of Bangladesh (CPB, the pro-Moscow communist party and close ally of the AL) took a stand against the ruling party and a wave of demonstrations including a spontaneous successful general strike rocked the cities.

The supporters of the ruling party took this opportunity to clamp down upon the opposition with lightening speed and in an organized manner. The offices of NAP-M and JSD were attacked, ransacked, and burned; the dais of a public meeting of the APAC was destroyed and respected leaders like Ataur Rahman Khan physically attacked. During counter demonstrations speakers claimed the protests were organized to "foil the conspiracy" of foreign powers including China and the United States and their agents in Bangladesh against the sovereignty of Bangladesh. Although the NAP-M and the CPB finally capitulated, the events made it clear that popular opposition against the regime was on the rise.

Some of the opposition parties (e.g., NAP and CPB) overestimated the popular discontent and went too far, while others (e.g., JSD, NAP-B) cautiously took a back seat to see whether the allies of AL were serious in

142

breaking away from their friends. Nevertheless, the events of the first week of January 1973 also revealed how brutal and ruthless the ruling party could be in countering opposition. A comment of Sheikh Mujib himself is enough to illustrate it. On January 4, 1973, while addressing a public gathering organized by the student wing of the AL, he said, "If I wish, *I can finish* these anti-social elements without police and *Rakkhi Bahini*. With the cooperation of the people *I can finish* them within five hours" (*Gonokantha* 1973:1).

It was against this backdrop that the first parliamentary elections were held on March 7, 1973. A total of 1078 candidates contested 288 seats.[3] Of them, 958 were nominated by 14 parties, including the AL, and the remaining 120 were independent candidates. The ruling party secured a landslide victory (292 seats, 72.4 percent of votes cast). Though the elections were rigged and results manipulated, the opposition parties failed to organize a united movement against the ruling party. But the discontent of the masses increased and pressure from opposition political forces intensified.

The progressive alienation of the ruling party from the student community was reflected in the student union elections held in the latter part of 1973. Student organizations generally represented the political parties on campuses. The student community, considered the most sensitive and progressive section of the populace, rallied with the AL in pre-independence Bangladesh and played a key role in the independence war. However, by 1973 the student front of the ruling party had lost almost all student union elections. The most embarrassing moment for the ruling party came on September 3, 1972, when its student front and allies faced a humiliating defeat in the Dhaka University Central Students Union Election (DUCSU). Although armed miscreants seized the ballot boxes before the final results were declared, it was obvious from preliminary results that the student front of the JSD had taken a more-than-comfortable lead.

Boosted by the election results of the DUCSU, the JSD began to organize demonstrations and mass agitations against the regime. After a successful general strike in February, the JSD adopted a drastic program of mass upsurge beginning with *gheraos*[4] of several important government offices. On March 17, 1974, the JSD organized a massive public meeting and marched toward the Home Minister's residence. The police and paramilitary forces confronted them. Indiscriminate firings not only resulted in the killing of at least six people, but it also led to the arrests of the top-ranking JSD leaders including its President and General Secretary. It was followed by an offensive by the ruling party and massive repression of JSD workers all over the country. The entire organizational network of the JSD was shattered and they were driven underground. Following the incident of March 17, the JSD changed its strategy and decided to launch an armed struggle against the regime. They raised their own armed group *Gonobahini* (People's Force) within a short time. Six other opposition political parties formed the United Front (UF) in April 1974 under the leadership of Maulana Bhasani and decided to launch a mass movement in July. The government made a preemptive move, arrested the leaders of the Front, and suppressed the ensuing movement. In subsequent months, the political opposition to the regime was transformed into one of violent armed conflict.

Opposition did not come from the political parties only, but also from military and freedom fighters. As mentioned in chapter 2, during the war a section of the military vehemently opposed the war strategy pursued by the government-in-exile and the conventional army. They insisted that the new army of Bangladesh should be more integrated with the people. Differences over the war strategy took a new form in post-independence Bangladesh. At the command level, Taher and Ziauddin actively opposed measures to restore and rebuild the army in accordance with the traditional concepts, practices, and colonial pattern of a conventional army. They argued that a conventional army either becomes an economic burden to the nation or compromises national independence in order to obtain foreign assistance and imperialist loans for their sustenance (Lifschultz 1979:38). Both Taher and Ziauddin ultimately lost the debate and had to leave the army; but their stance made a long-lasting impression on other members of the army.

The opposition from the freedom fighters (FF) who did not belong to the organized conventional army took a similar shape. After the liberation of Bangladesh, and before the arrival of Sheikh Mujib, the Prime Minister Tajuddin Ahmed drew a plan to incorporate both the members of the conventional army and the freedom fighters raised during the war into a "National Militia." This force, though trained to be the future defense force of Bangladesh, was also to serve as agents for the reconstruction of the war-ravaged country.[5] The plan was to bring all freedom fighters together, gradually disarm them and provide them with jobs for national reconstruction and development. Accordingly, an eleven-member "Central Board of National Militia" with the PM as Chairperson was constituted on January 2, 1972. It included leaders of other political parties including Moulana Bhasani. But after the arrival and assumption of power by Sheikh Mujib, the primary concern of the regime was to disarm the freedom fighters without delay. Sheikh Mujib ordered all freedom fighters to surrender their arms within ten days from January 17, 1972. However, he mentioned that a national militia would be set up (*Morning News* 1972:1). Within two weeks of the announcement a large number of freedom fighters laid down their arms through two ceremonies—one in Tangail and another in Dhaka. But many freedom fighters were disappointed to see that they were being disarmed while members of different forces, collaborating with the occupation forces, still possessed illegal arms. They suspected—with some justification—that they were being disarmed without being incorporated into any program that would enable them to contribute to the reconstruction and development of the country. These disgruntled freedom fighters refrained from surrendering arms and later joined the radical opposition parties including the JSD. Having failed to convince the freedom fighters to surrender their arms, the government banned the *Mukti Fouz* (Freedom Fighters) and all other *Bahinis* (Forces) including *Mujib Bahini* on February 24 and 27, respectively (*Morning News* 1972a:1).

Crisis of Governability

History demonstrates that major revolutions are often followed by varying combinations of civil war, political turmoil, and general chaos. The civil war after the Bolshevik revolution, the political turmoil after the Chinese revolution, and the chaos and disorder that followed the Iranian revolution are illustrative in this regard. Although the nature of the liberation war of Bangladesh was different from these other revolutions, the country suffered similar effects, such as the easy availability of firearms and absence of the so-called civil administration, which materially hindered the restoration of peace and order. The situation was worse in Bangladesh because of the absence of a single command over the freedom fighters and the presence of armed forces that were in collaboration with the Pakistani occupation forces. Although the government-in-exile provided leadership during the war, they did not have total control over the guerillas that had fought against the occupation forces. In fact, resistance forces evolved spontaneously all over the country. Most of them were neither organized hierarchically nor had any command structure. As a result, no one was sure about the total number of freedom fighters and the quantity of firearms under their control.

Furthermore, during the war a number of armed paramilitary forces (e.g., Razakars, totaling about 10,000) were organized by the Pakistani occupation forces. The occupation forces also supplied arms to members of the right-wing political party, Jamaat-i-Islami, which organized at least two politically motivated forces—*Al-Shams* and *Al-Badr*. The latter were the most ruthless and killed at least 50 intellectuals in planned attacks during the last three days of the war (i.e., 14-16 December, 1971).

While hundreds and thousands of people possessed all sorts of firearms—unlisted, unregistered, unknown, and unaccountable—the so-called law enforcement agencies such as the Police and the Bangladesh Rifles were in complete disarray. The situation was complicated because of the government's unwillingness to involve freedom fighters in post-independence reconstruction measures. In the adverse political situation a number of the freedom fighters became involved in antisocial activities. The armed members of underground, leftist political parties, though small in number, also became a threat to the restoration of peace.

It was against this background that the new government took office. In the initial stages they achieved commendable success in establishing control. Though large numbers of firearms remained in the hands of people with contending ideological convictions, or people with no political convictions at all, the government restored control over all parts of the country. The presence of the Indian defense forces helped them a great deal,[6] but it was the ruling party and the feeble civil service who ran the day-to-day administration. The government also succeeded in containing any possibility of civil war. There is no doubt that without the support of people from all walks of life, it would have been impossible for the fragile government to restore order.

However, the situation began to change dramatically. Law and order began to deteriorate in an unprecedented manner. According to figures presented by the Home Minister to the parliament, in the first sixteen months (i.e., January 1972-April 1973) 4925 persons were killed by miscreants, 2035 secret killings of a political nature took place, 337 women were kidnapped and 190 were raped (Morning News 1973:1).

According to a newspaper report, 23 police stations and outposts had been attacked by "anti-social elements" between January 1972 and July 1973 (Morning News 1973a:8). The number of attacks on police stations increased substantially over subsequent months. In October 1973 alone, 11 police stations and sub-stations were attacked and looted (*Daily Ittefaq* 1973:6).

The incidence of political murders also increased significantly. In February 1973, 20 Awami League workers were killed (*Daily Ittefaq* 1973a:12). On November 5 1973, a daily newspaper reported that in the first twenty months after independence more than 6,000 political murders had been committed (*Morning News* 1973b). The AL claimed that five of its MPs and 20,000 supporters were killed by "extremists." Sheikh Mujib, in a televised speech to the nation on December 16 1974, admitted that four of his MPs and 3000 AL supporters were killed. The opposition claimed that 60,000 activists had been killed in the previous two years. There is no way to evaluate the charges and counter-charges of the Awami League and the opposition as to who was responsible for the violence. While the government-controlled mass media carried accounts of opposition violence and killings of AL supporters, the only opposition daily and almost all the weeklies were full of reports of violence perpetrated by the government and the members of the ruling party. All of these created a grave sense of insecurity in the minds of common citizens.

The actions of the ruling party certainly accentuated the crisis. But the drastic increase of violence was also a result of the actions of leftist political parties, especially the underground pro-Peking leftists. In post-independence Bangladesh, the leftist political parties attempted to achieve what they had failed to do during the liberation war: emerge as the champions of the people's cause. The members of the newly converted left (e.g., the JSD) had attempted to gain prominence while remaining within the AL since 1966, but they failed miserably. They sought to seize power overnight.

The case of the pro-Peking leftists was more complicated and requires some elaboration. In the mid-sixties, following the split with pro-Moscow cadres, the pro-Peking leftists drew the attention of radical youth and students. They became the principal organization within the student community. Their efforts to unite and agitate the people resulted in the mass upsurge of 1969. But, ironically, they completely lost control after Mujib was released from jail in February 1969. The leftists wanted to further radicalize the movement while Mujib and the AL wanted to bring the movement within "constitutional politics." The question whether or not to join in negotiations with the Ayub regime (the Round Table Conference, RTC) was the turning point in terms of the leadership of the future movement. Mujib joined the RTC and carried the people along with him. The leftist parties opposed to the negotiations correctly pointed out that RTC would reap no benefits. However, they failed to suggest an immediate viable alternative. This failure was followed by the disintegration of the pro-Peking left. In 1970, when political activities resumed under the military regime of General Yahya Khan, the underground pro-Peking left was split into at least five small parties/groups.[7] Subtle theoretical differences and the desire for leadership caused these divisions. While the pro-Peking left leaders were engaged in bickering, the AL consolidated its support and finally won the elections of 1970.

Although most of the pro-Peking left parties were convinced that a revolutionary uprising in East Pakistan would eventually lead to the secession of East Bengal, it was a secondary issue on their agenda. Thus, although the pro-Peking left was the only political force talking about the inevitability of an independent Bangladesh, they remained outside the nationalist movement, which was gradually moving toward a secessionist uprising. The results of the elections of 1970, which was boycotted by the left, moved the latter further away from the people's vision. The boycott strategy ironically helped the AL secure a landslide victory, which had certainly not been the left's intention.

Soon after the liberation war began, the pro-Peking left faced another wave of disaffections. Some members of the East Pakistan Communist Party Marxist Leninist (EPCPML), the East Bengal Communist Party (EBCP), and the Coordination Committee of Communist

Revolutionaries (CCCR) crossed the border and formed the Coordination Committee of the Bangladesh Liberation Struggle with the support of the Communist Party of India-Marxist (CPI, M). When China overtly sided with Pakistan and showed no sympathy for the liberation struggle of Bangladesh, the pro-Peking left became utterly confused. Those who fled to India disavowed the Chinese attitude and sought to carve out a position for themselves in the war. A section of the EBCP (led by Abdul Matin and Mohammad Alauddin), who remained within the country and initially joined the war, changed their views to conform to the Chinese position. A section of the EPCP (led by Mohammad Toaha) disagreed with the Chinese but considered the war a conspiracy between Indian expansionists and Soviet social imperialists and, hence, engaged themselves in fighting with the AL-led Freedom Fighters as well as Pakistani forces. The East Bengal Workers Movement (EBWM led by Siraj Sikdar), who declared a national war of liberation against the Pakistani military junta as early as March 2, 1971, reorganized (naming themselves *Sorbohara Party*) and fought against the Pakistani forces, yet remained separate from the forces supported by India.

Nevertheless, the mutual recriminations during the late-1960s followed by the disorganized and confused actions of the pro-Peking leftists during the war made it impossible for them to emerge as a formidable political force and play any leading role. They made very little impression on the guerrilla forces as well.

Faced with the new reality of Bangladesh where they were a marginal political force, the pro-Peking leftists attempted to unite[8] and began to look for an issue that would enable them to emerge as an alternative to the ruling party. Calling the war of liberation "an unfinished and truncated revolution," they urged the people to join them and complete the task of the "unfinished" revolution. To them, the war was not over and, thus, a determined effort was made to destabilize the government. As such, their opposition to the ruling party was not entirely determined by the actions of the regime but was guided by their goal to take over the state. The crises, as well as the failure to contain them by the ruling party, only served as the precipitating factor. The crises of governability and the political situation were certainly enough to keep the regime busy, but ensuing economic crises would make the situation even worse.

Economic Crises

Aggravating the problems of an underdeveloped economy, the liberation war ravaged the entire country and practically destroyed the physical infrastructure. Furthermore, ten million refugees who fled to neighboring India began to return after the war was over. Hence, the regime was faced with three urgent tasks: provide immediate relief to the returning refugees; reconstruct the economic infrastructure; and ensure the future development of the country. The massive flow of aid into the country in the early days of independence helped the regime avert an imminent famine and mass starvation, even though the level of consumption went down considerably. The food situation did not improve much in the following year because of a shortage in agricultural production caused by drought. Nevertheless, the United Nations Relief Organization in Bangladesh (UNROB) and other affiliated organizations helped the regime face the situation. The initial performance of the regime in terms of reconstruction of overheads was commendable. The largest sea port of the country (Chittagong) was cleared, all damaged bridges, with the exception of one, were repaired, industrial production began to make a recovery, and exports increased. However, by the end of 1972 the situation began to take a turn for the worse. The cost of living jumped from Taka 208 in January to Taka 297 in October, nearly 50 percent. According to one account, the cost of living index of an industrial worker rose to 200.31 from the base of 100 in 1969/70 (Bose 1974:244).

In 1973, the failings of the economic policies of the regime began to become apparent. Production in both agriculture and industry failed to reach the level of 1969/70, the most recent normal year for Bangladesh. In the first year of the Five Year Plan, the total output in the industrial sector was 25 percent lower and in the agricultural sector 12-13 percent lower than in 1969/70 (Islam 1978:4). Food grain production surpassed the 1969/70 level (11.8 million tons compared to 11.2 million) but was well below the target (12.5 million tons). The balance of payments reflected a similar trend. It surpassed the projected deficit by 23 percent. The import bill was higher than the projected estimate by Taka 635 million ($79 million) and export receipts fell short of the projection by Taka 220 million ($27 million). The inflow of foreign aid fell from the projected amount of Taka

150

3700 million to Taka 3070 million ($463 million to $348 million) resulting in short term borrowing and drawing from the resources approximately $217 million. Exports of raw jute and jute goods, the principal foreign exchange earning commodities, were far below targeted levels: 2.7 million bales compared to the target of 3.6 million bales (GPRB 1974a:9).

The production level of the nationalized sector was decreasing, causing a huge loss. In the first eighteen months after independence, 12 corporations in this sector incurred a loss of Taka 930 million (*Daily Ittefaq* 1973b:1). The total liabilities of the sector stood at Taka 5375.8 million (*Daily Ittefaq* 1973c:12). The total money supply increased from Taka 387 crore to 696 crore, causing massive inflation. The prices of essential consumer goods rose by about 40 percent. Large scale smuggling from Bangladesh to India played a key role in driving up the prices of essential consumer goods. During the fiscal year 1973/74 an estimated 1.5 million tons of paddy and 800,000 tons of rice were reportedly smuggled to India (*Banglar Bani* 1974).

The economic situation further deteriorated in 1974-1975. The GDP registered a growth of 2 percent while population grew by nearly 3 percent resulting in a negative per capita growth rate (*Bangladesh Observer* 1975:4). The total production of food grains was 11.5 million tons, which was lower than the previous year and 12.6 percent less than the targeted amount. Production in the jute sector declined by 8 percent (GPRB 1975a:6). The balance of payments position worsened rapidly. Actual imports were valued at Taka 9710 million as opposed to the estimated amount of Taka 7660 million. The value of actual exports was Taka 2960 million while the target was Taka 3480 million. The price levels in 1974/75 increased by about 35 percent over the previous year while there was a declining trend in the index of real wages.

The economic crisis reached its apogee in the middle of 1974 when an early flash flood was followed by a devastating countrywide flood in July-August, considered to be the worst in the history of the region. The flood wiped out a considerable amount of food grains (estimated at 1.2 million tons) leaving the country with a deficit of 2.9 million tons. The Government's internal food procurement policy totally failed at a time when there were inadequate foreign exchange reserves to procure food from international markets with higher prices. Additionally, the United States declined to supply food grains for political reasons (see the previous chapter). Under such circumstances, the regime faced a difficult choice: either continue supplying subsidized food grains to the most articulate and volatile pressure groups (e.g., military, police, government employees, students, etc.) through the Public Food grain Distribution System (PFDS) or reduce the amount and divert some of it to the most vulnerable and poorer sections of the rural population. Faced with such a difficult choice the regime opted to continue to deliver food to the politically expedient groups, mostly from the intermediate classes. Hence, a large number of the poor, about 100,000, were pushed toward starvation and death. The famine helped add to the growing opposition to the regime and corroborated the opposition's claim that the regime was failing in all areas.

Economic crises faced by the regime were partly beyond their control, largely connected to the country's peripheral status. In the early seventies, the world capitalist economy itself faced some unanticipated shocks. The recession and inflation of 1973-74 had an impact all over the world including metropolitan countries. These were passed on to the peripheral countries making the latter subject to severe fiscal crises. Two prominent methods practiced by metropolitan countries to pass on the burden were charging increased prices for goods imported by the peripheral countries and imposing unfair terms of trade. These two features of trade are always present in the relationship between periphery and center, but they are usually well-disguised. At times of crisis in the center, these become obvious.

In 1973, Bangladesh suddenly faced both of these in a blatant way. The economy was facing price hikes in oil and food grains in international market, and import costs went up dramatically. The import price index rose 53 percent in 1973/74 and 115 percent in two years, 1973/75. While export prices improved by 33 percent in 1974/75, the terms of trade deteriorated by 32.1 percent, primarily because of rises in the price of food grains, rather than to the oil price hike. The price of food grains—for which Bangladesh was dependent upon metropolitan countries—was more crucial than the price of oil. Over a period of four years, purchases of food from Bangladesh's foreign exchange reserves accounted for $488 million compared to an expenditure of $388 million for oil and petroleum products (Sobhan 1980:161). According to the same estimate, Bangladesh, on average, had to spend an additional $227 million to cover its food gap compared to an increment of $84 million in its petroleum and crude oil bill. This pressure along with the serious lack of resources (again, a general characteristic of peripheral countries), compounded the problem. Bangladesh's situation is a glaring example of the unavoidable predicament of any peripheral country. The situation was intolerable because of the massive corruption of the regime and the greed of certain classes to the detriment of the majority of the population.

This, however, does not mean that the ruling alliance made no effort to solve the problems. In fact, the ruling party desperately searched for answers. Their search, however, was constrained by a variety of factors, including their class character and specific historical situation (e.g., rising post-war expectation and frustrations). Their failure to contain the proliferation of crises resulted in a gradual decline in social cohesion. The weakening of social cohesion made it evident that the capitalist mode of production has come under threat. Increasingly, the threat to the perpetuation of the capitalist mode of production became evident.

NOTES

1   Kamal Hossain, a prominent AL leader and the minister of law and constitutional affairs at the time, described the situation as follows: "The radicals had urged that the freedom fighters, instead of being disbanded, should have formed the nucleus of 'the party of revolution' headed by Sheikh Mujib. The party could then have led a 'class struggle' within the framework of a one-party system, and thus taken society forward towards the goal of social revolution" (Hossain 1979:107).

2   The ruling party envisaged that it could either pursue a politics of consensus or a politics of class conflict. Hossain (1979:107) recalls that "the alternative that had presented itself to the politics of 'class struggle' was the politics of 'consensus'. This policy would seek to

accommodate all contending groups within the framework of the system. It was envisaged that the Awami League could continue to be a de-facto one party, a coalition of contending factions, representing different tendencies, ranging from militant social revolutionaries on the left to conservative 'status quoists' on the right."

3   The total number of seats in the *Bangladesh Jatiya Sangsad* (The National Parliament) was 315. Of these, 300 members were to be elected through direct elections and the remaining 15 seats were reserved for women to be elected by the members of the parliament. In the 1973 elections, 11 AL candidates including Sheikh Mujib were elected unopposed. Elections in one constituency were postponed because of the death of one of the candidates.

4   *Gherao* is the political action of encircling a person or office to realize a demand.

5   The Cabinet approved the plan to raise the National Militia in its meeting on December 18, 1971—two days after the war was over.

6   The Indian forces were withdrawn from Bangladesh on March 12, 1972.

7   These are the East Pakistan Communist Party-Marxist Leninist (EPCPML); the East Bengal Communist party (EBCP); the Coordination Committee of Communist Revolutionaries (CCCR); the East Bengal Workers Movement (EBWM); and the *Mythi* Group (for details see Maniruzzaman 1973:242-249).

8   In early 1972, four pro-Peking left groups formed the Communist Party of Bangladesh-Leninists. These groups are the Coordination Committee of the Communist Revolutionaries; the East Pakistan Communist Party (ML); some communist workers of Khulna district led by Sayeed-ud-Dahar; and some communist workers led by Nasim Ali.

154

Chapter 4

Consent, Coercion, and the Counter Coalition

Gramsci (1971) reminds us that consent and coercion co-exist in all societies. The coercive elements inherent in a hegemonic system are laid bare if, and when, the ability of the ruling classes to organize consent weakens. Under normal circumstances, the elements of coercion are kept latent, concealed. The ruling classes seek and, of course, prefer the active and voluntary consent of the subordinate masses. But when the masses "do not 'consent' actively or passively" or the consent is not sufficient to reproduce capitalist relations, the apparatus of state coercive power "legally enforces discipline on those...who do not consent" (Gramsci 1971:12). That is why the ruling classes, in any society, attempt to impose a general direction on social life through their ideology and ensure social conformity to that ideology. If that fails, coercion becomes the principal tool to rule the masses. Gramsci's prediction came to life between 1972 and 1975 in Bangladesh. The responses of the Bangladeshi ruling classes were two-pronged—to seek "consent" and to "enforce discipline." In this chapter, I will examine these responses and show how a counter coalition with a definite political agenda emerged.

Seeking Consent

In the face of the gathering crises, the ruling classes sought consent and conformity through devising a new ideology, striving for conformity within the party and its allies, and, when necessary, through changes in their policies. Changes in various policies (e.g., investment policy) have been discussed earlier; here, I will discuss the efforts to devise a new ideology and to build new alliances.

New Ideology: Mujibism

To counter the growing popularity of the radical left and their ideology of "scientific socialism," the ruling party evolved a new ideology of its own—*Mujibbad* (Mujibism). Named after Sheikh Mujib, the ideology lacked any philosophical thesis and, as a matter of fact, even the promoters of *Mujibbad* at first did not know what it stood for. The ideology was essentially an admixture of populism and a personal cult and advocated "consensus" among people as opposed to "class conflict." The promoters insisted on the supra-class nature of this ideology, and the integration and accommodation of the various elements of social formations within a dominant party structure as its primary goal. This new "ism" (Mujibism), its advocates claimed, sought to correct the deficiencies of capitalism and socialism. In their view, it was a nationalist reaction against foreign "isms" and was deeply imbedded in the social, political, and cultural traits of the country.

The principal components of the new ideology were nationalism, democracy, socialism, and secularism. These were enshrined in the constitution as the principles of the Bangladeshi state. But, interpretation of these ideals remained open, as no specifics were ever provided by the ruling party. Mujib's own description only enhanced the scope of multiple interpretations. Sheikh Mujib said on one occasion:

> If "Mujibism" is to be considered an ideology, then it ought to be explained by philosophers. I can give my own understanding of what has come to be known as "Mujibism." In the first place, I believe in democracy—in the triumph of the will of the people, in the freedom of thought, of speech and in other freedoms which ennoble mankind. Together with faith in democracy, I am convinced that the development of democracy is possible only in conditions of a society which is free of exploitation. That is why in addition to democracy I speak of socialism. I also believe that all the religions that exist in Bangladesh should have equal rights. By this I mean secularism, the right to profess one's faith. And last, but not least, is the necessity for people to derive inspiration from Bengali culture, language and folklore and from the entire Bengali environment. This inspiration will rouse the Bengalis to work better for the sake of Golden Bengal. This is how I understand nationalism. (Mujib as quoted in Khan and Zafarullah 1980:86-7)

In spite of divergent interpretations, the state-controlled media began to propagate the ideology of Mujibism and gradually became the sole source for the propagation of this ideology. But, interestingly, these equivocations did not articulate the substance of this new ideology.

Nonetheless, one could deduce the meaning of this ideology from the actions of the ruling party and the regime. For example, the economic policies of the regime demonstrated what the ruling party meant by socialism. As I have pointed out in the previous chapter, the socialism of the ruling party was only beneficial to the intermediate classes through the extension of state property. The state enterprises were used by a small segment of the society to accumulate wealth at the expense of the larger section.

Bengali nationalism, as envisaged and practiced by the ruling party, marginalized the non-Bengali minority in general and the tribal nationalities/groups in particular. The debate in the Constituent Assembly on October 25 and October 31, 1972, especially the reactions of members of the ruling party, were indicative of this attitude. On October 25, while discussing Article 14 of the proposed Constitution, the question of ethnic minorities came to the fore. Article 14 stated that one of the fundamental responsibilities of the state would be to free the working population—peasants and laborers—and the "backward sections" of the population from all kinds of exploitation. The Article did not specify who these "sections" were. Manabendra Narayan Larma, an independent member from the Chittagong Hill Tracts, the home of several ethnic groups, moved an amendment to the above article proposing "a) the lawful rights of the minority and backward nations (nationalities) should be preserved; b) in order to improve their educational, cultural and economic standards they should be given special rights; and c) full opportunities should be given to them by the state to enable them to be at par with the advanced nations (nationalities)" (Bangladesh Parliament Secretariat 1972: 292). Larma also argued that because the Chittagong Hill Tracts were a tribal area, in order to ensure that its political, economic, and religious rights were not infringed upon, it should be classed as an autonomous tribal region. Larma was dismayed by the attitude of the ruling regime and expressed his discontent: "the framers of the constitution have forgotten my land, my people... We have been deprived of our rights, the country has become independent, but we continue to have a cursed life" (Bangladesh Parliament Secretariat 1972:295). Larma's amendments were rejected on procedural grounds, but his comments infuriated the ruling party members. They regarded these comments as a challenge to Bengali Nationalism, the *raison d'etre* of the new nation state. Some even described these comments as a conspiracy against the sovereignty of Bangladesh. A similar situation arose on October 31. Abdur Razzaque Bhuiyan, a member of the ruling party, proposed an amendment to Article 6 of the proposed Constitution. He argued that the clause regarding the citizenship should state that "the citizens of Bangladesh will be known as Bangalee [Bengali]" (Bangladesh Parliament Secretariat 1972:452). Manabendra Narayan Larma objected to this amendment saying that inhabitants of Chittagong Hill Tracts had been living there for centuries and had never been asked to be Bengalis: "I don't know why this constitution wants to make us Banglaee," he asked. Larma continued, "You cannot impose your national identities on others. I am a Chakma, not a Bengali. I am a citizen of Bangladesh, Bangladeshi. You are also Bangladeshi but your national identity is Bengali...(the hill people) can never become Bengali" (Bangladesh Parliament Secretariat 1972:452). Despite this plea, the amendment was passed, and Larma walked out in protest. Following Larma's walkout, the Deputy Leader of the House, Syed Nazrul Islam, requested he return to the session saying "I hope that he will accept this opportunity to identify himself and his people as Bengalis" (Bangladesh Parliament Secretariat 1972:461).

The fourth component of the ideology of Mujibism was secularism. The exploitation of Islam by Pakistani rulers to legitimize the perpetuation of colonial rule and the excesses committed by the Pakistani Army and the collaborating Islamic parties "to save the integrity of Islamic Pakistan" created bitter resentment among the people against the use of religion in politics. It was against this backdrop that the ideals of secularism gained support in Bangladesh. Article 12 of the Bangladesh Constitution reflected these secular aspirations. To achieve the ideals of secularism, the Bangladesh constitution called for the end of the following:

a) all kinds of communalism
b) patronization by the state of any particular religion
c) exploitation (misuse) of religion for political purposes
d) discrimination against, and persecution of, anyone following a particular religion. (GOB 1972:4)

In line with this principle, all religious political parties were disbanded after independence. Yet, at the same time that the regime took these bold and commendable steps, Sheikh Mujib categorically declared he was proud to be Muslim and that his nation was the second biggest Muslim state in the world (*Bangladesh Observer* 1972b:1). He not only frequently made use of Islamic expressions in his speech, but also repeatedly insisted that his vision of secularism did not mean the absence of religion. Mujib also led the *Munajaat* (Islamic prayer) on November 4 1972, inside the Parliament after the passage of the Constitution Bill.

The state-controlled media, especially radio and television, began to undercut the spirit of secularism when they adopted a policy of equal opportunity for all religions. Instructed by the government, they read extracts from the holy books of Islam, Hinduism, Buddhism, and Christianity. Their policy of distributive justice in terms of allocating time among the different religions, according to one newspaper, slowly poisoned the concept of secularism and injected religious fanaticism into the minds of the people (*Weekly Wave* 1972). The government not only extended indulgence to all religions but also buckled to religious pressure when it increased funding for religious education in 1973. The annual budgetary allocation for *Madrassah* (Islamic seminaries) was increased to Taka 7.2 million in 1973 from Taka. 2.5 million in 1971. Furthermore, in March 1975 the government revived the Islamic Academy, which had been banned in 1972, and elevated it to a Foundation to help propagate the ideals of Islam. The inherent self-contradiction of the ruling party in terms of its policy of secularism became more evident when Mujib joined the Islamic Summit held in Lahore in February, 1974. Two months later, Bangladesh took the lead at the Islamic Foreign Ministers' Conference held in Jeddah in establishing the Islamic Development Bank.

Thus, the ideology invented and propagated by the ruling party to counter the growing popularity of the radical left and the ideology of scientific socialism proved essentially barren. These drawbacks hindered the ideology of Mujibism from making any appeal to the general masses.

It is true that Mujib's name and charisma were not much help for the ruling alliance in creating a new legitimizing ideology, but it did help the ruling party remain intact. Most of the time, the presence of Mujib and his paternal form of leadership successfully contained internal feuds and cleavages. Yet, internal dissension proliferated and forced the party to take measures in this regard. The party devised their version of a "carrot and stick" policy—patronage and purge—to subdue the dissension.

Patronage and Purge within the Party

In order to pacify the disgruntled sections, patronage was extended, in some form or the other, but if the differences were too much or the group became a threat to the party hierarchy, they would be purged. Cabinet membership was one of the most significant forms of patronage the party could offer to any of its members. As a result, cabinet members were always chosen from different groups to maintain a judicious balance between the rival factions.

In September 1973, when factional tension within the party increased, the cabinet was expanded drastically. Fourteen state ministers were appointed to retain the support of some of the factional leaders. But this failed to satisfy all groups and some disgruntled factions continued to pressure the party for representation in the cabinet. Two months later, two more ministers were added. Such balancing acts between the different factions reaped some immediate benefits, but had adverse long-term effects. The cohesiveness of the party became the first casualty. The prime concern of the party leaders became the maintenance of their own groups and the dispensation of patronage to their supporters. The party as a whole became engaged in this kind of activity.

In the middle of 1974, an open conflict between the left-of-center faction led by Tajuddin Ahmed and the rest of the party surfaced concerning the question of dealing with the urgent socioeconomic problems of the country. Tajuddin made several critical remarks about government policies, holding them responsible for the famine. He urged that an all-party conference be convened to solve the food crisis. He also stated that the implementation of the development plan of 1973/74 would be impossible and that the economy of the country had almost broken down (*Weekly Holiday* 1974). As a result, 6 ministers and 3 state ministers of the Tajuddin group were asked to resign on July 7. On October 26 1974, Tajuddin Ahmed himself was asked to resign from the cabinet. He complied with the directives of the Prime Minister.

161

The differences between Tajuddin and Mujib were much more than the question of how to deal with the imminent food problem. The regime, at this point, was gradually moving away from its socialist policies. AL insiders reported that Tajuddin opposed the revision of the investment policy in July 1974. He was very much against the unconditional acceptance of foreign aid and, while still the PM, declared that Bangladesh was not eager to accept U.S. help because of the latter's opposition to the war of independence (Rahim and Rahim 2003:700). Some sources close to the AL allege that Tajuddin Ahmed was removed from office because of external pressures, especially by the United States. Pointing out how Tajuddin was ousted only a few days before Henry Kissinger paid his first visit to Bangladesh, they contend it was a hint from Mujib to the Western world that he was reducing the Indo-Soviet influence in his cabinet.

Thus, the ruling party, faced with internal feuds and dissensions, attempted to contain these by pursuing a policy of patronization and purges, instead of having an open debate and attempting to build a consensus. Maintaining the delicate balance between the different sections of the party enabled the party to manage its day-to-day affairs, but such a strategy fell far short of keeping the party in a leading position. But the ruling party was so content with the immediate success of the policy that it became the cornerstone of the political strategy of the ruling party, not only to as a means of dealing with internal crises but also for combating the growing opposition political forces.

The Precarious Balance of Right and Left

Having failed to mobilize the masses against the radical political parties, the ruling party moved to form a broad alliance with moderate leftists on the one hand, while taking a conciliatory attitude toward the right, especially the Islamists, on the other.

In October 1973, the ruling Awami League formed an alliance with two pro-Moscow left parties: the Communist Party of Bangladesh (CPB) and the National Awami Party (NAP) led by Muzaffar Ahmed. A Central Committee of the alliance known as *Gono Oikya Jote* (Popular United Front) was formed with the representatives of three political parties. Close cooperation between these three parties was nothing new. Barring the brief split and confrontation in the beginning of 1973, they had maintained a close relationship since the mid-1960s.

There were two previous attempts to build an alliance among these parties. Both initiatives came from the CPB and the NAP. The first was in 1971 during the liberation war.[1] The second attempt was made in May 1972 and led to the establishment of "a National Committee of Three Parties."[2] But the committee failed to get off the ground because of the "Awami League's sectarian policy of working single-handedly" (CPB 1974:256). After these two abortive attempts, came the third initiative, surprisingly from the Awami League.[3]

The joint declaration of the three parties issued on October 14 claimed "the purpose of the alliance would be to mobilize the working people, laborers, peasants, middle class intelligentsia, students and youth for continuing consistent struggle against all barriers on the way of Bangladesh's advance towards socialism" (CPB 1974:302). The declaration also noted that the immediate tasks of the alliance was "the establishment of law and order in the country; putting an end to the terrorism and robberies; struggle for the effectiveness of production; struggle against profiteering, smuggling and corruption; cleaning up the government machinery of corrupt pro-imperialist and anti-people elements" (*Bangladesh Observer* 1973a:1)

One of the principal objectives of this newly formed alliance was to combat the radical left parties. It was unequivocally stated in the joint declaration:

> It has become an urgent political task to resist, in the interests of the country's independence and progress, those parties and individuals within the country who are trying to foil the progressive domestic and foreign policies of Bangabandhu's government and are trying to mislead the people by carrying on vile propaganda against our friend-states particularly India, the Soviet Union and other friendly countries. In reality, these circles have taken up the role of the enemy of the country, nation and the interests of the people. They are engaged in conspiracies against the national interests in connivance

with those foreign powers who tried to foil our struggle for independence. This evil clique is conspiring to destroy the basis of progressive nationalism of Bangladesh and re-establish reactionary communalism. Actually they, in the interest of their foreign masters and national reactionaries, want to foil our national independence achieved at the cost of the blood of three million martyrs. So a countrywide intense struggle has to be developed to uproot these enemies from the sacred soil of Bangladesh. (CPB 1974:302-303)

The efficacy of the alliance was not as strong as the rhetoric. But it did send a clear signal to the radical left about the ruling party's feeling and their strategy to combat them.

The formation of the alliance signaled the ruling party's inclination toward the moderate left, but they did not want to isolate themselves from the right as well. The rightwing elements, especially the religio-political forces, were considered strong; it was believed they could neutralize the growing influence of the radical left (Umar 1973a). Furthermore, the government's increasing relationship with the Muslim world meant the ruling party needed to improve its Islamic image. Faced with such a situation, the government embarked on a policy of conciliation toward the Islamist forces. In addition to emphasizing Islamic values and the use of Islamic symbols, the government declared a general amnesty on November 29 1973, for all the prisoners held under the collaborator's act. Exceptions were made only in cases where there were specific criminal charges. Because of the limitations of the Evidence Act and inadequacies in the provisions of the Collaborator's Order, specific charges could be brought against only a few persons. Thus, almost all alleged collaborators were granted amnesty. Some 33,000 detainees were released over the following days. This conciliatory gesture from the ruling party was welcomed by the rightwing elements.

By the end of 1973, the government was playing a political game with two distinctly different sources of support: the secular moderate left and the Islamist right. All of them were, however, directed against the radical left forces. In the pamphlets and public speeches of the ruling party, these forces were portrayed as the enemy of the country, nation, and the interests of the people. The leaders of the ruling party alleged that the left was engaged in conspiracies against the national interests in connivance with those foreign powers.

Enforcing Discipline

Concurrent with the efforts of seeking consent, was the threat of coercion and, when necessary, the actual *use* of coercion through constitutional means and extraconstitutional measures. This means that on the one hand the ruling classes manipulated democratic processes and the constitution to give legitimacy to their coercive actions, while on the other hand they employed repressive apparatus to quell the opposition. The result was not only a rise in authoritarianism, but also contributed to the realization of their nemesis, a coherent counter coalition within the state.

Manipulation of Electoral Process

The constitution framed by the Constituent Assembly (CA) came into effect on December 16, 1972. On the commencement of the constitution the CA was dissolved and the government announced the first parliamentary elections under the new constitution would be held on March 7, 1973.

Following the announcement, almost all political parties expressed their willingness to contest the elections. But, at the same time, they alleged that the conditions for holding a free and fair election were completely absent. They maintained that the opposition parties did not have the freedom or the opportunities to present their programs and viewpoints to the electorate. Further, they noted that the intolerant attitude of the ruling party toward criticism by the opposition was a serious obstacle in participating in the upcoming elections. In order to remove these obstacles the NAP-M leaders Muzaffar Ahmed and Pankaj Bhattacharya demanded that the government resign (*Dainik Bangla* 1972a:1). Awami League leader A. H. M. Kamruzzaman responded quickly, saying that there was no need for the ruling cabinet to resign (*Dainik Bangla* 1972b:1). The All-Party Action Committee (APAC) led by Maulana Bhasani reiterated the opposition's demand in their 15-point charter and called for "the formation of an all-party government" (*Dainik Bangla* 1972c:1). Responding to the opposition parties' demand to resign, Mujib later said, "I have obtained votes for remaining in power for five years. Why should I resign? An all-party government could be formed but with whom should I form such a government?"(Gonokantha 1973a:1).

Election politics took a different turn after the incident of January 1, 1973. As described earlier, the close allies of the ruling party (the NAP-M and CPB) engaged in bitter conflicts with the government. The storm troopers of the ruling party rapidly turned against the opposition parties, including their former allies. As a result, a tense atmosphere prevailed. The opposition alleged that the ruling party was trying to sabotage the conditions of a free and fair election, while the ruling party charged that the opposition was responsible for the reign of terror. They also accused their opponents of trying to disrupt the election process (*Bangladesh Observer* 1973b:1), and contended that a foreign conspiracy was at work to create disorder in the country (*Bangladesh Observer* 1973c:1).

The situation began to ease after the NAP-M and CPB capitulated in the third week of the month. In the meantime, the election schedule was announced. Given the experiences of the preceding three weeks, the APAC called for a greater electoral unity among opposition parties to combat the ruling party in the elections, but in vain. The JSD, expecting a handsome victory, decided to follow a "go [it] alone" strategy. The opposition parties failed to forge a unity for a limited time and for a limited purpose even though they were subjected to the attacks of, and repression by, a common adversary—the Awami League. This raises an important question: why could the opposition not come to terms with each other, especially when it became clear, even to the critics of the Awami League, that it was, according to a *Weekly Holiday* report (1973:4), "rivalry between the opposition parties which was going to help the Awami League win the election"? The common response of the opposition was that they were not interested in a United Front victory because of the difficulties of governing a problem-ridden country with a heterogeneous and ill-assorted United Front. This explanation, indeed, had some merit. But, if the actions of the opposition were indicative of their state of mind, the reason was definitely quite different: they had an exaggerated notion of discontent among the electorate against the AL and thus expected to do extremely well. None of the parties were ready to share the glory of victory over the AL. Beyond the immediate reason of disunity, there existed a deeper cause: the class affiliation of the party leaders. Badruddin Umar insists, "these parties, in spite of their pretensions represent the interests of various sections of the same classes that form the basis of the ruling Awami League" (*Weekly Holiday* 1973a). With the exception of a few involved with underground radical left political parties, the leadership of the opposition came from the intermediate classes. Additionally, their support base was primarily within the urban middle classes. The JSD, for example, relied heavily on the middle class youth and students. The organizational ethos and the radical rhetoric of JSD demonstrated, what Lenin described as, "petty-bourgeoisie adventurism" (Lenin 1964:186-207).

Nevertheless, apart from the disunity among opposition political parties and their failure to present any pragmatic alternative program to that of the AL, the ruling party had a clear edge over its opposition. The entire administrative machinery was on their side; the state-controlled mass media, including radio and television, were being utilized almost as a "party-spokesman," with public transport such as buses, cars, trucks, jeeps, and helicopters available to the AL candidates. Finally, they had an asset no other political party could have: Sheikh Mujib. Although the Awami League was rapidly losing its popularity, Mujib still enjoyed the enormous confidence of the people. To the common people, Mujib was still their dream child who could perform miracles if given the chance. In their view, it was the party cadres and the men around Mujib who should be blamed for their misery, not Mujib; he was still their friend: *Bangabandhu*. Yet, as the elections approached,

> The Awami League took a course of intrigue and intimidation. The leaders of the Awami League plunged into a competition to prove their popularity to impress their leader. A rage of arrogance dominated their thoughts and an element of intolerance crept in their mind and they maintained an egoistic jingoism that they and they alone had the right to rule the country. So when the election strategy was worked out, democratic practices and norms were

167

disregarded and sometime deliberately violated on petty personal motivations with a general but erroneous notion there was actually no opposition in the country....They became irritant, intolerant and arrogant despite all the advantages they had on their side for a sure victory. (Ahmed 1984:141)

Beginning February 5, the last date for submission of nomination papers, the Awami League activists resorted to all sorts of violence and intimidation to perturb the opposition candidates and their supporters. In various places, they prevented the opposition candidates from submitting their papers; and later, in some constituencies, AL activists forced them to withdraw their papers. On election-day (March 7, 1973), a reign of terror was unleashed. According to the newspapers[4] and other informed sources, there was organized false voting in favor of the government party through-out the country, the opposition party polling agents were driven away from polling booths under threat of being shot, voters were terrorized by gunfire emanating from the ruling party's armed bands, while law enforcement agencies were rendered helpless in the face of directives and threats from above. The outcome of such massive rigging became obvious when the results began to come in: a landslide victory for the AL.

Despite the scare tactic, opposition nominees maintained their lead over the AL candidates in about 25 constituencies. Some of them were unofficially declared elected by the local officials, and at least three of them—the JSD President M.A. Jalil, prominent JSD leader Shahjahan Siraj, and NAP-M nominee Mustaq Ahmed Chowdhury—were announced by the state-controlled television commentators as having been elected.[5] But, soon the results were reversed allegedly on orders from the *Gonobhaban,* the official residence of the PM. Of 288 seats contested, AL won 281 and the opposition, including the independents, secured only 7.[6]

The exact magnitude of the rigging and manipulation was difficult to determine, and the opposition parties, in some cases, exaggerated the facts while the ruling party completely rejected any such charges. The polling officials remained silent for the same reasons they had allowed any malpractices to occur—for fear of their lives and jobs, and because most of them were government officials. Nevertheless, the commentary in the government-controlled newspapers, the allegations of AL allies, and the Awami League's attitude toward the opposition, manifested in the post-election discourse, reveal a trend that helps us understand the situation.

It was a foregone conclusion even before the elections that the ruling party would secure a respectable majority despite the growing discontent. The disunity of the opposition as well as the charisma of Mujib worked heavily in favor of the ruling party, but not to the extent represented by the election results. Three days before the elections, a correspondent of a government-controlled newspaper suggested that the opposition would secure at least 30 seats (*Bangladesh Observer* 1973d:1). Barua (1978:168) maintains that "a reasonably free and fair election would have returned to the first Parliament about 50 to 60 opposition members, and these would have included 15 to 20 major opposition party leaders." One day after the election the President and General Secretary of the NAP, Muzaffar Ahmed and Pankaj Bhattacharya, alleged that the government had forcibly defeated opposition candidates. They claimed that if the government had not resorted to election rigging, at least 70 opposition candidates would have won (Sangbad 1973:1). This statement, especially the allegations of rigging, carries some weight, for it came from a party that has maintained an excellent relationship with the AL.

Even more revealing than these estimations, allegations, and statistics is the discourse of the ruling party after the election. Two examples are enough to show the trend. Sheikh Mujibur Rahman, in his post-election press conference on March 8, 1973 not only claimed that the elections were free and fair but stated unequivocally: "the results of the election have amply demonstrated that there is nothing like an opposition party in Bangladesh." Additionally, he said, "the political parties expressed their views freely and openly. They could not prove their bonafides and they will disappear by themselves" (quoted in Umar 1973b:1). The statement clearly reflected an attitude of intolerance toward the opposition, which was antithetical to the spirit of democracy. Furthermore, this statement was clearly an indication as to how the government was going to view opposition politics. Badruddin Umar noted the trend:

> To say that there is no Opposition worth the name inside the newly elected National Assembly is one thing, but to say there is no polit-

ical opposition in Bangladesh is quite another. The Prime Minister has left no doubt about the sense in which he publicly denies the existence of any political opposition. The statement was a prelude to making Bangladesh a one-party state where no party other than the Awami League would be allowed to function. ...in the history of man a "there is no opposition" type of statement has always betrayed a determination on the part of the ruling party. And this determination can be expressed in the following terms: there shall be no Opposition. (Umar 1973b:1)

The second example is a comment made by a youth leader of the ruling party. On March 11, three days after the election and two days after Mujib made the remark about the opposition, Nur-e-Alam Siddiqui said in a public meeting that "those who have voted against the Awami League in [the] last election are *Razakars* and *Al-Badrs*.[7] These enemies of independence will be weeded out with the tool of Mujibism" (*Gonokantha* 1973b:1). Statements such as these, as Umar noted, were not incongruous with their previous statements. As a matter of fact, AL leader Shah Muazzem Hossain maintained in early January that those who were trying to oppose the AL in the forthcoming election were the same collaborators who had sided with the Pakistani military junta (*Bangladesh Observer* 1973e:1). Thus, in the view of the AL leaders, opposition to the ruling party signified opposition to the sovereignty of the country and hence severe punishment should be meted out to those "anti-state" elements.

With such perceptions, the Awami League established overwhelming control over the Parliament. This gave them the leverage to manipulate the constitution, if necessary, to consolidate and perpetuate their power and privileges and silence the opposition in a very "legitimate" way. And this is exactly what they did in subsequent days.

Manipulating the Constitution

One of the major accomplishments of the AL regime in the early days of independence was framing the constitution in less than seven months.[8] They should also be given credit for an extraordinarily democratic facade despite the inclusion of some highly undemocratic provisions that essentially took away the fundamental rights of the people. The salient features of the Constitution were the introduction of a Westminster-type parliamentary system, providing the Parliament with supreme authority on important issues like declaration of, or participation in, war and imposing and collecting taxes. Additionally, the Constitution apparently made provisions "guaranteeing" the fundamental rights of the people and "ensured" the separation of the judiciary from the executive organ of the state. But, notably, alongside these provisions there remained others that could enable the government to "legitimately" act to the contrary. A few specific examples will support this point.

Let me begin with the example of fundamental rights of citizens. Contained in Part III of the Constitution, Articles 27-29 and 31-43 provide a long and comprehensive list of the rights of the citizen guaranteed by the state[9] including freedom of movement, freedom of assembly, freedom of association, freedom of thought, conscience, and speech. Furthermore, in Article 44, a right has been guaranteed to move the Supreme Court for the enforcement of all the rights conferred in this part of the Constitution. The list is, of course, comprehensive enough to cover almost anything one could think of. But the problem is not that some rights were excluded, but the conditions included with those.

Article 35 grants the right to every citizen to have open, fair, and impartial trials in courts of law. But, the explanatory paragraph immediately following the provision states that on grounds of public safety, morality, and on any other *reasonable ground,* such trials may be held *in camera* through appropriate legislation of the Parliament. Articles 35, 36, 37, and 38 guaranteeing the freedom of movement, freedom of assembly, freedom of association, and freedom of thought, conscience, and speech are the most significant provisions in terms of democratic practice. All of these rights can be taken away on *reasonable grounds*. The question is—who would decide what is reasonable and what is not? The answer is unknown to anyone. Article 39 guarantees the rights of freedom of speech and press, which is again very conditional. According to the sub-clause (2), all of these rights will be suspended if any attempt is made to disrupt friendly relations with foreign countries, which essentially means that the foreign relations of the government cannot be discussed by the citizens—a significant point if one considers that a treaty had been signed with India for 25 years before the Constitution came into effect.[10] Moreover, there was a growing suspicion in many quarters that another "secret pact" was signed during the war.[11] Further, the foreign relations of a government are not, and cannot be, static in nature. Over time, friends change. Does this mean nothing can be said about anyone?

A second example relates to the suspension of the constitution. It is, indeed, true there was no provision *per se* that the constitution could be suspended by anyone at any time, rather the constitution was perceived to be the supreme law of the land. But, interestingly, a unique provision was inserted into the Constitution that practically empowered the Parliament to suspend it altogether. Article 63(3) contained a provision that for public safety and the protection of the state during war, aggression, and armed revolt, the Parliament would be able to enact any law and during such enactments the other provisions of the constitution would not, in any manner, restrain the Parliament from making any such laws. Essentially, this means the constitution can be suspended and the rights enjoyed by the citizens can be taken away if the Parliament feels it is necessary.

Apart from taking away the basic rights of the citizen, provisions were made to concentrate power in the hands of the Prime Minister. Apparently, there is nothing wrong with providing constitutional power to the PM under a parliamentary system. However, in Bangladesh the situation was somewhat different as manifested in the juxtaposition of Articles 55(4-6), 48(3), and 70(1-4) of the Constitution. Article 55(4-6) described the power and authority of the President. It stated the President shall be the highest authority for issuing executive orders on behalf of the government. In this matter, no one will be able to raise any questions in the court of the law—so far so good. But, according to Article 48(3), with the exception of appointing the Prime Minister, the President in all and every matter is to act with the advice of the Prime Minister including the framing of necessary rules. Thus, the PM remains out of the reach of the courts of law while performing his executive duties. Additionally, the PM has the power to control the judiciary indirectly because the Chief Justice and other Judges of the Supreme Court will be appointed by the President (Article 95) and, of course, on the advice of the PM. As a result, both the executive and judiciary come under the authority of a single person—the Prime Minister. This is in addition to his immense control over the members of Parliament elected as his party's nominees, and the fate of the Parliament in general. The extent of his control over Parliament members can be understood from Article 70(1-4). This Article contains the provision that if a Parliament member resigns, is expelled from, or votes against the party, he/she will lose the Parliament membership. The control also goes beyond the party, because if the PM ceases to retain the support of the majority of MPs, he would either resign or advise the President to dissolve the Parliament (Article 57). Hence, the party leader who is also very likely the parliamentary leader and the Prime Minister has control over all of the three organs of the government: the executive, the judiciary, and the legislature.

All of these provisions were incorporated in the original constitution enacted on December 16 1972, and provided ample power to the government. Nevertheless, the ruling party, faced with greater political opposition in the post-election situation, felt the need to amend the Constitution to include some further provisions that would give the government power to legislate and enact laws contrary to the provisions pertaining to the fundamental rights of the people. On September 22 1973, the ruling party introduced the *Constitution (Second Amendment) Bill,* which incorporated provisions relating to preventive detention and proclamation of a state of emergency. Article 33 was substituted with a new Article in order to make provisions for preventive detention, and Part IXA was incorporated to include emergency provisions in the constitution. The salient feature of this amendment was that the government could now detain anyone for an initial period of six months in order to prevent that person from engaging in any action which, in the opinion of the government, constituted a threat to the public safety and sovereignty of the state. An Advisory Board would be constituted to review each case separately and could extend the detention for an unlimited period if the Board was convinced that sufficient cause existed for such detention. This provision is self-explanatory and needs no further elaboration.

With the incorporation of Part IXA in the constitution, a provision was made that "if the President is satisfied that a grave emergency exists in which the security or economic life of Bangladesh or any part thereof, is threatened by war or external aggression or internal disturbances, he may issue a proclamation of emergency" (Article 141A(1)). By Article 141B, certain articles relating to the fundamental rights could be put under suspension and laws inconsistent to Article 36, 37, 38, 39, 40, and 42 could be made during the period of emergency. Furthermore, in Article 141C, provisions were made to have the enforcement of fundamental rights through the courts of law suspended during any such period of emergency. The Inclusion of these provisions in the constitution, on the one hand, restricted the fundamental rights of the people while, on the other hand, they dramatically enhanced the power of the executive branch of the government. The near monopoly of the Awami League in the Parliament ruled out any scope of discussion on the proposed amendment. As a result, the amendment was passed by the parliament, despite feeble resistance by the opposition and independent members.

With the power derived from the amended Article 33, the government moved further in early 1974. On February 5, Parliament enacted the Special Powers Act. The Act contained provisions for preventive detention. According to the Special Powers Act, a person was to be detained if the government was satisfied that it was necessary to do so with a view to preventing him from doing any "prejudicial act" (Section 3). The Act also dealt with sabotage (Section 15) and the prohibition of prejudicial acts including the publication of any prejudicial report (Section 16). The Act curtailed the freedom of association and authorized the government to impose control over such associations that would "act in a manner or to be used for the purpose prejudicial to the maintenance of public order"; it also gave the government necessary power to "direct the association to suspend its activities for such period not exceeding six months" (Section 19 and Section 20). The Act laid down that the persons engaged in hoarding, black marketing, sabotage, printing, possessing, or distributing any "prejudicial report" shall be tried by Special Tribunals created under the Act (Section 26-29). Anyone accused or convicted of an offence punishable under the Act could not be released on bail (Section 32). Furthermore, in the original Act, an appeal from the judgment of the Special Tribunal lay with the High Court Division, but, through an amendment on July 23 1974, the jurisdiction was taken away. The amendment also contained a provision for "firing squads" for the execution of persons found guilty by the Special Tribunals.

The Act clearly reflects the attitude of the ruling party. Combined with the provisions incorporated in the original constitution and the alterations made through the Second Amendment, this Act indicates an ominous trend. It is obvious that in the face of growing economic and political crises, especially the growth of the opposition, the ruling party drifted toward coercive measures rather than making efforts to co-opt the opposition and combat the underlying reasons for the crises. In addition, the ruling party utilized their overwhelming majority in parliament to manipulate the constitution. Parliament became a tool for legitimizing the coercive actions of the government instead of being a forum of discussion and debate about the future direction of the country. The views of opposition members were never taken into consideration.

The constitutional and legal measures discussed above contained special provisions to deal with dissenting voices, individual and media alike. Yet, legislation specifically designed to curtail the freedom of the press was passed and implemented vigorously.

Curtailing the Freedom of the Press

The distinctive features of the Bangladesh press at the time of independence were the prevalence of a number of gag laws, especially the Printing and Publication Ordinance (PPO) of 1960, and a total government control over the electronic media (i.e., radio and television). At the time, there were two dailies (*Morning News* and *Dainik Bangla*) under the control of the government through the National Press Trust (NPT), which was constituted in 1960s during the Ayub regime. The PPO, which journalists and politicians alike called a "black law," included several restrictive provisions including one of licensing. Under the PPO, publication of a newspaper without a proper license issued by the authorities would be considered illegal and thus liable for punishment. The Ordinance also empowered the government to arrest journalists. The Awami League promised to repeal the PPO and pledged to ensure the freedom of the press. After independence, a number of newspapers (e.g., *Bangladesh Observer, Daily Purbadesh,*

Weekly Chitrali, Daily Azad, Daily Paygam) owned by pro-Pakistani businessmen and politicians were abandoned and consequently brought under government control. Two wire services operating in the pre-independence period (i.e., Pakistan Press International or PPI, and Associated Press of Pakistan or APP) also came under government control. Thus, there was very little scope within mainstream journalism to oppose the government. The journalistic community failed to apply significant pressure on the government to ensure an environment conducive to the freedom of press. Even though the leadership of journalist unions reminded the ruling party of their pre-independence promises, some of the influential members of the union either joined the government or cooperated with it. The ruling party took advantage of this deep division within the community.

Nevertheless, an array of weeklies that began to come out in the early months of 1972 (e.g., *Hoq Katha, Spokesman, Wave, Nayajug, Chorompatra, Mukhopatra, Lal Pataka, Ittehad, Abhimat,* etc.) joined the band of pre-independence opposition weeklies (e.g., *Holiday, Gonoshakti*) and appeared as the principal critics of the ruling party. The JSD also brought out a daily: *Gonokantha*. These opposition newspapers—with a few exceptions—did not always behave responsibly. Some of them were full of venom and invective directed at the AL leaders combined with unrealistic propaganda spiced with revolutionary rhetoric. Their occasional irresponsibility provided the government with the opportunity to crack down on them.

While the leaders of the ruling party were declaring that securing a free press was one of their prime goals and the PM announced "the government of Bangladesh is aimed at establishing a free and responsible press" (*Bangladesh Observer* 1973f:1), the government began to use the PPO to close down newspapers, issue warrants, and arrest newspaper editors and others connected with their publication. They even used the ordinance to close down the printing presses used to print those newspapers.

The first indication of the ruling party's intolerance toward criticism was the dismissal of the editor of the government-controlled daily *Bangladesh Observer* in March 1972. Abdus Salam, a prominent and well-respected journalist, was removed from his office because of the opinion expressed in his editorial titled "the Supreme Test" (*Bangladesh Observer*

1973g:5). That, however, was only the beginning. Within the first six months of independence, two weeklies were banned (*Hoq Katha* and *Gonoshakti*), one of the editors was arrested, and a warrant was issued against another (DUJ 1973). On September 6 1972, editor of *Spokesman* and *Mukhopatra*, Fayzur Rahman, was detained. On January 2 1973, the editor and executive editor of the government-controlled daily *Dainik Bangla,* Hasan Hafizur Rahman and Toab Khan, were removed from their duties and made OSDs (Officers on Special Duty) in the Information Ministry. They were dismissed because they decided to bring out a special edition of the newspaper covering an incident of police opening fire in front of the United States Information Service (USIS) killing two students on January 1 1973. In March 1973, the government cracked down on the only opposition daily–*Gonokantha*.[12] By July, the government had acted against five newspapers, arrested two editors, and issued warrants against a publisher. In August 1973, the office of the *Deshbangla* (a newspaper published from Chittagong) was forcibly closed and 9 journalists including the news editor were arrested. Later, the editor was also taken into custody.

The PPO provided the necessary legal shield in cracking down on the opposition newspapers. Essentially, the ruling party was making use of the PPO in its extreme form to silence dissident voices. In terms of legality, one could hardly question the use of the PPO, but there remained a moral question: should the ruling party make such frequent use of a law that they themselves called a "black law"? Having faced this moral dilemma, the ruling party moved to make changes in the gag laws—but, ironically, only in name. The PPO was repealed at the end of August 1973. But the annulment came only after the government promulgated a new ordinance on August 28, 1973: *Printing Presses and Publication (Registration and Declaration) Ordinance, 1973*. The content as well as the form of the new ordinance was identical, a mere duplication of the previous one. No changes were made insofar as the restrictive provisions and punishments for violation of the law were concerned. The Ordinance found a safe passage in parliament when presented for approval on September 19 1973. It was accompanied by harsh criticism of the press by members of the ruling party, including the Home Minister.

The vilification of the journalists by the Home Minister and others in the Parliamentary debate was a prelude to a further crackdown on the freedom of the press. Armed with the new ordinance, the government began a campaign against opposition newspapers. Suspensions of newspaper publications, cancellations of newspaper declarations, the seizing of published materials, arrest of journalists and editors, and raids on newspaper offices became a part of life.[13] Within six months of the passage of the Ordinance came the Special Powers Act of 1974, which had, among other things, specific provisions to deal with the newspapers. The Act was a pointer to the ruling party's growing reliance on coercion in order to rule the country.

New Force of Repression: JRB

In early 1972, the government announced the formation of a paramilitary force named the *Jatiyo Rakkhi Bahini* (JRB, the National Defense Force).[14] The formation of the JRB grew out of two interrelated needs of the ruling party: administrative needs and political needs.

The administrative need arose from the lack of a strong law-enforcement agency. Immediately after independence, the government began to reorganize law-enforcement agencies such as the police, the Bangladesh Rifles, and the army. The question involving the future structure of the Army created a dilemma for the ruling party. On the one hand, they preferred the restoration and rebuilding of the Army in accordance with colonial precedents as opposed to the concept of a "people's militia" advanced by the radicals, while, on the other hand, the experience of Pakistan began to haunt them. Finally, the ruling party found a precarious balance between the two: the setting up of a small conventional Army with very little equipment and a low profile. The question that immediately followed the reorganization issue was whether to involve the defense forces in reconstruction and law enforcement. From the organizational standpoint, this was of little significance, because the forces were still in disarray. But the more fundamental point was political. The Army's involvement in law-enforcement so soon after independence was perceived as a prestige issue, an indication of the regime's lack of political authority. There was also skepticism from the ruling party as to whether or not the existing law enforcement would be able to meet the needs of the independent nation. Nevertheless, the regime was well aware of the need for a strong law-enforcement agency in a post-war situation where firearms were in the hands of many different factions.

The political imperative of the JRB involved internal feuds within the party as well as the ruling party's perception of opposition political parties. Contending factions within the party began to vie for power and set up private forces such as the *Lal-Bahini* (Red Force) and the *Awami League Sechhasebak Bahini* (AL Volunteer Force). Former members of the Mujib Bahini, led by Fazlul Hoq Moni (a nephew of Sheikh Mujib), insisted on a greater role in the government. The ruling party came to believe that the entire nation, except for a few Pakistani collaborators, was with the party. Hence, opposition to the party and the regime was deemed opposition to the sovereignty of the country and those involved in such acts should be dealt with severely. Furthermore, the prevailing skepticism of the ruling party about the existing law-enforcement agencies to meet the needs of an independent country convinced them that an organized legitimate force under the control of the party and its leaders would be a better solution.

Although these two needs were complementary, one question placed them in diametrically opposed positions: who would control the paramilitary force? To attend to the *administrative* need, the force had to be placed under the control of the state-bureaucracy, but to attend to the *political* need the force had to be placed under the control by the party hierarchy. If the newly created force was placed under the party's command, how would it acquire legitimacy?

When the JRB Order was promulgated in March 1972, it became obvious that the political needs of the ruling party superseded administrative concerns. Questions pertaining to the aim and purpose of the force, as well as control over the JRB, were kept vague leaving ample space for maneuvering. The Order was devoid of any specifics about the organization, its methods of operation, its powers and authorities, and its accountability as a law-enforcement agency. In terms of the objects and purposes of the JRB, Article 8 of the Order stated that it would be employed for the purpose of assisting the civil authority in the maintenance of internal security when required and it would perform such functions as the government would direct. In terms of the rules of its functioning, the Order only stated that the Government would make rules and regulations for functioning, including the conduct of its members and their powers and functions (Article 17). An organized force of 20,000 members equipped with sophisticated weapons was created, but it was not accountable to any specific institution of government. No one can doubt that this ambiguity was the result of a deliberate strategy of the ruling party to accord enormous power to the *Rakkhi Bahini* and its members.

The magnitude of power of the newly formed force was felt shortly after its creation. Reports began to pour in from different parts of the country about the atrocities committed by members of the *Rakkhi Bahini*. Apparently, they were up against "anti-social elements" such as smugglers, black-marketeers, hoarders, and *dacoits*, but essentially the political dissidents became their prime targets. Their methods were brutal, to say the least:

> It acted like a storm-trooper, a crack-force for a lightening strike. It would surround a whole village combing for arms, miscreants and political opponents and at times to recover 'fake ration cards.' In the process they would kill, loot and even rape—there was no regulation to control their conduct or make them accountable. Soon it assumed the name of a private Bahini working outside legal norms. They could enter any house, arrest anyone, detain any number of people including women and children in their camps all over the rural areas. (Ahmed 1983:56)

The harsh actions of the JRB evoked serious criticism in the opposition press. When some newspapers questioned the legality of such actions, the government introduced an amendment to the original order in October 1973 with retroactive effect from February 1, 1972 (*the Jatiya Rakkhi Bahini (Amendment) Ordinance, 1973*, October 30, 1973). The amendment legalized all acts committed by the JRB in the past or in the future by including the provision that no suit, prosecution, or other legal proceedings could be brought forth against any member of the JRB which was intended or carried out in good faith (Article 16A). The amendment also provided the JRB with the power and authority to search any place and arrest anyone without warrant (Article 8A). These provisions not only made the members of the JRB completely immune to legal proceedings, but also authorized them to operate beyond the reach of the law. Essentially, they were acting at the free will of their officers (who were called leaders) and followed no codes of conduct. The officers of *Rakkhi Bahini* also admitted that the JRB had no rules or procedures or codes of conduct (Mohsin Sharif vs. the State, 27 DLR, 1975 HC, p.186, popularly known as Shahjahan Case argued by Moudud Ahmed on behalf of the plaintiff in May 1974). The JRB officers acknowledged they "do not have to maintain any paper or document or record of their activities or conduct in the operations they used to undertake. There was no record of any arrest or search, or seizure they made." In response to a question as to how they worked, a Senior Deputy Leader told the court, "we work the way we decide" (ibid).

The numerical strength of the JRB reached 29,000 in subsequent years. A plan to raise the number to about 130,000 by the year 1980 was drawn up by the government. It was also planned that one regiment of the JRB would be placed under the command of the each district governor—a political appointee of the regime. The Bahini increasingly became the primary tool of the regime to counter law-and-order situations. The deployment of the JRB in various places for various reasons became common.

Alongside the JRB, the government began to call in the army frequently to aid the civil authorities. Sometimes this caused embarrassment to the ruling party, because the army occasionally went "beyond their jurisdiction" and caught party loyalists engaged in various unlawful acts. Nevertheless, the government's primary goal was to control the situation by employing whatever methods necessary.

The army was first called into action in the middle of 1973 to recover false ration cards and to evict the unauthorized occupants of abandoned houses left by Pakistanis. The operation, however, caused some tension between the army and the ruling party, because the army began to evict the illegal occupants indiscriminately including members of the ruling party. On the very first day, it was reported the army evicted 12 illegal occupants of houses in the Mohammadpur area of Dhaka but met with resistance from AL workers. Consequently, the central leaders of the party intervened and the subject of abandoned houses was taken out of the terms of reference of the army. But the operation continued for quite some time and, not surprisingly, it was the poor and lower middle class who became the chief targets of the army. Harassment in the name of fake ration card recovery became a part of their life.

The second time the armed forces were called into action was during the latter part of 1973. They were ordered to carry out localized operations against "miscreants and anti-social elements" in Barisal, Jessore, Khulna, Rangpur, and Rajshahi. According to a report published in the JSD-supported newspaper *Gonokantha*, some one hundred "communists" were killed in this operation. The regime claimed to have wiped out half of the miscreants from the 19 districts (*Gonokantha* 1973c:8).

The army was deployed for the third time in April 1974 on a national scale to deal with subversion, smuggling, the recovery of illegal arms, and black marketeering. Unlike the previous two occasions, the army was given the power to supersede the civil administration. The deployment of an army with such vast power was seen by some analysts, such as Enayetullah Khan, as the virtual abdication of civil authority to military rule. Khan commented "the irony is that the armed forces did not have to ask for it. It came to them in spite of their own selves and it is possible that they may be stuck with it for years from now" (*Weekly Holiday* 1974:1).

The deployment of the Army on a national scale through an executive order was nothing but the imposition of emergency rule without having it announced. Because of the very nature of the operations of the armed forces, even if it was to remain within the given terms of reference, it precluded basic human rights guaranteed by the constitution that could be suspended only under an emergency. Such Actions obviously revealed that the ruling party was desperately trying to make a compromise between the rule of emergency and a façade of parliamentary rule. But striking a complementarity between these two is practically impossible. Their inherent contradictions ultimately led to a clash between the respective institutions, even though an inimical forbearance might be achieved for some time. In the latter case, the only result that can be expected is limbo. Whatever may be the immediate repercussions, the ultimate result, as happened in all such cases, was the demise of even the semblance of parliamentary rule.

And that is what happened within eight months of the deployment of the army. On December 28 1974, the President, by an Ordinance, proclaimed a state of emergency in the country suspending the enforcement of fundamental rights during the period of emergency. The Ordinance stated that emergency rule was proclaimed because the "security and economic life of Bangladesh was threatened by internal disturbances" (*Dainik Bangla* 1974:1).

The proclamation of the emergency, of course, essentially brought an end to parliamentary rule and the constitutional state. But the facade remained. The supremacy of the parliament accorded by the constitution became discordant with the prevailing situation and, thus, was a source of contradiction. To eliminate the incompatibility, the concentration of power in the hands of the executive had to be legitimized constitutionally and the autonomous bases of power outside its jurisdiction had to be destroyed. These were inevitable, logical steps toward the completion of the process of establishing an authoritarian state. The ruling classes of Bangladesh advanced in this direction without any delay.

The One-Party State

Within less than a month of the promulgation of emergency rule, the Parliament hurriedly passed a constitutional amendment without any discussion or debate that brought an end to the last vestige of parliamentary rule in Bangladesh.[15] *The Constitution (Fourth Amendment) Act (Act No. II of 1975)* passed on January 25 1975, made sweeping changes. The country entered into a new constitutional arrangement where only one political party could exist and the executive branch with the President at its apex assumed supremacy over the legislative and judicial organs of the state. Additionally, by the amendment itself, Mujib was made the President for the next five years and with an opportunity to hold the office for an unlimited number of terms.

Contrary to the earlier constitutional provision that the President would be elected by the Parliament, the new system provided that the

President would be elected by the people in a direct election (Article 48) and the executive authority of the republic would be vested in him (Article 56). The amendment made it more difficult to impeach the President by increasing the number of members required to sign a notice of motion to initiate impeachment proceedings (a minimum of two-thirds as opposed to the previous one-third) and the number of votes required to pass the resolution (three-fourths as opposed to two-thirds). The "Council of Ministers" was made responsible to the President, not to the Parliament as under the original constitution. The ministers, including the Prime Minister, were to be appointed by the President and would hold office at his pleasure.

One of the principal features of the original constitution was the sovereignty of Parliament, which had supreme power and authority in law-making. Any bill passed by Parliament would become law and the President had no power of veto. But under the new system the President could withhold assent to any bill passed by the Parliament.

In Part II of the original constitution, where the fundamental principles of state policies were laid down, Article 11 contemplated that people would effectively participate through their elected representatives in the administration at all levels in order to ensure a democratic system. Accordingly, Chapter III of Part IV of the original constitution provided for local government at every administrative unit of the Republic composed of elected persons. The Fourth Amendment omitted the provisions and, thus, made it possible for the President to appoint local governments.

The separation of the judiciary and the executive is considered to be the one of the basic conditions, as well as the strength, of the democratic process. The primary function of the judiciary in a democratic society is to oversee the executive branch, strike a balance between the law and its application and administer justice. That is why any democratic constitution strictly prohibits interference by the executive in the functioning of the judiciary. But the Fourth Amendment severed the very root of the independence of the judiciary and made it subservient to the executive branch. As opposed to the original constitutional provision that "the Chief Justice of the Supreme Court shall be appointed by the President, and other judges shall be appointed by the President after consultation with the Chief Justice" (Article 95(1)), the new amendment empowered the President to appoint all judges without any consultation with the Chief Justice. In terms of the tenure of the office of judges, the President assumed total power as opposed to the previous stipulation "a resolution of Parliament supported by a majority of not less than two-thirds of the total number of members of the Parliament" would be required (Article 96(2)). Under the new condition, the President could remove a judge including the Chief Justice simply by an order on the grounds of misbehavior or incapacity. The President also assumed the authority to appoint additional judges to the Supreme Court without any consultation with the Chief Justice.

The power and authority of the Supreme Court was severely curtailed. The authority of the Supreme Court in matters of appointments to, and control and discipline of, subordinate courts was withdrawn and vested in the President (Article 115 and Article 116). The power of the High Court Division in respect of the enforcement of fundamental rights and to issue certain orders and direction was circumscribed.

While the Fourth Amendment established the supremacy of the executive over the legislative and judicial organs of the state and, thus, left no room for opposition to the concentration of power in a single hand, it also barred the dissidents from entering into the political arena through the introduction of a one-party system (Article 117A (1)).

The Counter Coalition, the Second Revolution, and the Martial Law

With these constitutional changes and consequent actions,[16] the executive branch and, consequently, the bureaucrats gained supreme authority. The chief executive held the power to control all institutions including the only legitimate political party. This was a dramatic development considering that at independence the intermediate classes had marginalized the bureaucrats and squeezed them to the peripheries of power. Within three years, the bureaucrats not only overcame some initial setbacks but also were on their way to the center stage of power. However, the bureaucrats were still under the dictates of a party that represented the intermediate classes; and the internecine quarrel among its factions was pulling them in different directions. In order to free them from the continuous tension and fulfill the necessary conditions for the realization of their potential autonomy, the

185

bureaucracy needed a constitutionally guaranteed supremacy. They were unable to do it alone. What they needed was an equal or junior partner.

In the preceding three years, a social class—the new rich—evolved as a direct beneficiary of state policies. Policies ranging from nationalization to licensing allowed them to accumulate wealth at an unprecedented rate. But the instability and the crisis of authority of the ruling classes was increasingly becoming a threat to their continued upward mobility. Moreover, the state had set limits to the reproduction of their capital. For them, the intermediate state had served its purposes and a new arrangement needed to be instituted to ensure their growth. It was not only that the wealth accumulated by this class needed to be protected, but, most importantly, avenues had to be provided to them for the reproduction of their capital. What they really needed, and aspired to, was a strong state that would come forward to help them ensure the much needed stability for their growth and extend financial support as the Pakistani state had in its early days. This class also found it necessary to establish a link, not mediated by the state, with the world capitalist economy. The situation pertained to the rise and actions of the burgeoning class, which had already come into being but was not yet "fixed"; their hopes and aspirations can be described by borrowing words from Marx's description of French small peasant proprietors between 1848 and 1851:

> They are...incapable of asserting their class interests in their own name, whether through a parliament or through a convention. They cannot represent themselves; they must be represented. Their representatives must appear simultaneously as their master, as an authority over them, an unrestricted governmental power that protects them other classes and sends them rain and sunshine from above. (Marx 1974:239)

The socialist postures and the democratic pretenses of the ruling party were not conducive to the realization of these goals of the new rich.

Thus, by the beginning of 1974, the need to fulfill the conditions of capitalist development, to accommodate the new rich class, and to ensure a highly visible autonomous role for the bureaucracy converged.

Interestingly, all these interests grew out of the political projects of the intermediate classes and as direct consequences of the policies of the intermediate state. But, the intermediate classes and the intermediate state could no longer serve their purposes. This gave birth to the counter coalition, and a new political project was defined. The democratic pretense became a hindrance in accomplishing the newly defined political project.

The final tussle between the emerging coalition and the intermediate classes became imminent: either the newly declared national party called BAKSAL would be able to deliver what the coalition expected or they would be replaced. Against this backdrop, Mujib initiated what he called the "second revolution"—a revolution to bring about "the democracy of the exploited masses" (quoted in Iliyas 1979:208).

Mujib's "Second Revolution"

Although a complete agenda for reform was never documented and made public, Mujib on various occasions referred to the changes set in motion in 1975 as the "Second Revolution." Three speeches delivered by Mujib between March and July, 1975, especially on March 26, shed some light on the principal features of his "second revolution."[17] These speeches, like the one delivered on January 25 in parliament while introducing the constitutional amendment for introduction of the one-party system, were unwritten and often lacked consistency. However, a broad outline of the changes Mujib envisaged can be gleaned from these important speeches.

The salient features of the agenda for reforms were the formation of compulsory, multipurpose co-operatives in every village; revamping the local-level administration; abolishing the highly powerful Secretary position; and establishing tribunals or courts at a *thana* (i.e., lowest tier of administrative unit) level.

According to Mujib, compulsory, multipurpose co-operatives would be formed in all 65,000 villages over the following 5 years, in phases. Each co-operative would be comprised of 500-1000 families and would bring together all the able-bodied persons of the villages, whether they were landowners or landless. The ownership of the land would remain with the current owners, but the produce would be divided into three parts: one to the owner, one to the local co-operative members, and the other to the government.

In terms of revamping the local-level administration, the prevalent structures of thana and district administration would be dismantled. The responsibility of the thana and district administrations would be assigned to a thana and district administrative council respectively. In contrast to the prevailing structure, where the civil servants enjoyed the supreme authority, these administrative units would be headed by the Chairman and the Governor, respectively. They would be appointed by the Central Government and the only required qualification would be party membership. Thus, anyone, including a government official, could be appointed to that position because government officials were also given the opportunity to be members of the "national party." The District Administrative Council was vested with immense authority with regard to planning and implementation of development projects. The District Commissioner, the highest-ranking civil administrator, would be the Secretary of the Council and work under the direction of the Governor. The Governor would control all government departments at the district level including the paramilitary forces.[18]

Mujib's speeches repeatedly mentioned the other two features (i.e., abolishing the highly powerful Secretary position and the establishment of tribunals or courts at the thana level) without any indication of what he was really intending to do. Mujib promised to abolish the secretariat, remove bureaucratic bottlenecks called red-tapism, and establish a people-oriented system. He, however, never mentioned how and when these would be done. The Fourth Amendment conferred powers on the President to establish court or tribunals at the thana level and Mujib frequently mentioned that he would exercise this power.

Besides these programs, no reference was made as to how the economy would be disciplined, the ills of corruption and inefficiency in the nationalized sector fought, or the proper functioning of the economic system ensured. One further point involving the composition of the new national party should be mentioned here. In spite of his call for "national unity," Mujib failed to attract much support from outside his own party. The old allies of the Awami League, the CPB and NAP (M), enthusiastically joined the bandwagon. But they were not included in the policy-making bodies of the BAKSAL. The 15-member Executive Committee, the highest policy-making body of the organization, had no members from outside the former AL. The former AL stalwarts dominated the 115-member Central Committee. Of the 28 members who came from outside the AL, 21 were senior bureaucrats.

Despite some elements of egalitarianism, the program of the so-called "second revolution" fell far short of a program for the socialist transformation of the society as its proponents insisted. Ironically, it was not a radical program of capitalist development either. In other words, the political project envisaged by Mujib appears to be different from the polit-ical project envisioned by the constituents of the emerging coalition: the new rich class, the bureaucracy and the military.

Organic Crisis and the Martial Law

The newly formed party, at its birth, made it obvious that it was incapable of bearing the responsibility history had put on its shoulders: to serve a new coalition. As such, the crises of the ruling alliance reached its zenith; it reached a level of an organic crisis wherein "the social classes become detached from their traditional parties...the traditional parties in that partic-ular organizational form, with the particular men who constitute, represent, and lead them, are no longer recognized by their class (or fraction of a class) as its expression" (Gramsci 1971:210).

Gramsci correctly points out that when such a crisis occurs, "the immediate situation becomes delicate and dangerous, because the field is open for *violent solutions*" (Gramsci 1971:210, emphasis added). Now, the question is: what might that solution be? Following Poulantzas (1976:72), we can say that situations like these necessitate a specific reorganization of the power bloc. This involves a modification of the relation of forces within the power-bloc and establishment of the hegemony of a new class within the power-bloc. It is understandable that the establishment of the hegemony of a new class within the power bloc cannot be achieved overnight; it defi-nitely requires some time. Without the direct patronization of state-power, a new class cannot acquire the material basis necessary for establishing its hegemony. As a result, the process of reorganization of the power bloc has to begin with a modification of the relation of forces within. Because the executive and coercive apparatuses of the state ascend to a preeminent position and wield enormous power by the time the organic crisis occurs, only they can substitute for the civilian political party in power. Thus, a military-bureaucratic oligarchy seizes state-power with a definite political and economic agenda whose ultimate goal is to establish the hegemony of a new class: the bourgeoisie.

This is precisely what happened in Bangladesh in 1975 after it gradually became evident that the BAKSAL was failing to adapt itself to the new tasks demanded by the classes it was meant to represent. The military-bureaucratic oligarchy took over state power through a violent *coup d'etat* on August 15, 1975. Early on the morning of that day, Sheikh Mujib and about 30 members of his family including his wife, a ten-year-old son, and his nephew, Fazlul Hoq Moni, were brutally murdered. Bangladesh had entered into an era of coups and counter coups, and prolonged military rule, and the Bangladeshi state had experienced a complete transformation.

NOTES

1 Despite the left parties' insistence on forming an alliance, the Awami League deliberately excluded members of the left political parties while recruiting guerrilla forces during the war. Some 6,000 members of the NAP and CPB, however, were enlisted. They also formed their own forces. The CPB and NAP continued to insist on a broader national alliance. Pressure also came from the Indian authorities in late August to build a broader forum where all other political parties could be included. The goal was to draw pro-Moscow forces into the decision-making process in order to gain support from the Soviet Union. The cabinet refused to do so, but authorized the PM to form an all-party consultative committee. The consultative committee was formed on September 8, 1971. The members of the committee were Tajuddin Ahmed and Khandaker Mushtaq of AL, Moni Singh of CPB, Muzaffar Ahmed of NAP, Monoranjan Dhar of Bangladesh Congress, and Maulana Bhasani.

Because of the absence of clear terms of reference and the reluctance of the AL leaders, the committee could not play a substantial role.

2   In post-independence Bangladesh, both the CPB and NAP (Muzaffar) decided to lend all-out support to the AL regime. In its First Plenum of the Central Committee of the CPB held on February 4, 1972 the party decided to "pursue a policy of cooperation with the government and the Awami League for the solution of the problems of people's life and for the reconstruction of country along the progressive line" (CPB 1974:256). The NAP in its first National Conference held in May 1972 adopted a program underlining the necessity of supporting the positive steps taken by the government (NAP 1972:24).

3   The Awami League called for unity of all patriotic forces in its public rally held on June 7. The CPB quickly responded to the call in its rally on June 10. On August 9, Sheikh Mujib called for the formation of an alliance of AL, NAP, and CPB. Leaders of these three parties met on September 1. Two days later Mujib met the leaders of the parties concerned and approved the decision of the formation of an alliance. After hammering out the differences and drafting the declaration the alliance was declared on October 14, 1973.

4   *Sangbad*, March 8, 1973; *Gonokantha*, March 8, 1973; and *Wave* March 10 and *Weekly Holiday*, March 11, 1973

5   Mustaq Ahmed Chowdhury's name had been published by the state-controlled *Bangladesh Observer* on March 9, 1973 as being elected.

6   Following the bye-elections and elections in the reserved seats for women the composition of the parliament stood as follows: AL: 306; JSD:2, BJL:1; Independent:6.

7 These are the two paramilitary forces organized by the Pakistani occupation forces during 1971. In the post-independence period these terms were used to denote anyone who was against the liberation struggle and hence the people's enemy.

8 The Constituent Assembly comprised of the representatives elected to the-then National Assembly of Pakistan and those who were elected to the Provincial Assembly in East Pakistan in 1970 was formed through the Constituent Assembly of Bangladesh Order 1972 (i.e, President's Order No. 22 of 1972). The Assembly had no other function except the framing of the Constitution (Article 7, P.O.22). The Assembly first met on April 10, 1972 exactly one year after the Proclamation of Independence and appointed a 34-member Constitution Committee headed by Dr. Kamal Hossain. Its second session began on October 12, 1972. A 91-page draft Constitution Bill with 153 Articles was presented on October 18, 1972. After three weeks of discussion the Assembly adopted the Constitution on November 4, 1972. The Constitution was authenticated by the Speaker on December 14 and was signed by 357 members. The three opposition members declined to sign. The Constitution came into effect on December 16, 1972.

9 These are equality before the law (Article 27); protection against discrimination on ground of religion etc., (Article 28); equality in public employment (Article 29); right to protection by law (Article 31); protection of right to life and personal liberty (Article 33); safeguards against arrest or detention (Article 33); prohibition of forced labor (Article 34); right to have an open, fair and impartial trial in the court of the law (Article 35); freedom of movement (Article 36); freedom of assembly (Article 37); freedom of association (Article 38); freedom of thought and conscience and speech (Article 39); freedom of profession or occupation (Article 40); freedom of religion (Article 41); right to property (Article 42) and protection of home and correspondence (Article 43).

10   On March 19, 1972 a "treaty of friendship, cooperation and peace" was signed between India and Bangladesh during the visit of the Indian Prime Minister Indira Gandhi. Ms. Gandhi and Bangladesh PM Sheikh Mujib signed the treaty on behalf of their respective countries. The treaty barred the countries involved from entering into or participating in any military alliance directed against the other (Article 8). The treaty also included a provision that in case either party is attacked or threatened with attack by a third party, the participants of the treaty will enter into mutual consultations "in order to take appropriate effective measures to eliminate the threat" (Article 9).

11   Lt. Colonel M. Ziauddin voiced that suspicion in August, 1972. He wrote: "This country is on the verge of falling into abyss. Everyone has to be united, infused with pride and made it move. Talking about pride, what has happened to our pride? Did we have it? Have we lost it or is it hidden? In this case, the nations pride remains hidden in 'secret treaty.' We had pride and we found it on 26th March. Those who are signatories to it must give it out to the people. The prize belongs to them. Those who know of such a treaty must tell the people that there is such an act of 'betrayal.' If they do not do it, they are enemies of the people and the freedom fighter have the right to demand it" (*Weekly Holiday* 1972a).

12   *Gonokantha* became the prime target of the government. Until its final closure in January, 1975, the newspaper faced several assaults from the government through "legal" means. Its editor was also incarcerated. The supporters of the AL attacked and burned the office building several times.

13   The final blow to the freedom of the press came in June 1975 after the introduction of the one-party presidential system. The government promulgated the Newspapers (Annulment of Declaration) Ordinance 1975 by which it allowed only 4 daily newspapers to continue publication and banned the rest. All four of these newspa-

pers were taken under the control and management of the government.

14   The Jatiyo Rakkhi Bahini Order, 1972 (President's Order no. 21 of 1972) was promulgated on March 7, 1972 with a retroactive effect from February 1, 1972.

15   The amendment bill, even though of great significance, was passed by the Parliament within less than an hour—at a speed, according to Ahmed (1983:235), unprecedented in the history of law-making.

16   In pursuance of the new constitutional stipulation, Sheikh Mujib declared the formation of the "national party"—"Bangladesh Krishak Srmaik Awami League" (BAKSAL) on February 24, 1975. The organizational structure of the party was announced on June 6, 1975.

17   These speeches were delivered on March 26 in a public gathering in Dhaka, on June 19 in the first meeting of the BAKSAL central committee, and on July 21 to the newly appointed District Governors.

18   The composition and function of the District Administrative Council was delineated in the District Administration Act, Act No. VI of 1975 and was approved by the Parliament on July 9, 1975 (*The Bangladesh Gazette Extraordinary*, July 10, 1975). Subsequently, 61 District Governors were appointed by the President.

Chapter 5

The New Bangladeshi State

B y the middle of 1975, the Bangladeshi state had begun to unravel. The ruling intermediate classes were wrecked by crises and their efforts to gain consent and impose discipline fell far short of regaining the hegemony they had once enjoyed. Their policies had fostered the rise of new social classes and had integrated the state into the global economic system as a dependent, peripheral, capitalist state. A coherent counter coalition within the state to represent an alternative ruling class had emerged and was becoming powerful enough to overthrow the regime. The counter coalition, consisting of the new rich class, the bureaucracy, and the military, was not a conglomeration of disparate forces tied together by their dislike of the intermediate regime, but a coherent force with a clearly defined political and economic agenda for the state. The state, which they aspired to, was, moreover, distinctly different from that which had emerged after independence. All these factors came together to produce the violent *coup d'etat* of August 15, 1975, with brutal killings and the subsequent transformation of the state. The political agenda of the new state was to consolidate the power and authority of the military-bureaucratic oligarchy as the central institution within the state and the economic objective was to ensure capitalist development in general and, specifically, to revert to the pre-independence policy of "sponsored capitalism," where the state would come forward to help private investors with financial support. In this chapter, I will analyze the composition of the state after the *coup d'etat* of 1975 and its political and economic agenda under the military-bureaucratic oligarchy in order to corroborate the above contentions. I also intend to show that the new state, especially its agenda, has remained unchanged to date, despite the dawning of a democratic era in 1990 through a popular uprising followed by credible elections.

We must, however, begin with a description of the events that followed the brutal murder of Sheikh Mujibur Rahman. The crises of the ruling alliance provided the necessary conjuncture for the elements supporting capitalist development to launch their assault and for the radical elements to make their bid for state power. Although the *coup de main* (surprise attack) of August 15 came from the conservative elements of the army, the radical elements were in the wings, waiting for a time when the balance of class and other contradictions seemed appropriate to take action toward a revolutionary seizure of power. And, added to these forces were the loyalists of the Mujib regime and supporters of the status quo, who were primarily concerned about the chain of command and hierarchy of the army. With the downfall of the Mujib regime, the contradictions between these different social forces shifted to the arena of military action—coups and counter coups—until the Bangladeshi version of Louis Bonaparte, Major General Ziaur Rahman, was found.

The Advent of Ziaur Rahman: A Bonapartist Solution?

The pre-dawn *coup de main* of August 15 1975 was engineered by about 50 army officers. Of them, six majors were in command.[1] Not all coup leaders were in service at the time of the coup. Some of them were retired, some had lost their jobs on charges of corruption, and some had been discharged on disciplinary grounds.[2]

Various accounts of the planning of the coup exist. Some claim it had been hatched over a long time with the acquiescence of some AL leaders and, perhaps, with the support of external powers such as the United States. Some accounts insist that it was organized with lightning speed, as a reaction to events, primarily by a group of disgruntled junior military officers (for various accounts of the coup and their implications see Riaz 1998). Whatever the real truth, on the morning of August 15 1975, a group of Army officers took power and killed Mujibur Rahman and his family. Following the coup, Khandaker Mushtaq Ahmed was installed as President and a cabinet was hastily organized. The cabinet consisted entirely of AL leaders. In fact, 11 of the 19 ministers and 8 of the 9 ministers of state of the Mujibur Rahman cabinet joined the government. No military officer was included, but the real power remained with the coup-makers, especially the six majors commanding the armored and infantry regiments.

The putsch came as a surprise not only to the public but also to senior military officers. Some were outraged at being left ignorant spectators of the events. Nevertheless, the chiefs of three services (i.e., the Army, Navy, and Air Force), the police, the Bangladesh Rifles (BDR), and the *Rakkhi Bahini* (JRB) endorsed the coup in their speeches. Most of the senior army officers were more concerned about the "chain of command" than the killing of Mujib and the unconstitutional acts of junior officers.

Clearly, three centers of power emerged out of the coup: constitutionally, the President and the civilian cabinet remained the supreme authority (even though they had very little control over the situation); the army, as a whole, remained under the command of its regular senior officers, who were caught off guard by the coup; and the third source of authority was the putsch-makers themselves, hiding in the safety of the Presidential palace (*Bongobhavan*) with loyal soldiers. They instructed the President on all matters. Soon after the coup, junior officers were asked by army command to return to their normal duties. They declined to do so because they feared a court martial for breaking the chain of command.

The chain of command question notwithstanding, the political affiliation of these majors became another source of conflict among army officers. After the takeover, the majors declared Bangladesh an Islamic state. Khandaker Mustaque himself, however, did not mention anything of that sort. Yet, it was known to the army command that the putsch-makers belonged to the conservative section of the army. A large number of army officers, especially those who had actively participated in the liberation war, found this extremely uncomfortable. They viewed it as a return of the "Pakistani" army, despite some of the coup-makers themselves having played a part in the war of independence.

While confusion, chaos, and tension were running high in the cantonment and in the Presidential palace, the Mushtaq government made some important decisions: it repealed a part of the Constitution that was related to the formation and the functioning of the BKSAL (the Presidential form of government, however, was kept intact); it rescinded the scheme to make changes in local government (i.e., to divide Bangladesh into 61 districts and run by district Governors); it annulled the Presidential Order no. 9 of 1972 (which enabled the government to dismiss any government officer without assigning any reason); it merged the Rakkhi Bahini with the Army; and it withdrew the ban on some of the newspapers imposed under the Fourth Amendment of the Constitution.

Ten days after the coup, a major shake-up in the military and civil bureaucracy took place. The Chief of Army Staff, Major General Safiullah, was replaced by Major General Ziaur Rahman. The Chief of the Air Force, A.K. Khandaker, was replaced by Air Vice Marshal M.G. Tawab. A. B. S.

Safdar was appointed Director General of Defense Forces Intelligence (DFI). Mahbub Alam Chasi was appointed Principal Secretary to the President. Shafiul Azam became the Cabinet Secretary, Keramat Ali became Establishment Secretary, and Kazi Anwarul Hoq became an advisor to the President.[3] General (Rtd.) Osmani was appointed Defense advisor to the President, a post created to handle the internal feuds of the army. Except Zia and Osmani, none of the new appointees had been involved in the liberation war. In fact, most of them had been associated with the Pakistan administration in different capacities. The only freedom fighter who benefited from these changes was Brigadier Khaled Musharraf. He was elevated to the position of Chief of General Staff. Hossain Mohammed Ershad (who was in India for military training at that time) and Kazi Golam Dostagir were also elevated in the ranks, and Ershad became the Deputy Chief of Staff. Both of them, we must recall, were repatriated to Bangladesh from Pakistan after the liberation war. These actions were welcomed by the section of the army that was repatriated from Pakistan, but caused fury among the freedom fighters and the Mujib loyalists. They saw it as the total return of the Pakistani command structure. Thus, on the one hand, a conflict between the junior officers who staged the coup and the senior officers who were in command surfaced, while, on the other hand, a tension between the former freedom fighters and the repatriates mounted. The Mujib loyalists and the radical elements had one thing in common: opposition to the new regime, who were, in their eyes, "pro-Pakistani."

Khandaker Mushtaq, in the meantime, sent envoys to different countries including the USSR and India to inform them that no major changes in foreign policy would occur. India allegedly assembled a large number of soldiers along Bangladesh's borders. The air was thick with rumors that India might intervene. In order to diminish the possibility of any pro-Mujib political move, the government began to arrest those AL leaders who either declined to join the government or were disliked by the coup-makers. By the end of the month, some 35 prominent AL leaders including acting President of the government-in-exile, Nazrul Islam, PM of the exile government, Tajuddin Ahmed, PM of the ousted Mujib regime, Mansoor Ali, a minister of ousted government, Kamruzzaman, and the political secretary of Sheikh Mujib, Tofail Ahmed, were all taken into custody.

Over subsequent days, it became evident that nobody was in control of the country. Mushtaq, in collusion with the bureaucrats, was trying to establish his authority; the majors, especially Rashid and Farook, were trying to exert their power; and senior army officers were annoyed by Mushtaq's "mistreatment" and attempted division among them. Mushtaq, convinced that a change was imminent, made some desperate attempts to rally public support and so indemnify himself and his associates against possible future punishments for their crimes, which included the killing of Mujib and his family members.

In order to legitimize the August coup on grounds of the economic hardship of the people, he appointed an Economic Task Force on September 12. The Task Force completed its report within a record time of twelve days. The report was then incorporated in a White Paper that was intended to show how miserable the situation had become under the former regime. But, ironically, it failed to stir any support for the regime as it failed to recommend anything different. As a matter of fact, the report even used the verbiage of the former regime. Mushtaq then addressed the nation on October 3. He promised that the restrictions on political activity would be lifted on August 15, 1976, and that parliamentary elections would be held on February 28, 1977. This move was acclaimed in some quarters, but a statement contained in his speech infuriated senior army officers. The seniors saw Mushtaq's reference to the Majors as "the valiant sons of the soil" (*Dainik Bangla* 1975:8) as an approval of the continued arrogance of the Majors. Additionally, he issued an ordinance on September 26 1975 to indemnify everyone involved in the August coup.[4] A meeting of the members of the parliament was then summoned on October 16 at Bangabhavan. But the meeting could not proceed because a parliament member declined to address Mushtaq as "President" and questioned the legality of Mushtaq's assumption of presidency.

By the end of October, it was apparent that the regime had no support base at all. It was around this time that the supporters of the status-quo began to plan a counter-offensive. Led by Brigadier Khaled Mosharraf and Colonel Safaet Jamil, the group hastily drew up a plan for takeover. The plan went into effect after midnight on November 2. Ziaur Rahman was put under house arrest and armored regiments moved to take control of

Bangabhavan from the majors.[5] Khaled Musharraf requested, by telephone, their surrender. The majors rejected such a notion and vowed to fight until the bitter end. But, in the early morning of November 3 they changed their minds and negotiated a compromise that would allow them to leave the country. The coup was ill-planned, hastily organized, and was strictly limited in its objective—bringing down the arrogant Majors. It was after the Majors' expulsion that the coup-makers begin to think about the changes necessary to establish their total control over the army. The next day (November 4) they forced Ziaur Rahman to resign as Chief of Army Staff and compelled Mushtaq to appoint Khaled to that position. On Mushtaq's insistence, the cabinet met that evening and approved these actions. But even before the meeting was over, the horrifying news arrived: four prominent AL leaders, Nazrul Islam, Tajuddin Ahmed, Monsoor Ali, and Kamruzzman had been brutally murdered by some army men in the early hours of November 3 inside the Dhaka jail. This news dramatically changed the entire situation. A section of coup leaders angrily demanded the resignation of Mushtaq and the Cabinet. The Chief Justice of the Supreme Court, Abu Sadat Mohammad Sayem, was hurriedly brought to the meeting from his home and was appointed President at 1:00 am on November 5.

Until the morning of November 6, when A.S.M. Sayem was sworn in and addressed the nation, people were in the dark as to who was in charge. In situations like this, rumors abound: a section of pro-AL army men in collusion with India had taken over, an Indian intervention was imminent. Whether or not these rumors were deliberately created is difficult to determine. But the consequence was evident: a complete rejection of the coup. Nationalistic feelings ran high and everyone began to talk about a possible retaliation by freedom fighters in the Army. The question of national sovereignty and independence acquired a new dimension and the fear of Indian hegemony loomed large (Ahamed 1988:79).

The radical forces that had been waiting in the wings for about three months for an opportune moment to strike and bring down the entire "exploitative social system" decided the time to act was at hand. On November 5, the *Biplobi Sainik Sangstha* (Revolutionary Soldiers Union), an organization of non-commissioned soldiers supported by the JSD and led by Lt. Col. Abu Taher, called upon the soldiers to revolt against the army officers who had been exploiting them for their own selfish and ambitious reasons, staging one putsch after another.[6]

The soldiers were moved by the call. On the night of November 6, they began to rise with a force that would eventually shake the state of Bangladesh; it was the first soldiers' mutiny on such a scale since that of 1857 against the British in colonial India. Khaled Musharraf with at least 33 other officers, some of their families, and nearly 100 enlisted men were killed.[7] Ziaur Rahman was freed by the Sepoys. On the morning of November 7, troops from Dhaka Cantonment poured into the city and paraded through the streets shouting slogans and firing their weapons into the air. An unprecedented situation emerged as common people and the soldiers participated in processions. There were, however, two different political strands involved: one that was in favor of the unity among the soldiers and the people, and another in support of Mushtaq and against India.

To the organizers of the soldiers' uprising it was a revolution, a revolution they had dreamed of for three years. And it did resemble a revolution in many respects;[8] there was a definite objective to bring about a social change, the organizers were dedicated to the cause, and it possessed a certain amount of spontaneity. However, it lacked two of the principal elements of a revolutionary uprising: powerful leadership and an organized mass movement outside the army. In order to fill the vacuum of leadership, the organizers fell back on Ziaur Rahman, an ambitious and seemingly nonpolitical man who lacked a progressive personality but had popularity among the soldiers as a patriot and war hero.[9]

On the morning of November 7, Ziaur Rahman was freed from captivity by the members of the Revolutionary Soldiers Union. Zia then delivered a brief speech on national radio proclaiming Martial Law and declaring himself as the Chief Martial Law Administrator (CMLA). However, he declined to join Taher and his followers at a public gathering organized by the JSD and *Biplobi Sainik Sangstha* at the *Shahid Minar* (Martyr's Memorial). Confronted by Taher and excited Sepoys, Zia signed a copy of the 12-point demand as a gesture of his commitment, but refrained from making any reference to it when he spoke again to the nation later on the day. He, instead, appealed to the troops to return at once to their duties. The differences between Taher and Zia began to be obvious. A meeting of the military high command attended by General Osmani, General Khalil, Air Vice Marshal M. G. Tawab, M. H. Khan, and Mahbub Alam Chasi took place at Zia's headquarters before noon. Col. Taher was also present at the meeting. It was decided in this meeting that Sayem would continue to be the President. It was also decided that for reasons of precedence Sayem should also be the CMLA. Zia was asked to be one of the three DCMLAs. Although the meeting decided to release all political prisoners, which met one of the 12 demands, it categorically declined to talk about the 12-point demand as such. The decision to release political prisoners was extremely beneficial to the JSD, for all its key leaders were in jail at the time of the coup. But after this meeting, it became clear Zia had taken advantage of the situation and began to shake off the coup-makers. A day that began with extreme hope for the revolutionaries ended with utter defeat. The only achievement was the release of its party leaders (i.e., A.S.M. Abdur Rab, Major Jalil) from jail.

Upon their release, the JSD leaders denounced Zia and asked the Sepoys not to surrender their arms until their demands were met, while Zia conversely ordered the soldiers to return to barracks, surrender the weapons looted from the armories, and refrain from attacking officers. On November 15 1975, a martial law regulation was promulgated, evidently aimed at JSD activists, instituting a death sentence against anyone encouraging mutinous actions. Eight days later, JSD leaders were again arrested on charges of sedition. Col. Taher was arrested on November 24 on charges of mutiny and treason. Thus, the revolution ended.[10]

Eighty-four days of chaos and confusion, coups and counter-coups, killings and counter-killings, conspiracy, and uprising finally paved the way for the rise of Ziaur Rahman as the strong-man.[11] A man who had participated in any of these coups became the ultimate beneficiary of all the changes. Contending groups within the army fought each other only to hire a "frontman," Zia, who cleverly took advantage of the situation. In the process, they exposed and exhausted themselves. The rise of Zia quite appropriately reminds us of the situation in France between 1848-1851 leading to the emergence of Louis Bonaparte (Napoleon III as he is more commonly known); "all fell on their knees, equally mute and equally impotent, before the rifle butt" (Marx 1974:236), and all that once seemed achievements "vanished like a series of optical illusions before the spell of a man whom even his enemies do not claim to be a magician" (Marx 1974:151).

These eighty-four days, however, not only brought Zia to the helm but also brought back the bureaucrats who were trained in leading a state capable of navigating through rough waters toward the goal of the capitalist shore. The bureaucracy as an institution had already secured a prominent position in the last days of the Mujib regime, and now it found leaders asserting their authority in collusion with the army. In other words, the final act of the transformation of the Bangladeshi state began. The state, we can say, borrowing Marx's (1974:149) words, began to return to its ancient form, "the unashamedly simple rule of military saber and clerical cowl."

Rule of Military Saber

In his first speech after the November 7 uprising, President Sayem dissolved the Parliament, suspended the constitution, and appointed three DCMLAs. The country was divided into nine martial law zones and nine Zonal Martial Law Administrators were appointed. The President was nominally in charge; the core of the central authority was composed of military officials.

A seven-member Council of Advisors was appointed on November 26, 1975. Four bureaucrats and technocrats were added to the three DCMLAs. Subsequently, the council was expanded to almost double its original size, but it maintained its essential character; it was full of "nonpolitical" bureaucrats and technocrats who had served in the regimes of Ayub and Yahya Khan during Pakistani colonial rule, and who knew the art of running a civil-military bureaucratic regime (Jahan 1980:210). The number of advisers then increased to 24, and of these 10 were from the civil bureaucracy (and not surprisingly, former CSP officers), 3 were military officers, and the rest were technocrats. The numbers of bureaucrats demonstrated their dominance and their positions within the cabinet reflected their control. The important ministries such as Planning, Finance, Industries, and Agriculture were headed by bureaucrats. Thus, their orientations had a significant impact on the future course of Bangladesh. Shafiul Azam is a case in point. Azam, who continued to serve as Chief Secretary of East Pakistan during the liberation war, left the civil service some time in 1972 because of his strong opposition to the government's nationalization policy. He was brought back during the Mushtaq regime as Cabinet Secretary. During Ziaur Rahman's rule, he initially headed the Planning Commission and was then elevated to the position of President's special adviser. He became the architect of Bangladesh's move toward privatization and private sector development (Humphrey 1990:59, fn 5). The preeminence of the bureaucrats in the cabinet remained unchanged throughout the Zia period. In 1981—the year Zia was assassinated in an abortive coup—there were 24 cabinet ministers and of them, 6 were military bureaucrats, 5 were civil servants, 6 were technocrats, 4 were businessmen, 1 was a landlord, and 2 were lawyers.

The bureaucrats were not only occupying cabinet memberships, they were also successfully usurping positions in public enterprises and the planning apparatus; they established a firm control over the institutions responsible for implementing government policies. Public corporations, Ahmed (1980) informs us, became the exclusive preserve of bureaucrats, both civil and military. By the end of 1975, of 38 public corporations, 11 were headed by former CSP officers, 2 by police officers, 5 by military officers, 6 were headed by former EPCS officials, and the rest were headed by members of other civil service cadres. In fact, an account of 1976 shows there was not a single person who was head of a public enterprise who came from outside the civil-military bureaucracy. A World Bank report noted that of 76 chief executives appointed in public sector corporations in 1972, not one was in place 3 years later; quite a few emigrated (IBRD 1984:140).

In the face of opposition and virtual non-cooperation from the bureaucracy, and because of disillusionment with the political regime, the original members of the Planning Commission had left before the coup d'etat of August 15, 1975. With the changes in the apex of state power, the Planning Commission experienced changes in terms of its composition and functioning. The National Economic Council (NEC), a colonial vestige abolished during the Mujib-regime, was revived and given enormous power. A five-member Executive Committee of the NEC was constituted with civil-military bureaucrats as its members. The Planning Commission, an eight-member body, was completely dominated by civil bureaucrats. The importance of the Commission itself was reduced drastically by reducing the status of deputy chairman, the members, and others further down the hierarchy. The external resources division had been reorganized several times. The monitoring function was taken away from the sectoral divisions of the Commission; the administrative division assumed bureaucratic control over the functioning and organizing of sector divisions. Essentially, the Commission lost its capability in respect to plan formulation, monitoring implementation, and even evaluation because of an increase in intervention by aid donors in these areas as well as by authoritarian decisions that emerged at the top. The function of the Planning Commission had been infructuous, often used for *post-facto* approval. The bureaucratic dominance over the planning mechanism also ensured control over scarce resources which, quite naturally, had far-reaching consequences. Indeed, the planning process is ultimately about allocating the resources at the disposal of the state.

During the period between 1975 and 1981, the control of the bureaucracy extended to the implementation level. Islam's (1988) calculations, based on government publications, show that the Investment Board of the government, which was the highest authority for implementing the development strategy, consisted of 15 members, and, except for one member, all of them were bureaucratic elites during the Zia period (Islam 1988:148).

Added to these were the strengthening of the supremacy of the executive and militarization of the administration. Despite the military regime's so-called "civilianization"—meaning general elections, the appointment of civilian politicians in larger numbers to the cabinet, and the installation of a parliament—the supreme authority remained with the chief executive, the President. The power and authority of the President was enhanced in subsequent years. The Second Proclamation (Fifteenth Amendment) Order, 1978, among other things, made the parliament completely subservient to the President. Furthermore, the President could draw one-fifth of his cabinet from among people who were not members of Parliament; he could enter into treaties with foreign countries without informing Parliament if he considered such action "in the national interest"; and he could withhold his assent from any bill passed by Parliament (Second Proclamation Order No. IV of 1978, December 18, 1978).

The military bureaucrats, during this period, increasingly began to occupy high-ranking positions in the civil administration and foreign services. On March 1 1979, 25 of 625 officers of the senior policy pool (SPP)[12] were military officers. At that time, 6 of 20 Secretaries came from the military. In June 1980, of 101 senior officers (i.e., Chairman, Managing Director, Director, General Manager) of public sector enterprises 42 were military officers or retired military personnel. Ten out of 20 top public corporations were headed by military officers. At the beginning of 1980, the number of military officers appointed to civilian positions (such as Secretary, Ambassador) was 41, but by the end of the year the number had increased to 79. Of them, 32 were in diplomatic missions abroad and 7 were ambassadors.

Occupying the key positions and dominating the planning and implementation mechanism, accorded the civil-military bureaucracy immense control over the country's scarce resources, which they used for their own benefit. Huque and Ahkter (1989) explained the situation:

> The military rulers of Bangladesh have consistently tried to keep the army and the bureaucracy satisfied by granting additional facilities to them. Armed forces personnel have received rations (foodstuffs) at very low prices, free furnished accommodation and attractive fringe benefits. On retirement or resignation from active service, officers have been rewarded with lucrative commercial facilities and contracts or appointments to important and well-paid administrative positions. (Huque and Ahkter 1989:174)

In order to enhance their benefits and coercive abilities, the military rulers increased the defense allocation substantially. The defense budget left over from the Mujib regime for 1975-76 was immediately revised upwards, with the original allocation raised from Taka 750 million (7 percent of the national budget) to Taka 1109.34 million (20 percent of the national budget) (Islam 1988:121). The increase, however, was not limited to defense expenditure alone, but was accompanied by an increase in general administration and police. In the first two years of military rule, there was an increase in defense and civil administration expenditure by over Taka 2 billion against the increase of less than 1 billion in the total expenditure on all other heads taken together (Hossain 1979:34). Table 7 shows the revenue expenditure of the Bangladesh Government on defense, police and justice, and general administration heads between the years 1973/74 and 1980/81. These figures, however, do not reflect the total expenditure on these heads because some expenditure for these purposes was concealed under other heads. It is alleged that money spent to build cantonments was covered either under the development budget or included under the head of civil works. Yet, these figures provide us with a clear impression of how resources were used for the benefit of the military-bureaucratic oligarchy. The expenditure on education is also included in this table to show the priorities of the regime in a country whose literacy rate was below 20 percent.

Besides these macro-statistics some micro-level data may assist in understanding the astounding amount of money spent on military personnel. According to Vivekananda (1986:324), in 1977 the regime was spending $1,606 per soldier. In 1979, this went up to $1,697. We should

Table 7.
Revenue Expenditure of the Bangladesh Government
on Selected Heads: 1973/74 - 1980/81
(In Crore Taka)

Year	General Admn.	Police & Judiciary	Defense	Education & Sports
1973/74	32.21	24.51	41.96	64.82
1974/75	35.15	22.45	70.85	82.21
1975/76	24.66	66.38	110.93	85.45
1976/77	35.33	87.10	151.39	98.21
1977/78	38.69	96.59	144.41	126.50
1978/79	47.57	125.86	207.21	154.19
1979/80	343.10	131.20	178.20	177.20
1980/81	292.00	77.30	211.80	209.80
1981/82	381.80	213.40	274.20	234.90

Source: Statistical Pocket Book of Bangladesh: 1978, 1979, 1980, 1981, 1982
Bangladesh Bureau of Statistics, Statistical Divisio n, Planning Ministry, GPRB.

recall here that the per capita annual income in Bangladesh at that time was less than $100. Available statistics show that during the period of 1976-1980 Bangladesh annually spent about $593 for each member in military.

Obviously, resource allocation favored defense service personnel. One glaring example is the food distributed under the Public Foodgrain Distribution System (PFDS). As I have mentioned previously, the Army, the Police, and other paramilitary forces included in the Essential Priority (EP) group received a larger share than any other section of the society, and this share increased from 13 percent in 1972/73 to 39 percent in 1980/81 (World Bank 1985:35). Additionally, they received it at a significantly lower price. The price of rationed rice for the EP group was Taka 58 per maund (about 80 lbs.) from July 1975, while it was Taka 229 per maund for SR (Statutory Rationing), MR (Modified Rationing), and other groups. There was a gradual price increase of rationed commodities between 1973 and 1985. In fact, the cumulative increase in the ration price of rice was 564 percent. This affected all categories except the EP.[13]

Following the coups and counter coups of 1975, the numerical strength of the defense forces and members of law enforcement agencies increased at a spectacular rate. The number of total defense forces personnel (including Air Force and Navy) was about 26,500 in 1974, which grew to 63,000 in 1976; by 1982, the number reached 80,000. The Army expanded from 5 divisions in 1975 to 8 divisions in 1981. Within the first three years of the military takeover, a new army division was created. Paramilitary forces grew from 29,000 to about 46,000. The strength of the Police force increased from about 40,000 to about 70,000, with a combat-ready Special Police Force of 12,500 men (Maniruzzman 1980:203).

With the attainment of prominent positions at different levels of the administration, the civil and military bureaucracy successfully consolidated itself as the central institution within the state. Along with the consolidation of power, the oligarchy moved forward to implement its economic project: to ensure capitalist development in general and, specifically, to revert to the pre-liberation policy of "sponsored capitalism," where the state would come forward to help private investors with financial supports.

The Economic Project of the New State

In order to ensure a capitalist development, the military regime took a number of significant steps during the period 1975-1981. These steps can be broadly summarized as follows: a) legalization of "black money"; b) disinvestment/denationalization[14] of state-owned enterprises; c) raising and subsequently abolishing the ceiling on private investment; d) withdrawal of restrictions on private foreign investment; and e) providing credit to private entrepreneurs.

One of the first acts of the military regime was to legalize the wealth earned by the new rich class through a variety of means. The military regime contended that the misery under the Mujib regime was a result of unprecedented corruption and rampant pilferage of public property. They claimed they seized power to bring an end to this corruption. But soon after assuming power they decided to provide an opportunity to legalize wealth earned through "unknown" means, commonly referred to as "black money" in Bangladesh. By the end of the year 1975, the regime declared that it would not ask any questions of any intending investor about the source of his wealth. The government decided that even for the purpose of income tax and wealth tax, the amount declared would not be taken into account at all and assessment would be made under the normal law as usual, as if no declaration of such funds were made, if the funds were utilized for the purchase of the disinvested units or for new investments before 30 June 1978 (*Weekly Holiday* 1976:1). The significance of the decision can be appreciated if one takes into account the estimated amount of black money accumulated by the new rich class after liberation. According to a weekly newspaper, during the three and a half years of the Mujib regime, at least Taka 800 crore had been accumulated by this new rich class. The newspaper maintained that people involved in the textile trade alone had made an illegal profit of Taka 138.50 crore (*Weekly Holiday* 1976:1). The decision, of course, was made to placate the new rich class and their allies.

It was at this time that the government delineated the basic principles of its economic policies. Shafiul Azam, the Commerce Minister at the time, stated that the government was ready to extend all possible support to the private sector for utilizing the full potential of the private entrepreneurs in increasing the productive economic activities of the country (*Bangladesh Observer* 1975:1).

The government declared a "Revised Investment Policy" on December 7, 1975. Though the policy was periodically amended, it remained the basic policy statement and guideline until a completely new and more liberalized policy was declared in June 1982 by the Ershad regime. Under the revised policy of 1975, the ceiling on private investment was raised to Taka 100 million. The new policy opened up opportunities for joint ventures between public corporations and private indigenous or foreign investors in all but eight categories.[15] The moratorium on nationalization, which had earlier been raised to 15 years, was altogether scrapped.[16] Tax holidays and other incentives introduced earlier were reinforced. The policy also announced the government's intention to set up the Investment Corporation of Bangladesh (ICB) to provide bridge finance.[17] The Dhaka Stock Exchange, which had been shut down in 1972, was reactivated. The policy made it permissible to repatriate foreign capital and profits. Additionally, the policy outlined the government's plan to disinvest and denationalize some industrial enterprises. As mentioned earlier, there were some amendments to the policy in subsequent years. One of them was related to the ceiling. In September 1978, the ceiling was altogether removed.

The policies of the military regime brought a fundamental change in the role of the private sector in industrial development. Hence, in accordance with the new policy, the regime went ahead with denationalization and disinvestment. By the end of 1977, 21 industrial units were disinvested and handed over to the new owners; 15 units were disinvested but not handed over; and 33 units were in the process of disinvestment (Rahim 1978:1185). The process intensified after 1977. By March 1982, a total of 236 industrial units were disinvested/denationalized. Between 1982 and 1989, another 156 units were disinvested.[18]

These figures do not include the commercial and trading entities. Clare Humphrey, a US-AID researcher and proponent of privatization acknowledges that there is no aspect of privatization in Bangladesh more shrouded in mystery, obfuscation, and a general lack of information than the issue of the privatization of commercial and trading entities. According to Humphrey (1990:50), estimates of privatized commercial enterprises have varied from 2000 to 8000. Comprehensive official figures are non-existent, or at least not available. Nevertheless, statistics pertaining to the share of commercial/trading enterprises in the private sector in 1974 and 1977 provide us with some indications. The share of private enterprises went up to 65 percent from 30 percent. The non-existence of data related to commercial enterprises is linked to the speed of disinvestment/denational-ization. In most cases, units were sold without any public bidding and primarily to those who could establish close contacts with the regime.

Two reasons were cited for the policy of privatization: first, the industrial units were grossly mismanaged; second, they were not at all prof-itable. Although the allegation of mismanagement is partially true, the claim that the performance of all public sector industrial units was dismal is factually incorrect. Sobhan and Ahsan (1984), in their study of the performance of disinvestment and denationalized units, show that 90 small and medium sized units disinvested between 1976 and June 1982 profited about Taka 6 crore even in the year prior to disinvestment. The performance of 32 units was "excellent."

In accordance with the government's policy of privatization in the industrial sector, similar initiatives were taken in the agrarian sector. Given that the government did not own land, privatization policies took a different form. The withdrawal of subsidy from supplies such as fertilizers, the increase of tube-well rent, and the privatization of irrigation equipment were some of them. Soon after the military takeover, the government began to withdraw subsidy from fertilizers and irrigation equipment. As a result, the price increased considerably over the period 1975-1984. For example, the price of Urea fertilizer increased 326 percent, that of TSP fertilizer 348 percent, and MP 340 percent (Osmani and Quasem 1985). This stunning increase, according to the study of Osmani and Quasem (1985), affected the poor and middle class peasants so much that they were virtually driven out of agricultural production. The situation further deteriorated because of the agricultural credit policy of the government. The study reveals that in 1981/82 peasants who owned more than 5 acres of land received about 31.2 percent of credit, while marginal farmers (owning land of 1 acre or less) received 3.2 percent of total credit disbursed by banks and other govern-ment agencies.

Additionally, since 1975, rent of irrigation pumps had been increased. In 1975/76, the price of rent for a 2 cusec power pump was Taka 600 and for a deep tube-well was Taka 1200. In 1983/84, the amount was raised to Taka 3600 and Taka 5000 respectively. Along with the increase in rent, the government began to privatize the pumps and tube-wells. The process of privatization began in 1979/80. By the end of 1983, 43 percent of deep tube-wells and 56 percent of power pumps had been transferred to private ownership. Privatization of irrigation equipment had virtually ended the access of relatively poor farmers.

The encouragement of the private sector did not stop at disinvestment and denationalization measures. The state provided further help in the form of bank loans to entrepreneurs. The total value of funds provided by the *Bangladesh Shilpa Bank* (BSB), the *Bangladesh Shilpa Rin Sangstha* (BSRS), the Investment Corporation of Bangladesh (ICB), and three Development Finance Institutions (DFI), between the period 1972 and 1982, reveals the trend. Prior to the changes of August 15, 1975, the private sector received 21.6 percent of loans provided by the DFIs. Conversely, after the military takeover, 93.4 percent of loans went to the private sector. Data available from these DFIs informs us that during the period 1971/72-1974/75, average disbursement per year to the public sector was Taka 23.83 million and Taka 6.54 million per year to the private sector. During the period 1975/76-1981/82, the corresponding figures were Taka 40.71 million and Taka 508.89 million respectively.

In order to encourage private enterprise, the military regime introduced some changes to the First Five Year Plan (1973-78) that was being implemented. Since two years of the plan were already over, the regime revised the plan targets for the remaining three years instead of changing the plan altogether. The "Three-Year Hard Core Plan," as it was called by the regime, allocated a larger share to the private sector, especially the industrial division. Private investment in industry increased from Taka 87.4 million in 1973/74 to Taka 2091.4 million in 1977-78 (Bangladesh Planning Commission 1980: Section IX, 6-7). In the Two-Year Plan that followed the Hard-Core Plan, the private sector was allocated 16 percent of the plan outlay as opposed to 11 percent in the First Five Year Plan (BPC 1978). Although the Second Five Year Plan recognized the limitation of the private sector, the allocation went up to 22 percent in the Second Five Year Plan (1980-85) formulated by the military regime (BPC 1980).

The economic project of the new state also included further integration with the world capitalist economy. With that end in mind, the government inspired the establishment of export-oriented industry and promoted foreign investment. During 1975-80, a total of 119 export-oriented industrial units were sanctioned involving a subsidy of Taka 1929 million (19,291.85 lacs) including foreign exchange components of Taka 1351 million (13,511.90 lacs). In addition to a wide range of privileges already offered such as tax holidays, general rules for depreciation of fixed assets, and "Free Zone" concessions, an act was passed by Parliament in 1980 to promote foreign investment and protect the interests of foreign investors (Foreign Private Investment: Promotion and Protection Act No. XI, 1980). The act stated unequivocally "foreign investment shall not be expropriated or nationalized" and "if any foreign enterprise is nationalized for a public purpose adequate compensation will be provided."

None of these measures brought any significant change in favor of Bangladesh. Because of the difficulties associated with capturing foreign markets by a country coming relatively late to industrialization, as well as the low quality of products, the export-oriented ventures did not reap any substantial profit during this period. The scheme to attract private foreign capital also failed to achieve success to any significant degree for two reasons:

> First, the existing weak industrial infrastructure, except cheap labour, was not enough to provide profitable grounds for investment. Second, the metropolitan investors were hesitant to invest, as they wanted to be sure that no radical regime would come to power and nationalize their investment. (Mannan 1990:403)

The legislation of the Foreign Private Investment Act of 1980 was an attempted remedy for the second problem. But the measure was apparently insufficient to gain the trust of metropolitan investors.

As opposed to this situation, there was an upward surge in import bills leading to a huge deficit in the balance of trade. It rose to Taka 3396.60 crore in 1981/82 from Taka 770.65 in 1974/75. There were two reasons for this: The first concerns the structure of industry in Bangladesh—there was (and still is) an almost total dependence on imports for raw materials. The second reason was the result of the sumptuous lifestyles of the new rich, which necessitated the import of consumption goods.

During the aforementioned period, the share of exports in GDP remained almost stagnant (6.33 percent in 1972/73 and 6.80 percent in 1981/82), while the share of imports increased from 17.14 percent in 1972/73 to 22.70 percent in 1981/82. During the fiscal year 1975/76, when the military regime took over, the share of exports in GDP was 5.17 percent and the share of imports was 13.68 percent. Over five years, according to the Bangladesh Bureau of Statistics, the share of exports increased 1.63 percent, whereas the share of imports increased 9.02 percent.

The regime's ambitious plans to revitalize the private sector and extend all sorts of credit to entrepreneurs necessitated further dependence on aid. Prodded by the donors, they embarked upon a policy of seeking more and more aid from Western countries. Depending on the foreign help lined up for the private and public sector, Zia repeatedly said that money was no problem and that entrepreneurs should be more creative and come up with new projects (the dimension of aid dependence and contribution of aid to the Bangladesh economy during this period is documented in Table 8 and Table 9).

Massive privatization, adherence to a policy of sponsored capitalism and infusion of aid along with an autonomous role of the civil-military bureaucrats brought dramatic changes in terms of the class composition of Bangladesh society. At the center of these changes was the consolidation of the class that had begun to grow under the previous regime. The class that we have so far described as new rich (*nouveau riche*), now with the help of the state functionaries, elevated themselves to the position of "lumpen capitalist," i.e., a class that is more interested in plundering as a means of accumulating capital than resorting to economic means of accumulation, namely "profit maximization through productive investments in various sectors of the economy" (Siddiqui et al. 1990:197). We will return to the discussion of the consequences of these policies on Bangladesh society. However, it is important to first consider the legitimation processes of military-bureaucratic rule and the crises of the state during the years 1975 to 1981.

Table 8.
The Dimensions of Aid Dependence
(1975/76 - 1981/82)

	1975/76	1978/79	1980/81
GDP	58,686	66,766	73,850
Aid Disbursed	6631.0	7723.0	10128
Aid as % of GDP	11.3	11.6	13.7
Aid as % of imports	65.70	71.17	61.06
Domestic Savings as % of GDP	1.8	3.0	0.9
Aid as % of investment	107.55	83.35	64.92
Disbursed Aid as % of Development Budget	141.18	97.83	78.26

Notes:
1. GDP at Market Prices of 1972/73 in millions of Taka.
2. Aid Figures in millions of Taka computed at 1972/73 prices using the import index of the World Bank.
3. Imports in 1972/73 market prices . Real value of imports taken from World Bank data.
4. World Bank estimate.

Legitimation of Military-Bureaucratic Rule

The legitimation process of the new state involved constitutional measures as well as an ideological shift. Constitutionally, the regime was illegitimate. However, they could claim that Zia neither engineered nor participated in the process of violation of the constitution and that the coups and counter coups, killings and counter killings, paved the way for his emergence but were not carried out with the intention to bring him to power.

Ziaur Rahman essentially derived his legitimacy from the uprising of November 7 1975, although he did not identify himself with the spirit of the uprising. The aim of the coup, according to the pronouncements of the organizers, was to stimulate social change, bring an end to social injustices, and build an army that would protect the interests of the poor (Biplobi Sainik Sanghstha 1975). However, there was clearly ambivalence: Zia had to separate the act from the spirit of the act. To do so, he attached a new

216

Table 9
Contribution of Aid in the Economy
(1975/76 - 1980/81)

A. **The % share of disbursed project aid to development expenditure in the Annual Development Plan in various sectors**	1975/76	1980/81
1. Agriculture	4.52	21.32
2. Rural Development	1.86	27.70
3. Water & Flood Control	11.14	23.47
4. Industries	32.76	33.97
5. Power, Scientific Research & Natural Resources	26.95	45.63
6. Transport	15.80	60.89
7. Communications	7.75	22.00
8. Physical Planning and Housing	12.60	30.29
9. Education	21.12	20.38
10. Health	37.80	39.79
11. Population Planning	27.32	52.82
12. Social Welfare	81.67	7.43
13. Manpower and Employment	4.95	43.57
14. Cyclone Reconstruction	32.30	—
Total	**19.62**	**38.64**
B. **The % share of disbursed food aid to total food availability**	10.6	6.0
C. **The % share of disbursed commodity aid to import of intermediate goods**	83.6	NA

Source: Sobhan (1982:26)

meaning to the uprising, interpreting it as nationalist, yet different from the nationalism of the Mujib regime. He thus explained that the purpose of the uprising was to safeguard the national sovereignty against foreign conspiracy (i.e., Indian hegemony) and to assert the independent identity of the people of Bangladesh.

There were three elements to this interpretation of the uprising: it marked a break with the radicals' claim of class uprising and hence attempted to reach all classes, shifting the political discourse from class contradiction to consensus and national building; it was justified on the basis of safeguarding national sovereignty—it was primarily led by the military, which took on the role of defender of national independence at a critical juncture and would thus play a paramount role in ensuring state security in the future; and thirdly, a new enemy against whom nationalism was pitted had emerged—India.

In accordance with this interpretation, Ziaur Rahman began to talk about a new nationalism, Bangladeshi nationalism. In April 1977, soon after assuming the office of President, Zia made some constitutional amendments through a proclamation (Second Proclamation Order no. 1, April 23, 1977). The amendment brought changes in Article 6 of the original constitution which stipulated that the identity of the citizens of Bangladesh would be known as *Bangalee*. Instead, the amendment proclaimed, the citizens would be known as "Bangladeshi." Thus, the identity of the nation was linked with the territorial limit in order to isolate it from the so-called "Bangalee subculture" of India. The amendment also brought changes in the Preamble of the Constitution. The words, "historic struggle for national liberation" were replaced by "historic war for national independence." The change, though it appears to be only semantic, reflected the regime's bias: it highlighted the war of 1971 in which the military played a role, rather than the political movements of the civilian population in the 1950s and 1960s that contributed to the growth of Bengali nationalism. Minimizing the role of the civilian population in "achieving independence" also minimizes their role in "safeguarding independence."

The word "secularism," appearing in the Preamble and Article 8 as one of the four fundamental principles, was substituted with "absolute trust and faith in the Almighty Allah"; and a new clause (1A) was inserted to emphasize that "absolute trust and faith in almighty Allah" should be "the basis of all actions." Article 12, which defined "secularism," was omitted and above the Preamble the words *"Bismillahir Rahmanur Rahim"* (In the name of Allah, the Beneficent, the Merciful) were inserted to give the Constitution an Islamic color. The principle of socialism was given new meaning—"economic and social justice" (Preamble and Article 8). A new ideological terrain was created by the regime to legitimize their rule. Religion, the territoriality of identity, and national security constituted the core of this new ideology.

Concurrent to the process of ideological legitimation, the regime initiated a process to gain constitutional legitimacy. President Sayem, in his first speech to the nation on November 6, 1975, promised the ban on political activities would be lifted by mid-1976 and that general elections would be held by February 1977. Accordingly, the Political Parties Regulation (PPR) was promulgated on July 28, 1976. Under the regulation, parties were allowed to function on a limited scale (e.g., organize small-scale, indoor meetings) provided their programs were approved by the government. A strict rule for licensing political parties was followed. Nevertheless, major political parties, including the AL, were approved for functioning. In the process, the pan-Islamic parties, banned under the Mujib regime, also gained permission to revive their organizations. At the beginning of these "indoor politics," President Sayem reiterated his pledge for the restoration of democracy. He declared the ban on politics would be totally lifted by August 1976 and the elections would be held as promised (Bangladesh Observer 1976:3). But later, on the grounds of a deteriorating law and order situation, the restrictions on open politics were continued and on November 21, allegedly because of pressure from Zia, President Sayem postponed the general elections. He, however, maintained that local-level elections would be held in February. On November 30 1976, Zia assumed the position of CMLA leaving President Sayem merely a ceremonial head. The non-partisan elections to the local-level bodies were held in early 1977, which generated considerable political activity. Having seen that the people were inclined to accept the regime and its authority, Zia took over the Presidency on April 21, 1977, and made the constitutional amendments referred to earlier. Shortly afterward, he declared a 19-point program for his administration and announced that he would seek a popular mandate to remain in power and implement his program. The program, among other things, called for preservation of "the independence, integrity and sovereignty of the state at all costs" and to "give necessary incentives to the private sector for the economic development of the country" (BNP n.d.)

The referendum, held on May 30 1977, was a mockery of the electoral process. No political party was allowed to speak out against him or his program. Strict censorship imposed on the newspapers made it impossible to make any evaluation of the program, let alone of Ziaur Rahman. The entire administration was employed in favor of Zia; all mass media were forced to propagate the program. Two separate ballot boxes—one with a picture of Zia and another without any symbol—were supposed to be placed in all polling centers. Thus, anyone voting against Zia would have had to identify himself publicly and expose himself to future intimidation by the administration and Zia's supporters. It is alleged that in a number of polling stations, the box without the picture was removed altogether by Zia's supporters. Additionally, organized mass rigging and false voting was rampant. Under such circumstances, the results were bound to be in favor of Zia; and so it was, with Zia securing 98.88 percent of votes.

Through this election Zia cultivated his supporters. On the other hand, opposition parties succeeded in reorganizing themselves and began to demand national elections. The attempted coup of September 30 and October 2, 1977 (discussed later), sent a clear signal to the regime that organized political support was needed to continue their rule. Accordingly, at the end of the year, Ziaur Rahman, who claimed he had no political ambitions, hinted at launching a political platform.[19] With his active support and encouragement, a political party named *Jagodal* (*Jatiyatabadi Gonotantrik Dal*, Nationalist Democratic Party) was launched by the Vice-President Justice Sattar on February 23, 1978. Although it was public knowledge that Zia was behind the party, he did not join. For the first time in the history of Bangladesh, a party was being formed by those who were already in power. Leaders and workers of different parties were enticed to join the new party, primarily through dispensation of patronage, bribes and hand-outs.

On April 21, 1978 Zia announced that Presidential elections would be held on June 3, 1978 and restrictions on political activities would be withdrawn in May. The Jagodal formed an electoral alliance (Nationalist Front) with five other political parties (the Muslim League, the United People's Party, the NAP-B, the Bangladesh Labor Party, and the Bangladesh Scheduled Caste Federation), appointed Zia the Chairperson of the alliance, and nominated him their candidate. Zia's main rival was retired-General M.A.G. Osmani, former C-in-C of liberation forces, nominee of an alliance (*Gonotantrik Oikkyo Jote*, Democratic United Alliance) of six opposition parties including the AL. Given that the opposition had not been allowed to function for the last three years and a large number of opposition leaders

220

were in jail, 40 days notice of the election and 23 days to campaign was insufficient time for the opposition to reach the voters. Additionally, Zia used all government resources and mass media. The government's information and broadcasting ministry was put in charge of Zia's publicity, while martial law restrictions on press were still in place. The manipulation of election results was also reported. The results were a foregone conclusion. Ziaur Rahman was elected as President securing 76 percent of the vote. Osmani, who had not even been able to buy the voter lists (cost $60,000) because of insufficient funds, gained 21 percent of votes.

Following the election, Zia took the initiative to integrate the Front into a single party. Accordingly, a new party was formed on September 1, 1978: the Bangladesh Nationalist Party (BNP). Shortly afterward, the date of Parliamentary elections was announced. The opposition political parties initially refused to join the elections unless their demands were met. The demands included the withdrawal of martial law and the Special Powers Act of 1974; the restoration of the constitution of 1972 except the Fourth amendment; the guarantee of press freedom; and the release of all political prisoners. After a few postponements because of the opposition's threat of boycott, parliamentary elections were held on February 18, 1979. The opposition parties failed to gain any concessions because of internal squabbles. Twenty-nine political parties participated in the election; 1703 candidates from different political parties and 425 independent candidates contested 300 parliamentary seats. The Bangladesh Nationalist Party (BNP) secured 207 seats. They were followed by the Awami League with 39 seats and an Islamist Alliance with 8 seats.

The newly elected Parliament met in its first session at the beginning of April 1979. An amendment to the Constitution was passed (The Constitution Fifth Amendment Bill) which incorporated all the resolutions, decrees, proclamations, and orders issued under the authority of martial law into laws and parts of constitution, where necessary. Thus, the actions taken after August 15, 1975, were legitimized including the indemnification of the killers of Mujib and the deletion of secularism from the constitution.

One may conclude from the preceding paragraphs that the military-bureaucratic regime led by Zia was extremely successful in legitimizing its rule. And, indeed, this is true to a great extent. In terms of constitutionality, the regime became a legal authority. In terms of changing the course of Bangladesh politics or, borrowing Zia's own words, making politics difficult, their success was immense. The regime, indeed, changed the entire discourse of Bangladesh politics. The secular politics of Bangladesh was dealt a serious blow. The core identity base of nationalism had been changed from language to religion. Since then, the emphasis on religious identity has grown so strong that the Islamist force has emerged as one of the principal political actors in Bangladesh. The pursuance of a growth oriented development strategy, prodded by donors and beneficial to the regime, not only pushed Bangladesh into a deeper debt trap and increased the incidence of poverty, but, more significantly, marginalized the question of public intervention to redistribute productive assets.

Redistribution with growth is no longer on the agenda in the economic planning of Bangladesh. The "success" must be attributed to the military-bureaucratic regimes, especially that which ruled Bangladesh between 1975 and 1982. The economic rationale for the political promotion of economic growth was advanced to ensure the absolute control of the bureaucracy over the planning process, not only for the time being but also in the future.

Though this regime did have some success, it would be wrong to say that the regime was free from crises and faced no opposition at all. At the initial stage, the regime encountered resistance from different factions of the Army, which were contained with remarkable brutality. At a later stage, intra-party squabbles and conflict between politicians and bureaucrats created considerable difficulty for the regime.

Crises and Opposition of the Regime

Political developments following the November 7 uprising evidently benefited the repatriated officers much to the annoyance of freedom fighters within the Army. The trial and execution of Col. Taher, who had lost one of his legs during the liberation war and was awarded the highest military award for his bravery, appeared to the latter section as an act of vengeance by the repatriated officers. The economic programs of the regime and rehabilitation of the once-ostracized, top-ranking bureaucrats corroborated their feelings that the history of Pakistan was being repeated. This gave the followers of Taher ample opportunity to bring a large number of freedom fighters together to make further coup attempts. Additionally, there remained supporters of the exiled six Majors, who felt they were being excluded from power. In order to gain salience and bring back their leaders from exile, they also conspired in a number of coups during the period 1975-1981.

Following the arrest of Taher and the JSD leaders, serious troubles began to erupt in several cantonments. Hundreds of soldiers were arrested and, allegedly, summarily executed. In March 1976, an Army unit in Chittagong was reported to have mutinied. Although it was not clear whether or not *Biplobi Sainik Sangstha* was involved, three officers were killed. Zia personally intervened to bring an end to the trouble. In April, Air Vice Marshal M.G. Towab, one of the DCMLAs, attempted to takeover through a right-wing coup d'etat. The exiled Majors were brought in by Towab and one of them joined a tank regiment stationed in Bogra to begin the assault. This short-lived coup attempt, staged on April 30 1976, cost Towab his job. He was thrown out of the country. Farook Rahman, who managed to reach his loyalists in Bogra, was convinced by his parents and sister to give in. He was then sent out of country again. Two months after the coup attempt, the tank regiment that rallied with Farook was disbanded and about 250 of its members were charged under the service act.

Bogra, hometown of Ziaur Rahman, ironically became a citadel of anti-Zia military activists. On July 17 of the same year, a day-long rebellion caused considerable problems for the regime. Rapid actions contained the rebels. But another rebellion began to stir. One year later, on September 29-30 1977, an uprising of soldiers took place in Bogra. Supposedly, the members of *Biplobi Sainik Sangstha* took over Bogra city and marched through the streets carrying their weapons and shouting slogans against the regime. Some members of the rebel group were involved in looting as well. Mutineers alleged that the government had "sold out" the country to foreign powers. The next day, they freed some political prisoners and exchanged fire with local police. According to the official account, the mutineers were dealt with without much trouble. Only one officer was killed. The police, with the help of local people, apprehended five of the runaways, referred to in the local papers as "miscreants." But insiders insist hundreds of soldiers were either killed or later executed.

Even before Bogra was brought under the control of government forces, Dhaka was shaken by another attempt to unseat the regime. On the night of October 1, a full-fledged soldiers' uprising took place, presumably organized by *Biplobi Sainik Sangstha*. According to one account, the Bogra and Dhaka uprisings were not isolated events but rather part of a grand design; the proximity of these two events gives credence to the claim, but substantial evidence has not been found to back such an assertion. Nevertheless, the Dhaka uprising was well-organized and more powerful than the Bogra attempt. The rebel soldiers—claiming to be members of *Gonobahini*— took control of the radio station for about three hours and announced that an armed revolution was taking place led by the armed forces, students, peasants, and workers. In the early hours of the day, in addition to the radio station, rebels captured some vital points of the cantonments and Dhaka city, advanced toward the President's residence, and attacked the airport where Air Force Chief A. G. Mahmood and some senior military officers were engaged in negotiations with international skyjackers (*Japanese Red Army*) of a JAL airliner. A large section of army and air force personnel participated in the coup and it almost toppled the government. This was the bloodiest coup attempt since the November 7 1975 uprising. Eleven senior air force officers, 10 army officers, and an estimated 200 other soldiers were killed in the battle between the rebels and the pro-government forces at the airport.

The failed attempt was followed by brutal executions. Martial Law Tribunals set up by the government hurriedly prosecuted the soldiers and airmen. According to the government account, within 25 days of the incident 92 persons had been sentenced to death, 34 persons received imprisonment for life, and 18 others received various terms of rigorous imprisonment (*Bangladesh Observer* 1977, 1977a). Ziaur Rahman himself confided to a reporter of the *New York Times* that 460 officers and soldiers were tried for their involvement in the October 2 coup attempt. Only 63 of them were acquitted (*New York Times* 1977). The *Times* of London reported on March 5 1978, on the basis of conversations with senior army officers, that more than 800 servicemen had been convicted by military tribunals.

Mascarenhas (1986) reckoned that 1143 men were hanged in the two months following October 1977.

Such a massive scale of repression, and the subsequent changes made in the army structure, eliminated and completely silenced all opposition within the army. Over the next two years, the situation remained remarkably calm and quiet. Meanwhile, presidential and parliamentary elections were held and the political party (BNP) was formed.

The BNP was composed of defectors from different political parties. An uneasy combination of the extreme right and extreme left, collaborators and freedom fighters, Islamic fundamentalists and pro-Peking leftists, was made primarily through the dispensation of privileges and, thus, the seeds of conflict were sown at the birth party. The conflict began to surface after the parliamentary elections of 1979. The selection of PM provided the opportunity for a showdown of strength. Much to the annoyance of the freedom fighters, Shah Azizur Rahman, a politician who actively supported the Pakistani regime in 1971, secured the position.

Personal rivalry and ideological differences became increasingly obvious. Zia, sitting at the helm, sometimes played one against another, and sometimes attempted to resolve the conflicts. The cabinet was expanded several times. Additionally, political elites were trying to gain some control over the state apparatus and engaged in conflict with the bureaucracy. At one point, the Deputy Prime Minister, Moudud Ahmed, alleged that the bureaucrats were defying the political ministers. As Moudud said, "The bureaucrats think that politicians are transient and if this government falls they will have the total power to rule the country" (*Sangbad* 1979:1). At the end of the year, Moudud Ahmed, who was calling for the "democratization" of the party, was dismissed from the cabinet. Corruption was then rampant within the party. Zia himself, in his speech to economists, recognized that "corruption and misuse of power have led to the wasting of almost 40 percent of the total resources set apart for development" (quoted in Puchkov 1989:133).

By 1980, the economic situation had deteriorated significantly. In spite of massive aid inflows, the incidence of poverty had increased and the number of rural landless had risen substantially. In 1977, 58.5 percent of rural households claimed ownership of one acre of land or less. In 1978, the percentage increased to 59.4 (Januzzi and Peach 1980). Personal income decreased[20] while the consumer price index increased by 19.3 percent as compared to the previous year. Labor militancy began to rise again because of economic hardship.

In the conflict between political elites and the bureaucrats, which intensified in 1980, Zia began to sway. Facing pressure from political elites for more power and authority, Zia created a position of District Development Coordinator (DDC) to coordinate and assist in the execution of development projects in district (GPRB 1980). Twenty MPs were appointed to this position. This measure irked bureaucrats and was viewed by them as a move to curtail their power.

Ardent supporters of the Zia regime and the international agencies were somewhat discontented by his slow progression toward deregulation. Although the World Bank was applauding that a new, more pragmatic policy orientation had been taking place since 1975, it contended, "despite moves towards pragmatism the Government still tries to exercise detailed control over many aspects of economic life...These restrictions lead to delays in production and investment, inefficiency in resource allocation and, frequently, abuse and corruption" (World Bank 1989:21). Tacitly, it was suggesting complete deregulation within a short period of time.

Meanwhile, a small section of the military comprised of radicals and supporters of the exiled Majors plotted a coup on June 17, 1980. But the government intercepted their communications and foiled the attempt at a very early stage. Nevertheless, the top-ranking military and civil bureaucrats were becoming increasingly disenchanted with, and critical of, Zia because of his reliance on party men. The DDC scheme appeared to be a distinct effort to shift the power-base away from the bureaucracy. In a meeting on May 20 1981, high-ranking military Generals suggested to Zia that he impose martial law in order to quell the internal strife of the party, arrest the deteriorating law and order situation, and bring down inflation. Nine days later, on May 30 1981, Zia was brutally murdered in an abortive coup attempt in Chittagong.[21] Within ten months of this killing, Lt. Gen. H. M. Ershad took over in a successful coup d'etat on March 24, 1982.

Despite a number of coup attempts and instability associated with these, the Zia regime was extremely successful in achieving its political and economic objectives. It consolidated the power and authority of the military-bureaucratic oligarchy as the central institution within the state; it ensured capitalist development in general and, specifically, a "sponsored capitalism," where the state helped private investors with financial supports. These policy measures, of course, brought changes in the class composition of Bangladesh society.

Consequences of State Policies

The primary result of the economic policies pursued since 1975 has been the consolidation and enhancement of the class that began to grow under the previous regime: rich in wealth, small in numbers, and influential in terms of political and social connections. They are popularly known in Bangladesh as a class of "industrialists without industry"; whom I will call—borrowing Andre Gundar Frank's (1972) term—"lumpen capitalists." They have established unbridled control over national resources and are engaged in plundering the country at an unprecedented rate. This privileged few—not more than 1000 families—were the recipients of industrial loans in Bangladesh (Sobhan and Mahmood 1981). Thirty-six of them, until 1981/82, controlled credits of approximately Taka 4,700 million (Sen 1988:19), i.e., 52 percent of the total credits disbursed by the state in the private sector. The personal income structure shows that the upper 10 percent of the total population control 32 percent of the national income (Sen 1988:25-26).

The enormous amount of credit this class received from Development Finance Institutions (DFIs) was never repaid and, in many cases, was written off. As of June 1990, the loans defaulted to the DFIs stood at Taka 10.5 billion as against a loan commitment of 10.4 billion (Sobhan 1991:5). The overwhelming part of the default accrued in the private sector whose loans defaulted to the DFIs accounted for 96.5 percent of the total default. As a matter of fact, 20 business houses owed Taka 457.5 million in overdue loans to the Bangladesh Shilpa Bank (BSB) and 24 business houses, mostly owned by the same owners, owed a debt of about Taka 670.4 million to Bangladesh Shilpa Rin Sangstha (BSRS). As Siddiqui et al. (1990) have noted, perhaps the most important way of getting rich in

Bangladesh has been to defraud and permanently default on loans taken from NCBs (Nationalized Commercial Banks) and DFIs (Siddqui et al. 1990:193).

The wealth accumulated by this class was not invested in the industrial development of the country but was invested or spent abroad. Essentially, the policy of channeling public resources to a privileged few had vitiated the entire structure of productive efforts. According to the report of a commission appointed by the government in 1985, the total amount of capital allotted to the private sector during the period 1980-1985 was Taka 1938.46 crore. A total of 7068 industrial units were supposed to be installed with this capital. However, the report noted that only 3051 units had been initiated (meaning 43 percent). The total amount of capital invested was only Taka 897.59 crore (i.e., 46 percent of allotted capital). The remaining money had been amassed by the beneficiaries of the "credit policy" (GPRB 1985). Siddqui et al. (1990), based on the data derived from interviews with the 68 richest persons in Dhaka, concluded that through various legal and illegal methods, a considerable part of the accumulated surplus was being continually siphoned off from an already capital scarce Bangladesh to countries with a relative abundance of capital (Siddiqui et al. 1990:197).

It is understandable that this new class of "lumpen capitalists" gained affluence through its access to state power. It is well documented in Rahman and Huq's (1987) study of 9 industrialists, who had outstanding loans amounting to Taka 2 billion as of 1987, that a close connection with the bureaucracy was a necessary condition for accumulating wealth. It is no surprise that Siddiqui et al. found that every one of the 68 richest persons of Dhaka had social ties to one or more of the top officials in the country (Siddiqui et al. 1990:182). The relationship between this class and the bureaucracy (both civil and military) was, however, lopsided. The former depended upon the latter. This resulted in the capitalist class being completely dependent on the bureaucracy leaving no maneuvering space for the former, which definitely enhanced the potential autonomy of the bureaucracy. As the transfer of resources was mediated through the bureaucrats, they themselves sought, and evidently received, a share of the pie.

In the rural areas, public policy had enhanced the social power of those who actually commanded assets. The process of privatization of agricultural inputs such as irrigation water, equipment, and fertilizers reinforced the monopoly over the land. A situation had been created wherein the poor farmers were doubly oppressed by the landowners and input dealers causing massive pauperization in rural areas.

In order to fulfill the perpetual appetite of the military-bureaucratic oligarchy and its junior partner, the lumpen capitalists, the country was plunged into debt. Over the years, foreign aid has increased and, indeed, now there is no possibility in sight to break the vicious cycle of aid-dependence. The proliferation of an "aid-regime" has created further intermediaries and vitiated any future possibility of self-reliant development in Bangladesh.

This exposé of the nature of the state and social structure of Bangladesh after 1975 demonstrates that the course followed by the military-bureaucratic regime after the coup d'etat consolidated the power and authority of the military-bureaucratic oligarchy as the central institution within the state. The regime initiated a process of dependent capitalist development beneficial to a small segment of the society who began to emerge under the previous regime. Furthermore, the capitalist development model, although generating a new class of capitalists, failed to unleash the productivity usually associated with capitalism because the new capitalists of Bangladesh were less interested in profit maximization through productive investments in various sectors of economy. Instead, they relied upon extra-economic methods of accumulation, i.e., theft, plunder, and embezzlement. Pursuance of a dependent capitalist model further integrated the country with the world capitalist economy, primarily as an aid-dependent nation.

These developments would seem more obvious to an observer of post-1982 Bangladesh politics. The processes of capitalist development and the concentration of power in the hands of the military-bureaucratic oligarchy initiated in post-1975 intensified after the third successful coup d'etat of March 24 1982, which brought Lt. General Ershad to power. The Ershad era (1982-1990), in all respects, was a mere duplication of the Zia period. The economic policies, political strategies, and ideological positions of the regime were aimed at the consolidation of the "achieve-ments" of the previous regime.

The cornerstones of the economic policies of the Ershad regime, for example, were denationalization/disinvestment and encouragement of private entrepreneurship. A total of 156 industrial units were privatized between March, 1982 and July, 1989. Additionally, a 49 percent share of 11 state owned industries was sold by June 1989 through public bidding. Out of six nationalized banks, 95 percent of the shares of two banks and 49 percent of another were sold to the public (Chowdhury 1990). In the name of encouraging private entrepreneurship and providing incentives to the private sector, state owned development finance institutions (DFIs) contin-ued furnishing huge loans and equity finance to individuals. In 1982/83, Taka 31.9 billion was disbursed as credit to the private sector. In 1985 86, the total amount increased to Taka 83.6 billion. In 1987 88, the amount reached Taka 108.9 billion (World Bank 1989: Table 6.1). The government's credit policy, like that pursued during the Zia regime, was highly skewed toward a small segment of the society. It is of no surprise, therefore, that the lion's share of this credit went to relatively few business houses. More than fifty-five percent of the loans disbursed by the Bangladesh Shilpa Bank (BSB), a leading DFI, between 1980/81 and 1984/85, went to seven busi-ness groups; while 82 percent of loans disbursed by Bangladesh Shilpa Rin Sangstha (BSRS), another leading DFI, went to eight business houses (Mustafa 1989).

This was all done in the name of economic reforms and under the auspices of the IMF and the World Bank, which have become the *de facto* policy makers of the Bangladesh economy since Bangladesh adopted the Structural Adjustment Program (SAP). It started with the World Bank structural and sectoral adjustment loans (SALs and SECLs) in 1980. In March 1986, Bangladesh resorted to the three-year structural adjustment facility (SAF) of the IMF. Bangladesh was also one of the first nations to make use of the Enhanced Structural Adjustment Facility (ESAF), which was launched by the IMF in December 1987. Since then, funding from the IMF and the World Bank has been provided under the umbrella of SAP. Significantly, since that time Bangladesh has had very little control over its development planning. The country's economy has become subordinated to the guidelines and targets laid down by the Policy Framework Paper (PFP) prepared by the IMF and the World Bank. The PFP, claimed by the Bank as the Government's own document, is essentially a blueprint prepared by the Bank staff. Syeduzzaman, who had been in charge of the ministry of finance from 1986 to 1988, acknowledges this fact: "Bank-Fund staff are very keen to draft it themselves" (Syeduzzaman 1991).

The process of militarization of the administration along with increased spending for the military intensified after General Ershad took power in 1982. Between 1982 and 1990, at least 294 military officers had been appointed to different key positions in the government, semi government and autonomous institutions, and public corporations.[22] The breadth of the militarization was substantial, such that the government appointed a military officer as the Secretary of the Bangla Academy, a semi government organization in charge of research on Bengali literature and language. During the period under review, 28 military officers were appointed in the Foreign Ministry alone. In 1984, Bangladesh had 46 diplomatic missions abroad. Of them, 16 were headed by military officers as Ambassadors and/or High Commissioners. Key positions in local administrations were also given to military officers. In 1984, 20 administrative districts were divided into 64; and, in those 64 districts, 53 military officers were appointed as the district superintendents of police. In the same year, there were 49 military officers occupying the positions of Chairman, Secretary, Director General, Managing Director, Director, etc., in different corporations, directorates, and other public/autonomous bodies. By 1988, the number had increased to 85. During the entire period of the Ershad regime, twenty four military officers had been absorbed into the Police department. The Civil Aviation Authority and Bangladesh Biman, the national airline, had 25 military officers. The Ershad regime attempted to enhance the control of the military over the civil administration. In 1987, a bill was passed by the hand picked parliament to include military officers in the local levels of administration. The government, however, had to back out in the face of massive popular protests. In considering military spending, one piece of information says it all: throughout the Ershad era, only 5 percent of the revenue budget was spent on development as opposed to 18 percent on the army. While $147 was spent on each citizen per year, $4,700 was spent on each soldier (Bergman 1991).

In conjunction with the military, the civil bureaucrats emerged as the key persons in the decision making machinery. The civilian cabinet of General Ershad, which provided the political legitimacy to the regime, had very little power and authority and was overshadowed by the secretaries. It is well known in Bangladesh that 10 secretaries of the government constituted the so called "inner cabinet" of Ershad and held immense power. On a number of occasions, General Ershad informed the cabinet members of his decisions after consulting with these bureaucrats.

The bureaucrats in general, and military bureaucrats in particular, wielded so much power between 1975 and 1990 that it became impossible to make any political decisions without them. An examination of the events leading to the resignation of General Ershad bears this out.[23] There is no denying that the seven week-long, urban popular uprising beginning in October 1990, forced General Ershad to consider resignation, but it was the withdrawal of the support of the civil and military bureaucrats that determined the final course. The resignation of the Deputy Commissioner of Dhaka—the linchpin of the administration-at the height of the agitation was a clear signal to General Ershad that his good weather allies were abandoning him. The military officials were initially divided as to whether to support Ershad or not. But the top level officers opted to be on the sideline. The Army Chief of Staff, Lieutenant General Nooruddin Khan, then "advised" Ershad to resign and, hence, Ershad resigned without even consulting his Cabinet colleagues. It is no surprise that on December 5, even as people were celebrating the end of the army era, the Awami League-the premier political party-and its allies, chose to send the names of their short listed candidates to the Army Chief Lt. Gen. Nooruddin Khan, instead of sending the list directly to the presidential secretariat (Kulkarni 1990). Shahabuddin Ahmed, the Chief Justice of the Supreme Court who was a consensus choice of all major political parties, consulted with three individuals before accepting the position of the Acting President: Khaleda Zia, leader of the Bangladesh Nationalist Party and a seven-party alliance; Sheikh Hasina, leader of the Awami League and an eight-party alliance; and Lt. Gen. Nooruddin Khan.

The ideological terrain of the Ershad regime was little different from that of his predecessor—religion, territoriality of identity, and national security were the central elements. General Ershad, from the outset, insisted that Islam would constitute a key element of his ideological position. By late 1982, he declared in a religious gathering that Islam would be the basis of the new social system and would be given its due place in the constitution. On January 15, 1983, Ershad declared that making Bangladesh an Islamic country was the goal of his struggle. He also articulated his intention to introduce "Islamic principles" into the "cultural life" of Bangladeshi Muslims (*Daily Ittefaq* 1983:1). The announcement was made at a gathering of *madrassah* teachers organized by Maulana Abdul Mannan, the head of the Association of Madrassah Teachers and a former minister in the Zia cabinet. In the face of the growing political crisis and united opposition of all political parties, Ershad secured support from a number of *pirs*,[24] or preachers, with large followings. He often visited them and addressed their *urs* (annual congregations). On several occasions between 1983 and 1987, the Ershad regime came close to being overthrown through popular uprisings. His success in creating rifts among opposition parties in 1986 saved him from being toppled. Despite his Islamic rhetoric and steps toward the further Islamization of society, Ershad failed to win the support of Islamic political organizations. The Jaamat-i-Islami, for example, maintained close links with two opposition alliances led by the BNP and the Awami League, respectively, and participated in street agitations. Embroiled in a political crisis that began in early 1983 and intensified in late 1987, Ershad attempted to woo the Jaamat away from agitators and to bring it in line with the government. To placate the Islamist forces, as well as prove his Islamic credentials, Ershad secured a constitutional amendment in June 1988 that declared Islam the state religion.[25] This measure not only provided the final blow to the secular nature of the Bangladeshi state, but also accorded religion a definite space in the political discourse of Bangladesh.

The Bangladeshi State in the Democratic Era

The ideological terrain created by the military regimes of Ziaur Rahman and H. M. Ershad not only remained intact but also obtained support from the civilian regimes that came to power through popular elections in the

1990s. Since then, Islamization has become the agenda of the state and Islam has become the *de facto* state ideology. The use of religious rhetoric and idioms has assumed a preeminent position in the political arena and in public culture. During the regimes of Khaleda Zia (1991-1996) and Sheikh Hasina (1996-2001), the state machinery either remained oblivious to the spread of various religio-social organizations or extended its support. It was not a surprising development under the Khaleda Zia regime because the Islamization process began under the first BNP rule led by her husband Ziaur Rahman in 1975. This, in essence, was BNP's agenda and its agenda was increasingly becoming the political ideology of the Bangladeshi state in the democratic era. However, the Awami League's shift in the 1990s surprised many. The changing global scenario and the dynamics of local politics contributed to this shift (Riaz 2004). But the consequences have been damaging in many ways; most importantly, the state has become an active participant in the production of symbols, icons, and discourses that have accelerated the Islamization process. The relentless acrimony between the Awami League and the BNP, since 1991, and the pursuance of the politics of expediency, by both parties, enabled the Islamists to rise as a formidable force in the political arena. The election of 2001, the third credible election since 1991, brought Islamists to power as a coalition partner of the BNP.

One of the significant developments of this decade has been the growing trend within Bangladeshi society of tolerating and accepting a particular interpretation of Islam, which is being continually redefined by the state and the socio-religious organizations linked to the Islamists. The increasing presence of religion in everyday life can be recognized by looking closely at the dress codes, the extent of silent censure, the sensibility about acceptable female behavior, and the efforts to curtail particular modes of comportment (Feldman 2000:231). A particular reading of religious texts is being naturalized with the active participation of various institutions linked to the state. This has permeated the society to the extent that everyone must conform to avoid social denunciation (for details see Riaz 2004).

Equally significant are the proliferation of militant Islamist groups, many of which have been engaged in seditious acts, and the government's

234

capitulation to the intolerant behavior of small militant groups. It is estimated that about 30 militant groups have emerged over the late-1990s and early-2000s. One of these groups, *Jagrata Muslim Janata Bangladesh* (JMJB, The Awakened Muslim Masses of Bangladesh), headed by a man calling himself "Bangla Bhai" (Bengali Brother), unleashed a reign of terror in rural western and northwestern Bangladesh in 2004. Press reports claim that this gang has been responsible for at least ten deaths and various newspapers have described the abduction and imposition of Taliban-like rule in villages linked with the JMJB (Mortoza, and Islam 2005; Griswold 2005). Despite the Prime Minister's call for the leader of the JMJB— Bengali Bhai—to be brought to justice (*New Age* 2004:1), police have made little progress. Moreover, a cabinet member, and leader of the Jammat-i-Islami, denied the existence of any such individual (*Daily Star* 2004). In January 2004, yielding to the demands of the *Islamic Oikya Jote* (IOJ, Islamic United Alliance), an Islamist partner of the coalition, the government banned the publications of the Ahmadiyyas, a Muslim sect. The IOJ, in collusion with other small Islamist groups, desecrated and demolished Ahmadiyya mosques in various parts of the country (*Daily Star* 2004a).

This however, does not mean that Islamist ideology has emerged as the hegemonic ideology or that the ruling party is enjoying unequivocal moral support from the masses. Instead, both the Awami League and the BNP have resorted to extra-judicial means to maintain their power. During the Awami League rule between 1996 and 2001, harsh new security laws were introduced in addition to the existing Special Powers Act of 1974. The Public Safety (Special Provisions) Act, rammed through parliament with unusual haste in January 2000, was used not only against the criminals but also against political opponents. The BNP regime in its first term in power in the democratic era enacted anti-terrorist laws and used them to silence its critics. Despite a two-thirds majority in the parliament, since 2001, the BNP regime has exhibited paranoia and used the coercive machinery of the state to a degree unthinkable in any democratic environment. The so-called "Operation Clean Heart" and the creation of a new force are cases in point.

In October 2002, the government deployed armed forces to assist police in launching a joint drive called "Operation Clean Heart" designed to augment the effectiveness of law enforcement. Armed personnel, along with the other law enforcement agencies of the country, conducted this operation continuously for 85 days between 16 October 2002 and 9 January 2003. Although the law and order situation in the country improved significantly, some 11,000 persons were arrested. In addition, the Army perpetrated brutal tortures, inhuman and degrading treatment, and cruel punishments that resulted in 42 deaths in custody and rendered many victims mentally and physically incapacitated.[26] The government withdrew the army from the operation on 9 January 2003, followed by the promulgation of the *Joint Drive Indemnity Ordinance 2003*, exonerating all army actions arising out of, and in the course of, Operation Clean Heart.[27] This was followed by the creation of an elite security force named the Rapid Action Battalion (RAB) in April 2004 to combat criminal activities. By early February 2005, it had been responsible for the deaths of 230 people. The battalion claimed that most of the deaths had taken place in "crossfire," while human right organizations and members of the international community have described them as "extra-judicial killings" (*Daily Star* 2004b:1; *Daily Star* 2005:1)[28]

On the economic front, the post-authoritarian decade is marked by the continuation of the policy of liberalization and privatization. For example, the government closed down the Adamjee Jute Mills, the biggest jute mills in the world, in 2002. A staggering 25,000 workers lost their jobs as a result of the closure. The mill was closed so that it would receive the "jute sector adjustment credit" of $247 million from the World Bank under an agreement signed in February 1994. This jute sector reform project, the World Bank's attempt to "help" industrialization in Bangladesh, however, involved closing down nine of the 29 public mills and downsizing two large public mills, a reduction of the workforce in the public sector by about 20,000 employees, and the privatization of the remaining 18 public mills.

The economic policies, while they have produced growth, have also contributed to rising inequality. Economic analysts agree, "In the nineties...the pattern of growth became increasingly inequitable" (Sen, Mujeri, and Shahabuddin 2004:14). The amount of aid received by the country has fallen significantly. For example, the amount of foreign aid received in 1991 was equal to 5.9 percent of GDP, while in 2003 it fell to 2.8 percent of GDP. But that does not necessarily mean that the burden of aid has decreased. For example, in 1972 the per capita debt burden was Taka 67, while in 2004 it reached Taka 7200. In 1991, the per capita overseas loan was $119 while at the beginning of 2004 it stood at $122. While overall reliance on aid decreased, some of the projects of various sectors are still highly dependent on foreign aid. The projects in health, population, and family welfare sectors, for example, have a dependency rate of 74 percent; and almost 73 percent of the public administration sector projects remain dependent on the availability of aid. Having said that, it must be acknowledged that the overall picture in regard to aid dependence is far better than what it was in the 1980s.

The outward orientation of the Bangladesh economy, which intensified in the 1990s, made the country extremely vulnerable to the vagaries of the international market. The Ready Made Garments (RMG) sector proves this in a dramatic fashion. From a modest beginning in the 1980s, the RMG sector had by the late 1990s assumed a leading position in the Bangladesh economy: "In 1990/91, there were fewer than 1000 units, but by the end of the decade nearly 3000 units were in operation" (Sen et al. 2004:44). RMG exports grew to a staggering $4857 million in 2001 from a meager $865 million in 1991. This represents 75 percent of export earnings and 48 percent of total foreign exchange (Khondker and Raihan 2004:6). The industry employed around 1.8 million workers—mostly women from low income, rural backgrounds. The Multi Fiber Agreement (MFA) that provided captive markets in the United States and in the European countries spurred this phenomenal growth. But, it also made the sector dependent on those markets and the protection it enjoyed. The government, as well as private entrepreneurs, has failed to create any backward and forward linkages. Furthermore, it is obvious from the figures above that Bangladesh's export basket is very much concentrated around the RMG sector. In these circumstances, the expiration of the MFA on January 1, 2005 is bound to have a significant impact on the economic and social fronts.

The relationship between the state and non-governmental development organizations, commonly referred to as NGOs, in Bangladesh illustrates the tension between the state's desire to exert control over society and its deliberate choice to retreat from its welfare role. With a growing number of NGOs in the 1990s, this tension became visible in the conflicting attitudes of the state toward these organizations. The NGOs, present in Bangladesh since independence, came to the fore as agents of development in the late1980s owing to two factors: first, the failure of the state to deliver basic services to marginalized, poor segments of the society, especially in rural areas; and second, pressures from the donor countries and agencies to subscribe to a "gender-sensitive development agenda." To achieve the latter goal, Western development agencies provided funds for NGOs to initiate projects to involving poor women in economic activities. The growth in the number of NGOs—both local and foreign funded—was matched by their roles in the political sphere. As the NGOs began to seek a higher public profile and take active roles in national politics from the mid-1990s, the state became worried about losing control over the society. One can explain this within the general framework of the perennial conflict between the state and civil society. Here, in this particular case, however, the Bangladeshi state is standing on very shaky ground because in the previous decade it had relied on the NGOs to supply social welfare provisions to a large segment of society, especially the most vulnerable sections. The NGOs became involved in a broad range of areas beyond the initial venture of providing credit to the poor. They have not only become the providers of education, health care, and family planning, but also, to a great extent, became a substitute of the state in these areas. Wood (1997) has described this as a "franchising out" of key functions of the state to NGOs and the private sector. The aid conditionality of the IMF and the World Bank had forced the state to roll back from these services, but the state has yet to discard its interventionist pedigree.

Two factors have complicated the situation further in recent years: The first concerns the donors insisting their funds be channeled through the NGOs and the unstated scheme of the Islamists within the government to reign in the NGOs. Packaged within the rubric of "good governance," accountability, and transparency, the donors insist that the "civil society" should be an active partner of the government in sociopolitical issues; while the Islamists, who have never concealed their disdain for the NGOs, strive to install a system of control over them. It has not been very difficult for the Islamists, for understandable reasons, to find friends within the bureaucracy. An illustrative result is the regulatory measures implemented by the government in 2002.

Our discussion has demonstrated that the new Bangladeshi state that emerged in 1975 through a dramatic transformation has remained on course throughout the last three decades. The agenda of the state was set by a new ruling bloc with the military and bureaucracy at its core, but the agenda has been implemented by military and civilian regimes alike. Urban uprising and popular elections have changed the governments but the state, to a large part, remains unchanged.

NOTES

1   According to the available accounts and documents, the key planners of the coup were Syed Farook Rahman, Khandaker Abdur Rashid, Abdul Aziz Pasha, Sharful Islam Dalim, Bazlul Huda, and Shamsul Islam Nur. Captain Khairuzzaman and Captain Abdul Majed and Lieutenant Muslehuddin, Lieutenant Kismet Hashem, and Lieutenant Nazmul Ansar also played prominent roles. Some of them subsequently denied their involvement.

2   Major Sarful Islam Dalim, for example, was discharged from the army on disciplinary grounds. It is alleged that his dismissal was a result of an untoward incident involving an Awami League leader. Apparently, Major Dalim's wife was insulted and intimidated by two sons of a close associate of Mujib, Gazi Golam Mostafa, at a social gathering. Following the incident, the Chief of Army Staff Major General Safiullah went to Mujib and placed the matter before him requesting action against those involved. Mujib, however, expressed his annoyance and later, in August 1974, dismissed Dalim from the service.

3   Some more rearranging of the administration took place at this time. All of these changes brought back the once-ostracized, pro-Pakistani bureaucrats. For example, Salehuddin, who had been Home Secretary of East Pakistan provincial government in 1971 was brought back from a foreign job and appointed Home Secretary. Tabarak Hossain, a close associate of Yahya Khan who was dumped

as an Officer on Special Duty, became the Foreign Secretary of the new regime.

4   "The Indemnity Ordinance 1975" (Ordinance No. XLX of 1975) was promulgated "to restrict the taking of any legal or other proceedings in respect of certain acts or things done in connection with, or in preparation or execution of any plan for, or steps necessitating, the historical change and the Proclamation of Martial Law on the morning of the 15th August, 1975" (GPRB 1975b). The law remained in place until the Awami League came to power in 1996. On November 12, 1996, the Parliament repealed the Ordinance. This enabled the trials of those accused of killing of Sheikh Mujibur Rahman.

5   Some analysts, for example Khan (1984), characterized this coup as a pro-Mujib coup. This interpretation is common in Bangladesh. Some concurrent events and massive propaganda between November 4 and 7 against Khaled helped characterize the coup as such. The presence of Khaled's mother and a brother in a pro-Mujib demonstration on November 4 is one of the reasons why common people believed it to be a pro-Mujib move. However, I have found very little evidence to support this notion though some Mujib loyalists were involved in the coup. Khaled himself was concerned with restoring the chain of command in the army.

6   A leaflet distributed by the *Biplobi Sainik Sangstha* on November 5 contained a 12-point demand of the sepoys, which included a call for changing the structure as well as functions of the army; the abolition of colonial practices such as the Batman system; recognition of the Revolutionary *Sainik Sangstha* as the central policy-making body of the army and entrusting the supreme authority to this organization; the immediate release of all political prisoners; the confiscation of the properties of all corrupt officials and individuals; ending discrimination between officers and sepoys in the armed forces; and increasing the salaries of sepoys.

7   The conflict between the soldiers and their officers spread to some other cantonments in subsequent days resulting in indiscriminate killings. In Rangpur cantonment, more than 15 officers were killed on November 8. Later, it spread to naval bases as well. It is reported that in an uprising in the Navy between 13 and 15 November, 7 officials and 40 others were killed in Chittagong.

8   The opening sentence of the leaflet distributed by the *Biplobi Sainik Sangstha* on November 5 termed the uprising a revolution and succinctly described the goal: "Our revolution is not for changing the leadership only; this revolution is for the interests of the poor class." The leaflet further said, "For many years we have served as the soldiers of the rich classes. The rich classes have used us for their interests...This time we have revolted not for the rich and not on their behalf. We have revolted this time along with the masses. From this time onward the armed forces of the country will build themselves as the protector of the interests of the masses."

9   This is how the JSD later described Zia and justified their decision to bring Zia in the forefront (JSD 1976).

10   The arrests came right after an attempt to stage a coup on November 24. Seven months after the arrests, 33 persons including Col. Taher and the JSD leaders were charged with treason. Twenty-two of them were members of the defense services, the remaining 11 were prominent JSD leaders. In a trial held on camera, Col. Taher was sentenced to death, Jalil and Rab to life imprisonment, and 14 others were sentenced to imprisonment for various terms. On July 21, 1976, Taher was hanged at dawn in Dhaka Central Jail. Sporadic actions of Taher's followers, nevertheless, continued even after Taher's arrest. In December, 1975, "disturbances" were reported from Chittagong naval base and in March, 1976, Chittagong Brigade experienced a significant movement.

11   On November 19, 1976, the post of CMLA was handed over to Zia by Sayem in the "national interests" through a Presidential Proclamation. Later, on April 21, 1977, Sayem relinquished the office of President because of "failing health" and Zia became President as well.

12   A Senior Policy Pool was constituted by the Zia regime in March 1979 in order to streamline the bureaucracy and open the policy-making positions to new civil servants as opposed to the former CSP system practiced in Pakistan era. The pool consisted of the posts of Secretary, Deputy Secretary, Joint Secretary, and Additional Secretary. Qualifications for membership in the pool were the following: ten years of service in class I posts, less than 45 years of age, and successful completion of promotion tests conducted by the Bangladesh Public Service Commission (GPRB 1979).

13   In December 1975, the government increased the price of rationed commodities drastically (GPRB 1975c). But, the Secretary of the department issued a separate memo (No. 2374/87(91)MFCS-II dated December 17, 1975) saying that "the revised issue price of the commodities under reference shall not be applied to Army, Navy, BDR, jail Staff, Ansar staff and embodied Ansar and Police." He reiterated that they would continue to obtain their rations at the existing rates (i.e., rates prevailing before December 20, 1975).

14   The terms "disinvestment" and "denationalization" are used here to refer to policy measures taken by the government toward what is commonly known as privatization. In the context of Bangladesh, with reference to the industrial sector, "disinvestment refers to the process of selling off abandoned units through public tenders, while denationalization refers to the return of the units to their Bangladeshi former owners on administratively determined ground" (Sobhan and Ahsan 1984:7).

15   The following eight categories were reserved exclusively for the public sector: arms, ammunition and allied defense equipment; atomic energy; jute (sacking, hessian, and carpet backing); textiles (excluding handlooms and specialized textiles); sugar; air transport; telephone, telephone cables, telegraph, and wireless apparatus; and the generation and distribution of electricity.

16   The policy stated "In view of the misgivings that have been created in the minds of the investors by the reference in the New Investment Policy (of 1974) to the moratorium on nationalization for a period of fifteen years, this provision has been deleted" (GPRB 1975d:2).

17   Bridge finance is the amount of equity support provided by special institutional arrangement to meet the gap in finance needed by the private entrepreneur in establishing new industries. The ICB was established in 1976.

18   The numbers of disinvested units may, however, create some confusion and provide the wrong impression that a large-scale privatization began during the Mujib-regime. During the period, the units disinvested were small in size (i.e., industrial enterprises having fixed assets up to Taka 2.5 million). The units disinvested during 1975-82 were either medium (i.e., fixed assets of Taka 2.5 million-10 million) or large (i.e., fixed assets above Taka 10 million). But the units disinvested between 1982 and 1989 were mostly large. In the 1982/83 fiscal year, the average sale price of an industrial unit was about Taka 32.65 million (Sobhan and Ahsan 1984).

19   The first indication that Ziaur Rahman was planning to launch a political organization came in a meeting with leaders of different political parties on December 8, 1977. Later, in his speech on the eve of the victory day celebration of December 16, Ziaur Rahman maintained that there was a "political vacuum" and, in order to fill that vacuum, a party was needed.

20   According to government accounts, the rate of personal growth was negative during the year 1976/77, 1979/80, and 1980/81. They were -0.7 percent, -1.2 percent, and -1.5 percent respectively (*BBS* 1986:582).

21   The events surrounding the killing of Zia remain a mystery to date. The regime claimed it was conspired by Major General Abul Manzur, GOC of Chittagong, solely for personal vengeance as he was transferred from active command to an obscure position as Staff College Principal. Manzur was also killed mysteriously by soldiers after the mutiny was quelled. Thirty officers were tried by General Court Martial for mutiny, not for killing the President! Only four of them were acquitted. Thirteen of them were convicted and hanged. Seven others initially received the death penalty but later their sentence was reduced to life imprisonment. Six were sent to prison for various terms. The events took the lives of 15 officers including Zia and Manzur. Surprisingly, all of them were freedom fighters. The "White Paper" published by the government failed to provide enough evidence to show that Manzur was the key planner. There are enough reasons to believe that the events of Chittagong were designed by some others and that two birds were killed with one stone. With the killings, all the high ranking officers involved in the liberation struggle were eliminated.

22   These figures are calculated on the basis of government documents made accessible to me during my visit to Bangladesh in early 1991 and early 1993, and Uzzman's (1991) study on militarization of the administration.

23   For a detailed description of the events leading to the resignation of Lt. General Ershad, see Rizvi (1991) and Riaz and Rahman (1991).

24   *Pirs* (literally saints) are a very common feature of political-religious life in Bangladesh. The tradition grew out of a specific mode of preaching Islam in the subcontinent. Some of these early preachers

drew the attention of the local people irrespective of their religious beliefs through their spiritual power, morality, and principles of tolerance. These *pirs* originally represented mystic Islam and one or more mystic orders. Following their deaths, their graves are turned into *mazars* (shrines) and are visited by their *muridan* (disciples). But over the years, the practice has degenerated and has created cult-like organizations headed by *pirs* who exert influence over their disciples and their residential/worship compounds have become headquarters of complex social networks and places where patronage is exchanged between high-ranking people.

25   The State Religion Amendment Bill, commonly referred to as the *Eighth Amendment of the Constitution*, was introduced in Parliament on May 11, 1988, and passed on June 7.

26   These figures are widely reported in the media (for a complete list of those killed in custody see *Jugantor* 2003:1).

27   The indemnity ordinance drew widespread criticism both at home and abroad. The British House of Commons criticized the Ordinance as anti-human rights because it denies the constitutional guarantees of the citizens (*Janakantha* 2003:1). In December 2002, the European Parliament adopted a unanimous resolution on the consistent violation of human rights during Operation Clean Heart (*Janakantha* 2002). The Secretary-General of Amnesty International termed it a reflection of the "culture of impunity and lack of accountability" and demanded an independent probe into deaths occurring in army custody (*Daily Star* 2003).

28   The head of Delegation of the European Commission in Bangladesh, Ambassador Esko Kentrschynskyj, described the deaths as "extra-judicial" and expressed deep concern (*Daily Star* 2005:1).

Chapter 6

State Transformation:
A Comparison

Case studies, especially those that document changes over a long period of time, are exciting in their own right. But, they can also be narrowly focused. Often case studies are criticized for failing to draw the line between exceptional and general lessons. It is important to be aware of this danger and necessary to ask, in our context, can the analysis of state transformation in Bangladesh provide us with conceptual tools to understand states in other postcolonial peripheral societies?

The particularity of the Bangladeshi experience notwithstanding, it is my contention that the framework used for analyzing the formation and the transformation of the Bangladeshi state is valid for others. I will support this claim in this chapter through a comparison between Bangladesh and Tanzania, a postcolonial peripheral country in Africa that has also experienced a dramatic transformation over the last three decades. It is, however, by no means intended to draw grand comparative conclusions, which would require more extensive and probing case studies covering more time. The comparison will, however, make my arguments a little more persuasive and hopefully draw others into the debate.

To comprehend the comparison between the Tanzanian and the Bangladeshi state we must begin with a brief overview of Tanzania's recent history.

An Overview of Tanzania

Tanzania is essentially a colonial creation. The area now known as Tanzania is the result of the unification of Tanganyika and Zanzibar in 1964. Tanganyika was occupied by the Germans in 1885 and named "German East Africa." After the First World War, in 1919, the area came under British administration and remained so until 1961. The small state of Zanzibar was also a British colony until 1963. A year later, when Zanzibar joined the larger mainland territory Tanganyika, the federal state of Tanzania came into existence. Following independence, the Tanganyika African National Union (TANU), which had spearheaded the nationalist movement, became the ruling party.[1] In the early days of independence, there were no major changes in economic policies. The policies pursued by the colonial powers—mild, import substitution industrialization and reliance on private investment—remained the cornerstone of industrial policy. The economy depended heavily on the revenue from commodity exports, especially coffee and cotton—the two major cash crops of the country.

In February 1967, the ruling party, headed by Julius Nyrere, announced drastic changes in their economic policies and the constitution. The salient features of what became known as the *Arusha Declaration* included the nationalization of banks, insurance companies, businesses, and industrial units; the beginnings of a strict price control regime; the pursuance of a self-reliance policy moving away from over-dependence on foreign assistance in development; the organization of extensive compulsory cooperative villages (*ujamaa* or villagization); and the establishment of a one-party state. Nationalization resulted in the creation of hundreds of government-owned enterprises called *parastatals*. These policy changes were heralded as the beginning of the era of "African Socialism"—an indigenous way of establishing an egalitarian society.

The country experienced some economic growth and reasonably high investments in the first decade, but external debt increased substantially (Table 10). The drought of 1973-74 and the sudden rise of international oil prices in 1974, often described as the oil shock, adversely affected the Tanzanian economy. In the early 1970s the International Monetary Fund (IMF) and the World Bank began criticizing the Tanzanian policies and putting pressure on the government for change. However, bilateral donors remained supportive and this helped the government take a firm stand in negotiations with the IMF and the World Bank. By 1979, the situation began to change. The break up of the East African Community in 1977, the end of the coffee boom, war in Uganda in 1978-79,[2] and depleted foreign exchange reserves put the regime under severe strain. As the dialogue with the IMF broke down, bilateral donors started to pull out and foreign inflows fell dramatically. In an attempt to block reforms prescribed by the World Bank and the IMF, Tanzania tried its own structural adjustment programs in the early 1980s (the National Economic Survival Program (NESP) in 1981-1982 and the Structural Adjustment Program (SAP) in 1983-1985), but they were unsuccessful. In 1984, the government moved toward limited economic liberalization; by then most of its socialist programs had been rolled back. Following the resignation of Julius Nyrere

248

in 1985, the Tanzanian government reached an agreement with the IMF and a structural adjustment program with the World Bank in the following year. The economic reforms agreed upon included the massive privatization of the *parastatals* and allowing foreign investment in various sectors. On the political front, Tanzania introduced legislative reforms in 1992 and has held two elections (1995 and 2000) since then.

Table 10.
Tanzania, External Debt, 1970-1995
(in million dollars)

Year	Debt
1970	212
1971	284
1972	407
1973	619
1974	900
1975	1170
1976	1380
1977	1700
1978	1970
1979	2070
1980	2450
1981	2880
1982	3130
1983	3390
1984	3620
1985	4030
1986	4610
1987	5490
1988	6010
1989	5850
1990	6410
1991	6540
1992	6620
1993	6800
1994	7260
1995	7430

State Transformations Compared

Evidently, within a span of three decades the Tanzanian state underwent two major transformations, as did the Bangladeshi state. The similarities between Bangladesh and Tanzania are even more evident if one looks closely at the political and economic developments before and after independence. In order to perform such an analysis, one needs to consider the impact of colonial rule on society, the characteristics of the postcolonial ruling class, the political and economic agenda of the ruling bloc, the conditions for state transformation, and the nature of the new state that emerged after 1985.

The Colonial State and Social Classes

Both Tanzania and Bangladesh have experienced colonial domination which has left indelible marks on their society and economy. In both cases, the local economy was mediated through the colonial state and the production structure was geared toward the needs of the colonial society and economy. The Tanzanian economy was highly dependent on agricultural production and the colonial rulers preferred the cultivation of cash crops like coffee and cotton for the global market. After the Second World War, the British rulers encouraged limited industrialization in East Africa, but Tanganyika never benefited from these plans because neighboring Kenya had been selected for preferential treatment. This limited the possible emergence of any significant industrial capitalist class. The number of manufacturing companies in Tanzania immediately after independence illustrates the point: in 1962, there were only 137 local companies and 61 foreign companies registered in the country (GOT 1968). While colonial economic policies impeded the rise of the bourgeoisie, they fostered an array of intermediate classes. One of these has been the mercantile class of Asian origin. Stein (1985) explains: "In 1961, there were an estimated 10,000 non-African retailers and 3,900 wholesalers. Of the former, 7,500 were Asians, along with almost all the wholesalers. This is fairly significant considering that there were only 133,000 Asians and Arabs in Tanzania in 1961, as against 9.25 million Africans" (Stein 1985:114). The state also encouraged the growth of African licensed traders. In 1961, the number stood at 34,500 but they were largely concentrated in rural areas and had a very limited influence on the economy as they handled a small fraction of trade (Hawkins 1965:37). The education policy, which favored Asians over Africans and restricted African education to primary levels, also contributed to the rise of the intermediate classes. These classes were directly dependent on the colonial state and acted as its agents. We have noted similar policies in Bangladesh during Pakistani rule. The analysis of the state and social formations of Bangladesh under Pakistani rule show that the state impeded the rise of the indigenous bourgeoisie. Instead, the colonial state deliberately promoted a range of intermediate classes to serve the state apparatus and to act as the political agents of the state in its drive for expropriation of economic surplus (Chapter 1). Owing to the general requirements of colonial domination, and the specific nature of the Pakistani state, the intermediate classes of Bangladesh were kept on the periphery of power.

While these policies helped the colonial state perpetuate its rule and continue surplus expropriation, they also created a space for the emergence of a counter-hegemonic force from within these classes. The Awami League, a political organization of the petty bourgeoisie and the middle classes of Bangladesh, capitalizing on the popular discontent of the masses, evolved a counter-hegemonic ideology and utilized nationalist rhetoric in the construction of its own power base. Hence, an alliance of intermediate classes, outside the economically dominant groups, became prominent political actors engaged in a conflict with the colonial state, which finally resulted in the emergence of independent Bangladesh in 1971. The Tanzanian experience is consistent with that of Bangladesh and other colonial societies in their construction of "nationhood." In his discussion on state formation in Latin America, Oszlak (1981:6) underscored this point:

Historically, nation-building has entailed...at the ideal level, the creation of symbols and values that—to use O'Donnell's appropriate image—throw an arc of solidarities over the various and antagonistic interests in civil society. This arc of solidarities provides both the main integrating element of the opposing forces produced by the material development of the society itself as well as the main element differentiating it from other national units.

The intermediate classes' chances of succeeding in manipulating these symbols are much higher where other social classes are either non-existent or extremely weak. The absence of a bourgeoisie and a weak working class provided such an opportunity to the intermediate classes in Bangladesh and Tanzania. Like the Awami League in Bangladesh, the Tanganyika African National Union (TANU) leadership came from the middle classes. TANU, which had its origin in the African Association founded in 1929 by a small group of well-educated African civil servants to promote their self-improvement relative to local Europeans and Asians, assumed the leadership of the nationalist movement in 1950s. The leaders of TANU came from three sources: the civil services, the unions, and the cooperatives (Coulson 1982:108). The latter two had been co-opted by the colonial administration by the late 1930s and these organizations were deeply linked to the patronage of the state. Thus, the nationalist movement was organized and led by the intermediate classes, who emerged victorious in 1961 and established an intermediate state.

The Postcolonial Ruling Class

The characterization of the class that took over the Tanganyika state in 1961 had evoked serious debate among scholars in the 1970s. Issa Shivji describes it as a "bureaucratic bourgeoisie" (Shivji 1976). He insists the class emerged from the struggle between the commercial and petty-bour-geoisies for economic control in the postcolonial period and cannot be considered an independent class: "within the world capitalist system, the 'bureaucratic bourgeoisie' is a *dependent* bourgeoisie—dependent on the international bourgeoisie" (Shivji 1976:85, emphasis in original). Stein also makes reference to a "bureaucratic class" but argues "this is not some faction breaking off from a petty-bourgeoisie, as Shivji and others have suggested. They are not a class with small quantity of capital that is politi-cally somewhere between the workers and the bourgeoisie. They arose neither from capital nor from labour but a fourth factor of production, organization" (Stein 1985:113). Despite some differences, one consensus seems to be apparent: "those who took control of the state in 1961 were not the capitalists" (Coulson 1982:108).

Our analysis has shown that at the outset of independence, the emergent Bangladeshi state became an intermediate state in the sense that its apparatus was captured by the alliance of intermediate classes led by the petty bourgeoisie. The composition of the cabinets of both countries is instructive in this regard. The first full-fledged cabinet of ministers of the Bangladesh government, formed in 1972, had 23 members, of which 13 were lawyers, 4 were businessmen, 3 (including Mujib) were professional politicians, and the remainder included a college professor, a landholder, and a former military official (i.e., the C-in-C of *Mukti Bahini*) (see Chapter 1 of this volume). The 1963 Tanganyika Cabinet had 15 members, of which 5 were local government administrators, clerks, or policemen, 4 were teachers, 3 were co-operative leaders, 2 were labor union leaders, and there was 1 businessman (Stein 1985:117). The Tanganyika Cabinet was markedly different in composition from other African countries. More than one-third of the Kenyan Cabinet during the same period, for example, came from the business community.

The Agenda and Crises of the Ruling Class

In postcolonial Bangladesh, the intermediate regime pursued a "non-capitalist path of development," wherein the potential for development of an indigenous bourgeoisie was frustrated and cooperation between local and foreign capital was restricted. At the heart of the economic policies approved by the new regime between 1972 and 1975 was the expansion of the role of the state, and nationalization became the principal tool in achieving the goal of "socialism." Through the *Arusha Declaration* of 1967, the Tanzanian ruling class began the same journey.

Here, the objective of the ruling classes of both these countries seemed to be control of the means of production through the institutions of state. It became necessary because the ruling class did not have the power to establish control over the means of production. *Parastatals* in Tanzania, like the nationalized units in Bangladesh, provided the intermediate classes

253

with control of state property, and, employing the authority of the state, they accumulated a vast amount of wealth through both legal and illegal (e.g., corruption, smuggling) means. They exploited the state and received extensive protection and patronage. The expansion of state activities necessitated an increase in the number of state personnel. Between 1961 and 1974, the number of middle and upper level civil servants and their equivalent in the *parastatals* increased tenfold, from 1,596 to 15,182. They constituted 5 percent of the total public sector work force (Stein 1985:121, fn. 2). Nationalization contributed directly to the creation of job opportunities for the urban educated intermediate classes. In the late 1980s, *parastatals* contributed nearly 25 percent of non-agricultural wage employment and generated some 13 percent of total GDP with monopolies over utilities, railroads, and ports, and a strong presence in agriculture, mining, and banking (Due 1993).

One of the pronounced goals of the *Arusha Declaration* was to reduce external dependency. But data shows that dependency instead increased substantially (Table 10). The external debt rose from $212 million in 1970 to $1970 million in 1978 and to $4030 million in 1985. This dependency added to the vulnerability the nation already suffered as a supplier of raw materials to the global market. Like Bangladesh, the post-colonial regime of Tanzania faced pressure from international financial institutions to reform its economy and permit further foreign investments. The Bangladeshi ruling class folded within less than two years while the Tanzanian leaders succeeded in withstanding the pressure for almost two decades.

The program of establishing compulsory cooperative villages called *ujamaa* (or the *villagization* program) on the surface seems novel and socialist, for they were conceived of as agricultural producers' co-operative institutions. Mujib also declared a similar program of establishing cooperatives in the rural areas as part of his "second revolution" in mid-1975. The plan did not materialize because of the changes in August 1975. However, during the preceding three years, the agrarian policies of the government, especially the control and distribution of agricultural inputs (e.g., fertilizers) and the provision of credit to producers, established a firm control over the rural areas. At the conclusion of Operation Tanzania in 1977, an esti-

254

mated 79 percent of the mainland population and 90 percent of all rural dwellers—more than 13 million people—were living in 7,300 villages with an approximate average membership of 1,849 (Mapolu 1990). One must ask, however, what benefits it brought to the rural population. The government argued that this program would provide the rural population with essential social services, such as schools, dispensaries, and water facilities. But, in fact, this was an attempt to bring rural production under the control of the state. The ruling class was trying to tackle smallholder production in which almost 90 percent of the population participated through resettlement in chosen localities with government officials overseeing production processes.

The establishment of the one-party state in Tanzania and in Bangladesh attests to how the centralization and consolidation of power are key elements of the political agenda of the new ruling classes. Prior to the establishment of the one-party state, the Awami League manipulated electoral processes and the constitution, and silenced political opponents through violence and intimidation. With regard to rural administration, the Bangladeshi regime removed the constitutional provision that allowed the local level administration to be elected. TANU took similar steps with the local institutions in Tanzania:

> In the 1970s...almost all the local institutions with grass-root level participation were overhauled and new bureaucratic institutions, with direct central control, established in their place. In 1972, in accordance with an American consultancy firm's recommendations, district and town councils were abolished and central administration was devolved into the regions and districts to assume all the roles formerly played by the local government bodies. Until then these councils were directly elective with a degree of autonomy from central government. With the 'centralization' measures all powers were transferred to the central government bureaucracy, which was grossly expanded for the purpose. (Mapolu 1990)

These steps could not fend off, either in Bangladesh or in Tanzania, the crises faced by the ruling classes. The crises were both economic and political. Between 1978 and 1982, revenue fell by 15 percent in real terms, while government final consumption expenditure fell 39 percent and public service expenditure per capita fell 25 percent (IMF 1992; United Nations 1992). For the Bangladeshi ruling class, the economic crisis came a little early, within a year of independence. As discussed in chapter 3, in late 1972 the cost of living skyrocketed, there was a shortfall in production of food in the following year, and, in 1974, the GDP registered a negative growth. Although the immediate causes of economic hardship can be attributed to international economic conditions and climatic disturbances, they are also indications of the fiscal crisis inherent to the peripheral capitalist state. The situations in Bangladesh and Tanzania support what I have described as a general principle: "the socialist posture subjects the state to the pressure of international capitalism and different varieties of sanctions - overt and covert. This, in consonance with the structural economic crises of peripheral states, serves as a source of continuous economic crisis. The pursuance of such policies also impedes the development of the society's productive forces, a necessary condition for the perpetuation of a capitalist economy" (see Introduction). The economic crisis either serves as the source of, or contributes to, the political crisis. In Tanzania, "the decrease in resources was not merely an economic problem, but also a decline of state legitimacy. Weakened state capacity brought into question the ability of the state to fulfill the promises of Arusha. As people grew disillusioned, they began to avoid the state by selling their goods outside the state channels, neglecting projects within *ujamaa* villages and not responding to state-sponsored campaigns" (Costello 1996:138-9). The decline in state legitimacy led to a deterioration in law and order as the police faced challenges from local vigilante groups (Abrahams 1987). Similar kinds of incidents have been noted in Bangladesh in the early days of independence. According to the figures presented by the Home Minister to parliament, in the first sixteen months (i.e., January 1972-April 1973) 4925 persons were killed by miscreants, 2035 secret killings of a political nature took place, 337 women were kidnapped, and 190 women were raped. According to a newspaper report, 23 police stations and outposts had been attacked by "anti-social elements" between January 1972 and July 1973. The number of attacks on police stations increased substantially over subsequent months. In October 1973

256

alone, 11 police stations and sub-stations were attacked and looted. A decline in legitimacy not only creates problems in terms of governability and authority, but also indicates the rupture of the hegemony of the ruling classes, in this case the intermediate classes. The rupture, as we discussed in the introduction, can be attributed to three reasons: erosion in the fundamental basis of ideological hegemony; schisms within the ruling classes; and failure to represent the universal interests of the society. All three factors were at work in the Bangladeshi and Tanzanian contexts. This should come as no surprise because similar situations have been identified in postcolonial societies in Latin America (Oszlak 1981). As we know, the fundamental basis of the ideological hegemony of the intermediate classes in colonial societies, especially during the anti-colonial struggle, has been nationalism or some variant of nationalism. But the new political realities of postcolonialism can, and do, undercut the relevance of an overarching "nationalist" ideology. Were the ruling classes aware of it? Their efforts to devise new ideologies—"Mujibism" in Bangladesh and "African Socialism" in Tanzania, both with egalitarianism as the guiding principle, indicate that they were. But these were not enough to maintain their hegemony over the masses. This is because, as Oszlak (1981:28) has concluded about Latin American state formation, "identification with the struggle for emancipation, a precarious idealistic component of nationalism, was insufficient to produce stable conditions for national integration."

The Crises and State Transformation

The political and economic crises, described above, destabilized the equilibrium necessary for maintaining property relations and preserving social order, and, in so doing, threatened the traditional role of the state. However, although crises are necessary factors they are not sufficient for state transformation, meaning these crises contribute to but do not determine whether a transformation of the state would ensue. In addition to the crises, the existence of a sufficiently coherent counter-coalition within the state to represent an alternative ruling elite is required for state transformation (Costello 1996). In both Bangladesh and Tanzania, the bureaucracy provided leadership and was the central element of this emerging coalition.

The history of Bangladesh shows that a coalition of the bureau-cratic-military elite emerged as the ruling elite through the *coup d'etat* of August 1975. After independence, the civilian political regime apparently established its control over the two other components of the state (the bureaucracy and military) despite internal factionalism and a lack of consensus among the members of the ruling party. The internal feud within the bureaucracy, its close connections with the colonial power, and the inconsequential size of the military made it possible for the political regime to curb both of these forces. Although these institutions lost their authority in the course of the independence war, they were neither destroyed nor completely immobilized. These contenders for power were temporarily rendered impotent at the moment of triumph, but the dynamics of transition provided new opportunities for their remobilization. Furthermore, retaining the structures of the state, even augmenting its role, enhanced bureaucratic power and helped establish control over all social classes. The regime attempted to undercut some of the privileges enjoyed by both civil and mili-tary bureaucrats without any restructuring of the state apparatus. Two other factors that enhanced the power and relative autonomy of the bureaucracy were the degree of aid-dependency, and the ruling classes' reliance on coer-cion. As the principal functionaries in aid negotiations, bureaucrats assumed greater importance in policy formulation. Additionally, by secur-ing the unremitting flow of aid, bureaucrats became free from the slightest dependence on the indigenous social classes for the surplus necessary to maintain the state. In Tanzania, the *Arusha Declaration* established the party as the sole authority for decision-making and made adherence to the "Leadership Code" mandatory for bureaucrats. The leadership code required all state actors to undergo political training by the party and prohibited them from owning rental property, investing in business, or drawing a salary outside their state employment. The ruling party thought these measures would undermine the elitist attitude of the bureaucrats and ensure their compliance with party directions. However, throughout the 1960s, disagreements between the party (representing the intermediate classes) and government bureaucrats flared, and bureaucrats frequently expressed their disdain at the "amateurism" of party officials (Hopkins 1972:121). Costello's study of two central Tanzanian agencies—the National Development Corporation (NDC) and the Ministry of Agriculture and Livestock Development (Kilimo)—shows that "bureaucratic autonomy remained high" and was bolstered by, among other factors, "ties to foreign actors" (Costello 1996:123). Thus, in the backdrop of the crises, a coalition capable of articulating and implementing a new political and economic agenda emerged as the ruling bloc.

Policies and Priorities of the New State

After the *coup d'etat* of August 1975, the political and economic agenda of the new Bangladeshi state focused on the consolidation of power and authority of the military-bureaucratic oligarchy as the central institution within the state (in a society whose central institution is the state). In addition, capitalist development was accelerated; specifically, the state reverted to the pre-independence policy of "sponsored capitalism" providing financial support to private investors. The composition of the cabinets and policymaking bodies in subsequent years demonstrated that bureaucrats had established significant control and used the scarce resources that existed to their own benefit (Chapter 4). In the Tanzanian context, the rise of Ali Hassan Mwinyi, a career bureaucrat, to the Presidency is the clearest evidence in this regard.[3] By the late 1980s, policymaking power has been, in effect, transferred from the ruling party to the bureaucracy. Created and supported by the IMF, and staffed by economists and bureaucrats with few ties to the party, the President's Planning Commission and Economic Recovery Program (ERP) Secretariat have become the supreme authorities in formulating policies. The role of the party's highest body, the National Executive Committee (NEC), has become insignificant, mostly rubber-stamping the decisions by those bodies. Events surrounding the foreign investment code formulated in 1990 indicate this change. The bill regarding foreign investments and their protection was formulated by the president's planning office in consultation with the IMF. The NEC initially rejected the draft because, in their view, it failed to protect the national interests. But later, after some cosmetic changes, the NEC approved it without any reservations.

The economic project of the new Tanzanian state has focused on increased investment in the private sector and the privatization of the *parastatals*. Shares of the private sector in GDP have increased substantially since the 1980s. During the period of 1967 to 1980, the share of the public sector in GDP was 13.2 percent; during 1981-1985, the share declined to 8.1 percent because of an economic crisis; and during 1986-1995, the share gained modestly rising to 10.3 percent. The shift towards private sector investments has increased the share of the private sector in GDP over the years: 1967 to 1980—11.3 percent; 1981 to 1985—12.5 percent; and 1986 to 1995—17.6 percent. Along with the policy of increased private sector investment, the government has embarked on a massive privatization scheme. In March 1992, the Parastatal Sector Reform Commission (PSRC) was established to assess the assets, liabilities, and economic viability of the government-owned enterprises; to establish guidelines as to which enterprises should be reserved; and to initiate processes for selling and liquidating and then closing the enterprises. A total of 413 public enterprises (of which 339 were commercial and 56 were noncommercial) and several holding companies were selected for privatization over the following ten years.[4] According to Due, Temu, and Temu (2000), by the end of 1999, there were 299 units that had been sold, liquidated, closed, transferred under private management, or leased. Surveys conducted on a sample of 83 units privatized between 1993-97 show that 28 percent were bought by multinational and foreign firms, while indigenous and local buyers bought 53 percent of the units (PSRC 1997:13; Due and Temu 1999). These steps demonstrate that the new Tanzanian state's economic agenda is to ensure capitalist development and integrate Tanzania as a dependent capitalist state enabling international capital to exploit its market and resources with the support of the state. The structural adjustment program of the IMF and the World Bank, to which the Tanzanian economy has been subjected, entrenched the Tanzania state's subordinate position within the global capitalist network.

The economic policies of the Ziaur Rahman regime (1975-1981) and the Ershad regime (1982-1990) in Bangladesh demonstrate objectives similar to the Tanzanian state. Over a period of fifteen years, at least 850 units of various sizes were privatized, restrictions on foreign investments were rescinded, the ceiling on private investment abolished, and the state-owned banks and development finance institutions provided credit to private entrepreneurs. These policies not only accelerated the integration of Bangladesh into the world capitalist economy as a dependent capitalist state but also bred a new class of capitalists who were more interested in plunder as a means of accumulating capital than they were in profit maximization through productive investments in various sectors of the economy. Further, it established the IMF's and the World Bank's unbridled control over the economy of Bangladesh.

NOTES

1   The Tanganyika African National Union (TANU) and the Afro-Shirazi Party (ASP) of Zanzibar merged together in February 1977 to form Chama Cha Mapinduzi (CCM, Revolutionary State Party).

2   Ugandans temporarily occupied a piece of Tanzanian territory in 1978. This was followed by retaliation by the Tanzanian forces leading to the invasion of Uganda. The forces, in 1979, occupied the capital Kampala and helped oust Ugandan President Idi Amin.

3   After the resignation of Julius Nyrere in 1985, Ali Hassan Mwinyi became the President. He remained in power for ten years. The first multi-party elections held in 1995 brought Benjamin Mkapa of the CCM to office. Mkapa was elected for a second term in 2000.

4   The number of enterprises privatized varies by sources. According to one account, the PSRC had 383 enterprises on the books when it started and 230 units had been dealt with by June 1998 (Bigsten and Danielsson 1999:97).

Chapter 7

The Road Ahead

The tale of the transformation of the Bangladeshi state narrated in the previous chapters does not have an ending, for the process has not reached its finale, and, it never will. State transformation is a complex, continuing process and the factors that contribute to this process constantly change, causing new dynamics at different times under different circumstances. Structural as well as conjunctural developments, individuals and the passing of time, affect this multifaceted process. My objective in this book was to identify some of the major factors and examine their interactions over a period of time when part of the transformation process took dramatic shape. This investigation has documented the journey of a nation-state, but also provided an opportunity to reexamine the state transformation process in a peripheral society and, in so doing, contributes to our understanding of states in the Third World.

It became obvious over the course of this study that state transformation is dependent on the state-society relationship and the structural limitations of the state. It is also influenced by exogenous elements such as global capitalist institutions and the global geo-political environment. I argue that in societies where the state is the central institution and strong polar classes are absent, the state becomes relatively autonomous and the intermediate classes can capture the state. The relative autonomy gives the state enormous power in shaping the class configuration of society and in determining the course of history. The capacity of the state is, however, not unlimited, especially in peripheral societies. Instead, it is conditioned by legitimacy and its location within the global economic system. The state that fails to maintain, nurture, and improve the conditions of its citizens loses its legitimacy and, thus, becomes ineffective. Needless to say the relationship between legitimacy and state capacity is reciprocal: one reinforces the other. In some ways, their relationship can be described as symbiotic. The location of the state within the global system, as the Bangladeshi and Tanzanian cases demonstrate, significantly affects the state's ability to function in certain ways. Though the situation is now far more complicated than the period discussed in the book, the logic remains the same: nation-states are vulnerable to the vagaries of the global capitalist system as represented by a number of supranational bodies and multinational corporations. The processes of "thick" globalization—"faster, deeper, and cheaper," characterized by "long-distance flows that are large and continuous, affecting the lives of many people" (Keohane and Nye 2000:7)—are making this obvious all over the world.

Autonomy makes the state less accountable to the society at large, restricts popular participation in politics, and stifles democracy. Evans's (1995) study has demonstrated how "embedded autonomy," a necessary condition for the success of a developmental state, is also fraught with this problem. The Bangladesh case is illustrative in this regard. It took more than 15 years to return to some semblance of democracy. When Bangladesh entered into the democratic era, the representative institutions remained weak and fragile. Under such circumstances, the political parties have relied more on the state apparatus than on their moral leadership to govern. This has made the state an instrument of domination and coercion. The prolonged use of the state in this fashion diminishes its capacity to govern. The deterioration of law and order, the emergence of vigilante groups in rural areas, the relentless persecution of minorities, the targeted killings of political leaders, and extrajudicial killings by special forces in Bangladesh are all evidence of the governmental shortcomings (Riaz 2005).

Granted, the idea of the intermediate classes as a dominant class may reignite the debate about the definition of middle classes and the problems of drawing a boundary around the category. They will also raise a host of other questions. How to describe "those who stand between the workman on the one hand and the capitalist and landlord on the other," in the words of Marx, has remained an unresolved issue to date. Davis (2004) described the definitional quandaries as "the most contentious and controversial themes in the study of society." She insists,

> Drawing boundaries around any class category is fraught with difficulties, as is theorizing their bases for action in the context of this boundary drawing. To be concerned with a class whose so-called objective foundations are considered fluid and unstable and which is characterized by extensive occupational diversity is to invite further controversy. (Davis 2004:363).

Although the debate is welcome, the Gramscian notion of "intermediate" class seems more appropriate in the context of peripheral societies, both analytically and empirically. Waterbury identifies other important questions that should be considered: "if this putative class is small in its undertakings, how [does] it become dominant? If it is internally diversified and seldom aware of itself as class, why [do] other classes, particularly landowners and foreign economic interests, collapse...in its face? If it [is] strong enough to seize political power, why [does] it need an interventionist state to organize its economic interests?" (Waterbury 1991:8-9) The specifics of both the Bangladesh case and the Tanzanian case respond to these questions, but they must be answered at a general level as well. This is where Gramsci, especially his notion of hegemony, becomes relevant. The rise of the intermediate classes is a result of their ability to establish ideological hegemony over other social classes. As they lack the material bases to maintain their hegemony, they use the state as an agency of domination/hegemony, on the one hand, and as a means of gaining the material base they need to continue their domination, on the other. Therefore, to comprehend state transformation processes in peripheral societies, the examination of the state as an agency of hegemony and the role of ideology are crucial.

Discussions of Third World states, especially in the 1990s, have neglected the state's role as an agency of hegemony and its production of ideology. Often the discussions are skewed toward the state's role in economic growth. However, the issues of hegemony and ideology require urgent attention, especially as we are witnessing the rise of what is often inaccurately described as the "fundamentalist movement" in the Third World. States in various countries—from Iran to India to Sudan—have played an instrumental role in producing or accommodating confessional ideologies. I have briefly touched on this issue here (and have addressed it at length elsewhere—Riaz 2004), but more research must be done.

It seems obvious to say that state policies create and reinforce social classes. In peripheral societies, however, the significance of such a statement is heightened. Both the Bangladeshi and Tanzanian experiences discussed in this study demonstrate how the economic policies of the intermediate state engendered a class that eventually became its "gravediggers."

According to Marx and Engels in *The Communist Manifesto*, the bourgeoisie essentially and inevitably dig their own grave. Capitalism itself creates the instrument of its abolition–an oppressed class with both the capacity and the interest to fight for the overthrow of the existing system. If we accept Evans's (1995:229) argument that "successful transformation, not failure, is what produces gravediggers" we can say that the intermediate state succeeded at least on this account. But then the question remains has the new Bangladeshi state created its own gravediggers? The administrative state that emerged through the transformation processes of the mid-1970s has pursued policies of liberalization, deregulation, and marketization. These policies, prodded by the World Bank and the IMF, have remained in place to date, irrespective of the political party in power. And, indeed, these policies have created a new class, "a class of businessmen who survive on state patronage as well as default on their loans and a rent-seeking bureaucracy" (Sobhan 2002:26). The class is not only a creature of the state, but its interests and agendas lie with the perpetuation of the status quo. Thus, the successful transformation has not created, nor is it going to create the gravediggers. Rather, those described by Sobhan (2002) as the "most productive sectors" of society, who have been excluded and marginalized from the process of governance, may become the source of the pressure to change. They are the small farmers, the micro-credit beneficiaries, the creative professional classes, the workers of the export sector, and the successful members of the business community. Some of them, for example the latter two, are the product of Bangladesh's interaction with the global economy.

We can never predict accurately what the future holds for any country. This is as true for Bangladesh as for any other nation. Conflicts and contestations, struggles and the resistance of social forces mediate sociostructural change and political development. Thus, there is no inevitable trajectory of history. But it may be fitting to close the book with a concern about the future of the Bangladeshi state. In recent days, concerns have been raised, at home and abroad, about the future of democracy in Bangladesh.[1] Some have even noted that, perhaps, Bangladesh should already be considered a failed state.[2] The latter is indeed a contentious issue, but the former is not. Even those who passionately argue against characterizing Bangladesh as a failed state, accept its shortcomings:

> While the country most certainly cannot be branded as a 'failed state' or a 'rogue state,' at least not yet, one perhaps cannot completely rule out the apprehension that the state apparatus is increasingly weakening under the dead weight of multiple crises of governance. Few observers of the recent developments in Bangladesh would disagree that the obsolescence of almost all state institutions is more than palpable. Worse still, all of them seem to be malfunctioning simultaneously, often betraying a sort of competitive bid to outdo each other. (Dowlah 2004)

Add to this the rise of militant Islamists since the mid-1990s who have been seeking to establish an Islamic state in Bangladesh. Notably, their rise is not limited to the political arena; their reach has extended to the rural power structures as well. Islamists have used social institutions and practices, such as *salish* (village arbitration) and *fatwa* (religious edict), to further their cause, establish their authority, and naturalize a particular social order. This becomes a matter of great concern in the context of the crises of governance. Crises enhance the possibility of the emergence of a counter-coalition, which can transform the nature of the state. Whether this force will emerge as a counter-coalition to transform the state is an open question, but is not something that can be discounted altogether.

While the state is being weakened by the crises from within, it is also under pressure from the outside. In the wake of the state's failure to provide services to its citizens effectively and in a transparent manner, the donors are increasingly using Non-Governmental Organizations (NGOs) to replace the government as development contractors for the delivery of their aid, particularly to the poorer sections of the society (Sobhan 2002). The trend, which originated in the late1980s when Bangladesh was ruled by a military autocracy, has intensified in the 1990s, a period of democratically elected governments. The donors, euphemistically called "development partners," including the United States and Britain, are now keener to induct civil society organizations (CSOs) in the development process and improve their standing as an alternative to the state. These efforts are packaged

267

under the rubric of "good governance," accountability, and transparency, all of which are essential for the effective functioning of the state. Such efforts are justified on the grounds that civil society must act as a watchdog to protect and preserve the rights of the people. However, it is also necessary to examine whether this trend might eventually contribute to what Wood (1997) has described as the "franchise state"—a state that only serves a small clique and leaves the larger segment of the society to the vagaries of the international capital and the compassion of the NGOs.

Whether or not we call it the franchising of the state, the scenario obviously suggests an absence of the state. Such an absence, either in certain geographical areas (e.g., rural areas) or in regard to certain social services (e.g., education), would obviously accentuate the crisis of governance. The absence of the state is bound to create a void, which, in turn, leads to the establishment of a parallel structure of authority. One can easily see this coming to pass in various parts of rural Bangladesh where militant Islamist groups have a strong influence.

Two other factors likely to influence the future course of the Bangladeshi state are the insurgencies in the vicinity of the country and the so-called "war on terror" launched by the United States after the attacks at the World Trade Center and Pentagon on 9/11. A number of insurgent movements are continuing in and around Bangladesh. The Rohingya insurgency in Myanmar has already affected Bangladesh via the refugee crisis.[3] The southeastern hill tracts of Chittagong in Bangladesh are being used as a safe haven by the *Rohingya Solidarity Organization* (RSO) and *Arakan Rohingya Islamic Front* (ARIF). The rebels of the northeastern states of India, for example the *United Liberation Front of Assam* (ULFA), have allegedly received support from the Bangladeshi governments during the period of military rule and the BNP regimes. Furthermore, it is now evident that Maoist militants, commonly referred to as *Naxalites* in India, have become major sources of instability in the states of Andhra Pradesh, Jharkhand, Bihar, Orissa, Chattisgargh, Uttar Pradesh, Madhya Pradesh, and Uttaranchal. Some 170 districts of 15 states are experiencing what the Indian Prime Minister Manmohan Singh has described as "a virtual collapse of law and order" (*India Times* 2005). These militant groups have close ties with the Maoists in Nepal who have been engaged in an armed resistance, with formidable power, since 1996. These insurgencies have little support and sympathy among the Bangladeshis. However, the nation may be drawn into these insurgencies by the lack of border control and the lawlessness in the border areas. The border problems make it easy for outsiders to infiltrate and operate from within the country. Most significantly, a combination of weak governance, a corrupt system, and a porous border may invite these rebels to use Bangladesh as their base.

This is equally true in the context of the ongoing "global war on terror." The foreign policy of the U.S. administration, especially the strategies adopted in the "global war on terror," has not only fueled "anti-Americanism" among Muslims around the world, but also seems to have contributed to the growing alliance between homegrown Islamists and the transnational terrorist organizations. The militant Islamists within Bangladesh may, over time, move beyond their circumscribed objectives and become partners in the so-called "global jihad." Should that happen, the country will become the new frontline of the "war on terrorism" and the nature and the role of the state will be redefined.

NOTES

1   U.S. Deputy Assistant Secretary of State, Torkel Patterson, for example, commented during his visits to Bangladesh in March and September 2004 that the international community is worried about the political situation in Bangladesh (Daily Star 2004c:1; Daily Star 2004d:1). British MP Oona King, while visiting Dhaka in September of the same year, said "democracy in Bangladesh is eroding daily" (Daily Star 2004e: 1). *Time*, in April 2004, described Bangladesh as "Asia's most dysfunctional country" (Time 2004). The British weekly T*he Economist* asked, "Is Bangladesh slithering into anarchy?" (*Economist* 2004:37).

2   A commentary in the daily *Prothom Alo* in June 2004 stirred the debate that went on for months (see *New Age* 2004a; *Daily Star* 2004f).

3   More than 200,000 Rohingya (Muslims from the northern Burmese state of Arakan) fled to Bangladesh alleging widespread brutality, rape, and murder by the Burmese Army. In late 1991, Bangladesh saw another influx of Rohingya refugees when more than 250,000 fled their country.

References

Abdullah, Abu. 1972. "The Class Basis of Nationalism: Pakistan and Bangladesh." In *West Bengal and Bangladesh: Perspectives from 1972,* edited by Barbara Thomas and Spencer Lavin. East Lansing, Michigan: Michigan State University.

———. 1976. "Land Reform and Agrarian Change in Bangladesh." *Bangladesh Development Studies* 4(1).

Abdullah, A., M. Hossain, and R. Nations. 1976. "Agrarian Structure and the IRDP - Preliminary Considerations." *Bangladesh Development Studies* 4(2).

Abrahams, Ray. 1987. "Sugusungu: Village Vigilante Groups in Tanzania." *African Affairs* 86:179-96.

Ahamed, Emajuddin. 1988. *Military Rule and Myths of Democracy.* Dhaka: University Press Limited.

———. 1980. *Bureaucratic Elites in Segmented Economic Growth, Bangladesh and Pakistan.* Dhaka: University Press Limited.

Ahamed, Iftikhar. 1980. "State and Politics in Pakistan: 1500-1970." *Pakistan Progressive* 3(1).

Ahamed, Q.K. 1974. "Aspects of the Management of Nationalized Industries in Bangladesh." *Bangladesh Development Studies* 2(3):675-702.

Ahmad, Aijaz. 1985. "Class, Nation and State: Intermediate Classes in Peripheral Societies." In *Middle Classes in Dependent Countries*, edited by Dale L. Johnson London: Sage.

Ahmad, Nafis. 1966. "Urban Centers in East Pakistan." Occasional Papers, No. 12. Michigan State University.

Ahmed, Firoz. 1973. "The Structural Matrix of the Struggle in Bangladesh." In *Imperialism and Revolution in South Asia*, edited by K. Gough and H. P. Sharma London: Monthly Review Press.

Ahmed, Moudud. 1984. *Bangladesh: Era of Sheikh Mujibur Rahman.* Weisbadan: Franz Steiner Verlag.

Ahmed, Mushtaq. 1963. *Government and Politics in Pakistan.* Karachi: Pakistan Publishing House.

Ahmed, Raisuddin. 1979. "Foodgrain Supply, Distribution and Consumption Policies within a Dual-Price Mechanism: A Case Study of Bangladesh." Research Report No. 8. Washington: International Food Policy Research Institute.

272

Ahmed, Wakil. 1983. *Unisha Stakera Banali Musalmaner Chitachetanara Dhara* (The Trends of Muslim Thoughts of Bengali Muslims in the 19th Century), Volume I. Dhaka: Bangla Academy.

Akash, M. M. 1987. *Bangladesher Arthaniti O Rajniti, Sampratik Probonotasamuha.* (Bangladesh Economy and Politics, Recent Trends). Dhaka: Jatiyo Shahittyo Prokashani.

Alavi, Hamza. 1982. "The Structure of Peripheral Capitalism." In *Introduction to the Sociology of the 'Developing Societies',* edited by Hamza Alavi and Teodor Shanin. New York: Monthly Review Press.

_____. 1982a. "State and Class under Peripheral Capitalism." In *Introduction to the Sociology of the 'Developing Societies',* edited by Hamza Alavi and Teodor Shanin. New York: Monthly Review Press.

_____. 1980. "The Colonial Transformation in India." *Journal of Social Studies.* No. 7 (January):1-26 and No. 8 (April):32-69.

_____. 1976. "The Rural Elite and Agricultural Development in Pakistan." In *Rural Development in Bangladesh and Pakistan,* edited R. D. Stevans et al. Honolulu: University of Hawaii Press.

_____. 1973. "The State in Post-Colonial Societies: Pakistan and Bangladesh." In *Imperialism and Revolution in South Asia,* edited by Kathleen Gough and Hari P. Sharma. London: Monthly Review Press.

Anderson, Perry. 1974. *Lineages of the Absolutist State.* London: New Left Books.

Awami League. 1970. *Manifesto.* Dhaka: Abdul Mannan, Publicity Secretary, All Pakistan Awami League.

Azad, A.K. 1972. "The Saga of Bangladesh Army." *Weekly Holiday,* July 30.

Azfer, Jawaid. 1971. "The Income Distribution in Pakistan, Before and After Taxes." Ph.D dissertation, Harvard University, Cambridge, Massachusetts.

Ayoob, Mohammed. 1971. "Background and Developments." In *Bangladesh: A Struggle for Nationhood.* Delhi: Vikas Publications.

Bangladesh Bureau of Statistics (BBS). 1986. *Bangladesh Economic Survey 1985-1986.* Dhaka: BBS.

_____. 1975. *Statistical Yearbook of Bangladesh.* Dhaka: BBS.

_____. 1972. Report on the Survey of Small and Household Industries in Bangladesh (Rural Areas Only), 1970. Dhaka: BBS.

Bangladesh Gazette (Extraordinary). 1972. Presidential Order No. 135 of November 4, 1972.

———. 1972a. Presidential Order No. 154 of December 15, 1972.

Bangladesh Jatiya Sangsad. 1975. *Proceedings of the Jatiya Sangsad Debates*, Vol. 2, No. 7, July 2, 1975.

Bangladesh Nationalist Party (BNP). n.d. "19 Clauses of BNP" (in Bengali) at http://www.bnpbd.com/19_clause.html; accessed on May 12, 2005.

Bangladesh Observer. 1977. News Report. October 19.

———. 1977a. News Report. October 27.

———. 1976. "Full Text of President Sayem's Speech." July 28.

———. 1975. News Report. July 12.

———. 1975a. News Report. December 7.

———. 1974. News Report. March 26, 1974.

———. 1973. News Report. July 7.

———. 1973a. "The Declaration of the Three-Party Alliance." October 15.

———. 1973b. "Opposition Conspiring to Disrupt Election: Bangabandhu." January 3.

———. 1973c. "Foil Foreign Conspiracy: Bangabandhu." January 4.

———. 1973d. News Report. March 4.

———. 1973e. "Collaborators will be dealt with: Shah Moazzem." January 12.

———. 1973f. News Report. March 3.

———. 1973g. "The Supreme Test." Editorial. March 15.

———. 1972. "Brief Life Sketches of the Ministers." January 20, January 29, April 14 and April 15.

———. 1972a. News Report. February 2.

———. 1972b. "Bangabandhu's speech: Full Text." 11 January.

Bangladesh Parliament Secretariat. 1972. *Parliamentary Debates.* 2, No. 13. Dhaka: Bangladesh Parliament Secretariat.

Bangladesh Planning Commission (BPC). 1980. *The Draft Second Five Year Plan.* Dhaka: Bangladesh Planning Commission.

———. 1978. *The Two-Year Plan, 1978-80.* Dhaka: Bangladesh Planning Commission.

———. 1975. *Economic Review, 1974/75.* Dhaka: Bangladesh Planning Commission.

———. 1974. *IRDP — An Evaluation.* Dhaka: Ministry of Planning.

_____. 1974a. "Report of the Working Group of Officials' Committee on Distribution of Essential Commodities," Unpublished Memorandum.

_____. 1972. "Policy Options and Recommendations for the Nationalization of the Industries." Mimeograph. Dhaka: Bangladesh Planning Commission.

Banglar Bani. 1974. News Report. September 29.

Bardhan, Pranab. 1984. *The Political Economy of Development in India.* Delhi: Oxford University Press.

Barnett, Michael. 2002. "Historical Sociology and Constructivism: An Estranged Past, A Federated Future?" In *Historical Sociology of International Relations,* edited by Stephen Hobden and John M. Hobson. Cambridge: Cambridge University Press.

Barua, Tushar Kanti. 1978. *Political Elite in Bangladesh.* Bern: Peter Lang.

Bates, Robert H. 1989. *Beyond the Miracle of the Market: The Political Economy Agrarian Development in Kenya.* Cambridge: Cambridge University Press.

Bergan, Asbjorn. 1967. "Personal Income Distribution and Personal Savings in Pakistan, 1963-64." *Pakistan Development Review* VII, Summer.

Bergman, David. 1991. "Bangladesh's Opening for a New Beginning." *Economic and Political Weekly (EPW),* February 16.

Bigsten, Arne and Anders Danielsson. 1999. *Is Tanzania an Emerging Economy? A Report for the OECD Project "Emerging Africa."* OECD. Accessed at www.oecd.org/dataoecd/40/30/2674918.pdf accessed on October 12, 2004.

Biplobi Sainik Sanghstha. 1975. "Call for Uprising." Pamphlet. November 5.

Blair, H.W. 1978. "Rural Development, Class Structure and the Bureaucracy in Bangladesh." *World Development* 6(1).

Block, Fred. 1987. *Revising State Theory, Essays in Politics and Postindustrialism.* Philadelphia: Temple University Press.

Bose, Swadesh Ranjan. 1974. "The Price Situation in Bangladesh." *The Bangladesh Economic Review* 1(3).

_____. 1968. "Trend in Real Income of the Rural Poor in East Pakistan 1949-66." *Pakistan Development Review* 8(3):452-88.

Bottomore, Tom et al. eds. 1983. *A Dictionary of Marxist Thought.* Cambridge: Harvard University Press.

Braibanti, Ralph. 1966. *Research on the Bureaucracy of Pakistan.* Durham, NC: Duke University Press.

Burki, Shahed Javed. 1977. "Economic Decision-Making in Pakistan." In *Pakistan: The Long View,* edited by Lawrence Ziring et al. Durham, NC: Duke University Press.

Byers, T.J. 1996. "State, Class and Development Planning in India." In *The State, Development Planning and Liberalisation in India,* edited by T.J. Byers. New Delhi: Oxford University Press.

Carnoy, Martin. 1984. *The State and Political Theory.* Princeton: Princeton University Press.

Choudhury, G.W. 1972. *The Last Days of United Pakistan.* Bloomington: Indiana University Press.

Choudhry, Saud A. 1986. "Food Policy, Inequality and Underdevelopment: The Anatomy of an Agrarian Economy in Bondage." *Journal of Contemporary Asia* 16(2).

Chowdhury, Jafar Ahmed. 1990. "Privatization in Bangladesh." Working Paper No. 92. Institute of Social Studies (mimeograph). Hague: ISS.

Chowdhury, Rashid A. 1989. "United States Foreign Policy in South Asia: The Liberation Struggle in Bangladesh and the Indo-Pakistan War of 1971." Ph.D. Dissertation, Department of History, University of Hawaii.

Chowdhury, Shamsul Huda. 1982. *Muktijudhya Mujibnagar* (Mujibnagar During the Liberation War). Dhaka: Ahmed Publishing House.

Cohn, Bernard. 1967. "Regions Subjective and Objective: Their Relation to the Study of Modern Indian History." In *Regions and Regionalism in South Asian Studies: An Exploratory Study,* edited by Robert I. Crane. Durham, NC: Duke University, Comparative Studies on Southern Asia.

Communist Party of Bangladesh (CPB). 1974. "Political Report." *The Speeches, Messages and Documents, Second Congress of the Communist Party of Bangladesh.* Dhaka: Jatiya Shahitya Prakashani.

Constituent Assembly of Pakistan (CAP). 1956. *Debates*, January 1, 1:52.

Crow, Ben. 1987. "U.S. Policies in Bangladesh: The Making and the Breaking of Famine?" *Journal of Social Studies* No. 35, January, Center for Social Studies, Dhaka University.

Costello, J. Matthew. 1996. "Administration Triumphs over Politics: The Transformation of the Tanzanian State." *African Studies Review* 39(1):123-148.

Coulson, Andrew. 1982. *Tanzania: A Political Economy*. Oxford: Oxford University Press.

Daily Ittefaq. 1983. News Report. January 15, p. 1.

———. 1975. "Country would be run according to Islamic principles: Ershad." January 15.

———. 1973. News Report. November 1.

———. 1973a. News Report. March 2.

———. 1973b. News Report. June 3.

———. 1973c. News Report. July 23.

Daily Star. 2005. "EU worried over 'crossfire' deaths". February 14 at http://www.thedailystar.net/2005/02/14/d5021401033.htm.

———. 2004. "Dhaka's tradition as moderate Muslim state going off-track", May 20, 2004 at http://www.thedailystar.net/2004/05/20/d4052001033.htm.

———. 2004a. "Ahmadiyya mosque razed, 12 houses robbed in B'Baria", October 30, 2004 at http://www.thedailystar.net/2004/10/30/d4103001044.htm.

———. 2004b. "Rab accused of extra-judicial killings, violation of constitution". October 14 at http://www.thedailystar.net/2004/10/14/d4101401022.htm.

———. 2004c. "International community worried over political situation." March 15 at http://www.thedailystar.net/2004/03/15/d4031501033.htm.

———. 2004d. "Democracy faces derailment", September 15, 2004 at http://www.thedailystar.net/2004/09/15/d4091501022.htm.

———. 2004e. "Democracy erodes daily here", September 23 at http://www.thedailystar.net/2004/09/23/d4092301055.htm.

———. 2004f. "Failed State and Bangladesh." Editorial. June 11.

_____. 2003. "Impunity Encourages HR violations in Bangladesh." January 13 at http://www.dailystarnews.com/200301/13/n3011301. htm#BODY6.

Dainik Bangla. 1975. "Full Text of President Mushtaq's Speech." October 4.

_____. 1974. "Emergency Proclaimed throughout the Country." December 29.

_____. 1973. News Report. May 12.

_____. 1973a. News Report. January 2.

_____. 1972. News Report. December 31.

_____. 1972a. "Government Must Resign: NAP(M)." November 22.

_____. 1972b. "Resignation Demand Ridiculous." November 23.

_____. 1972c. "Form All-Party Government: Bhashani." December 31.

Davis, Diane. E. 2004. *Discipline and Development: Middle Classes and Prosperity in East Asia and Latin America.* Cambridge: Cambridge University Press.

Degnbol-Martinussen, John. n.d. "External Constraints on Policy-Making in Developing Countries: How Autonomous are the States?" In *External and Internal Constraints on Policy-making in Developing Countries: How Autonomous are the States?* Edited by John Degnbol-Martinussen. Occasional Paper No. 20, International Development Studies, Roskilde University.

Dhaka Union of Journalist (DUJ). 1973. *Annual Report of the Secretary General.* Dhaka: DUJ.

Doornbos, Martin. 1990. "The African State in Academic Debate: Retrospect and Prospect." *The Journal of Modern African Studies* 28(1):179-198.

Dowlah, CAF. 2004. "The State of Affairs in Bangladesh." *Weekly Holiday*, November 11, 2004, accessed at http://www.weeklyholiday.net /2004/anni40/s11.html#01 accessed December 5, 2004.

Due, Jean M. 1993. "Liberalization and Privatization in Tanzania and Zambia." *World Development* 21(12):1981-1988.

Due, Jean M. and Andrew E. Temu. 1999. "How Successful Have Newly Privatized Companies Been? Some Evidence from Tanzania" *Canadian Journal of Development* 19(2):315-341.

Due, Jean M., Andrew E. Temu, and Anna A. Temu. 2000. "Privatization in Tanzania: A Case Study 1999." Accessed on March 21, 2004, at http://www.ace.uiuc.edu/faculty/emeriti/due/tanzania.pdf.

Economist. 2004. "A bomb too far." August 28.

Engels, Frederick. 1975. The *Origin of the Family, Private Property and the State.* New York: International Publishers.

Evans, Peter. 1995. *Embedded Autonomy: States and Industrial Transformation.* Princeton: Princeton University Press.

Faaland, J. 1981. "The Bangladesh Aid Group." In *Aid and Influence,* edited by J. Faaland. London: Macmillan Press.

Fagen, Richard R. 1983. "Theories of Development: The Question of Class Struggle." *Monthly Review* 35(4).

Feldman, Shelley. 2000. "Gender and Islam in Bangladesh: Metaphor and Myth" in *Understanding the Bengal Muslims: Interpretative Essays,* edited by Rafiuddin Ahmed. New Delhi: Oxford University Press.

Franda, Marcus. 1982. *Bangladesh: The First Decade.* New Delhi: South Asian Publishers.

Frank, Andre Gunder. 1972. *Lumpenbourgeoisie, Lumpendevelopment, Dependence, Class, and Politics in Latin America.* New York: Monthly Review Press.

Gankovsky, Y.V. 1972. "The Social Structure of Society in the People's Republic of Bangladesh." *Asian Survey* 16(3) March.

Gardezi, Hassan and Jamil Rashid, eds. 1983. *Pakistan: The Unstable State.* Lahore: Vanguard Books.

Ghosh, Shyamali. 1990. *The Awami League: 1949-1971.* Dhaka: Academic Publishers.

Gonokantha. 1973. News Report. January 5.

_____. 1973a. "Mujib Dismisses Opposition Demands." January 5.

_____. 1973b. News Report. March 12.

_____. 1973c. News Report. December 19.

Government of Bangladesh (GOB). 1975. *The Bangladesh Gazette Extraordinary*, July 18.

_____. 1975a. "The District Administration Act." *The Bangladesh Gazette Extraordinary*, July 10.

Government of Pakistan. 1970. *Report of the Panel of Economists on the Fourth Five Year Plan, 1970-75.* Islamabad: Planning Commission.

_____. 1969. *Report of Pay and Services Commission 1959-60.* Karachi: Printing Corporation of Pakistan Press.

_____. 1966. *Pakistan Economic Survey 1966-67.* Economic Adviser to the Government of Pakistan, Rawalpindi: Ministry of Finance.

_____. 1958. *The First Five-Year Plan 1955-60.* Karachi: National Planning Board, Government of Pakistan Press.

_____. 1953. *Pakistan Year Book.* Karachi: Government Printing Press.

_____. 1951. *Economy of Pakistan.* Karachi: Ministry of Economic Affairs.

Government of the People's Republic of Bangladesh (GPRB) 1985. *Report of the Committee for Industrial Finance.* Ministry of Finance, Government of the People's Republic of Bangladesh. September.

_____. 1981. *Land Policy Report.* Dhaka: Ministry of Land Reforms and Land Revenues.

_____. 1981a. "Flow of External Resources into Bangladesh." Ministry of Finance, External Resources Division, November, 1981.

_____. 1980. Memo of the Establishment Ministry. ED/SAIV-57/80-112 dated 23 April 1980.

_____. 1979. Memos of Cabinet Secretariat, Establishment Division No. ED(IC) SII-6/78/5 dated March 1, 1979 and ED(IC) SII-6/78/20 dated April 9, 1979.

_____. 1975. *Land Revenue Committee Report.* Dhaka: Ministry of Land Revenue and Land Reforms.

_____. 1975a. *Economic Review, 1974-75.* Dhaka: Planning Commission.

_____. 1975b. "The Indemnity Ordinance 1975 (Ordinance No. XLX of 1975)." *The Bangladesh Gazette Extraordinary*, September 26.

_____. 1975c. Memo Nos. 2372-MFCS-II and 2373-MFCS-II dated December 17, 1975, Ministry of Food and Civil Supplies.

_____. 1975d. *Revised Investment Policy.* Dhaka: Ministry of Industry and Commerce, Industries division.

_____. 1974. *Revised Industrial Policy.* Dhaka: Ministry of Industries.

_____. 1974a. *Memorandum for the Bangladesh Consortium, 1974-75.* Dhaka: Planning Commission.

_____. 1973. *Investment Policy, 1973.* Dhaka: Ministry of Industry.

_____. 1973a. *Report of the Administrative and Services Reorganization Committee. Part I: The Services.* Dhaka: GPRB.

_____. 1973b. *First Five Year Plan.* Dhaka: Bangladesh Planning Commission.

_____. 1972. "Report of the Land Revenue Committee." Dhaka: Ministry of Land Revenue and Land Reform.

_____. 1972a. *Industrial Investment Policy 1972-73.* Dhaka: Ministry of Industry.

_____. 1972b. *The Constitution of Bangladesh.* Dhaka: Ministry of Law and Parliamentary Affairs.

_____. 1971. Cabinet Division, Memo No. 391(8)/Cab, Dated Nov 25, 1971.

_____. 1971a. Establishment Division, Memo No. 3179(19)/Est. Div., dated December 16, 1971.

Government of Tanzania. 1968. *Background to the Budget: An Economic Survey.* Dar es Salam.

Gramsci, Antonio. 1985. *Selections from the Cultural Writings 1921-1926*, Edited by David Forgacs and Geoffrey Nowell Smith, translated by William Boelhowler. London: Lawrence and Wishart.

_____. 1979. *Selections from the Political Writings 1921-1926*, Translated and edited by Quintin Hoare. London: Lawrence and Wishart.

_____. 1978. *Selections from the Political Writings 1910-1920*, Selected and edited by Qunitin Hoare, translated by J. Matthews. London: Lawrence and Wishart.

_____. 1971. *Selections from the Prison Notebooks.* Edited and translated by Quintin Hoare and Geoffrey Nowell Smith. New York: International General.

Griswold, Eliza. 2005. "Next Islamist Revolution." *New York Times Magazine.* Sec 6 (35-39). January 23.

Habibullah, M. 1976. "Social Origin of Business Executives in Bangladesh." *The Dhaka University Studies.* Part A. Vol. 24.

Hamid, M.A. and M.A. Rahman. 1977. "An Evaluation of Natore and Gaibandha Projects." Mimeograph. IRDP/Department of Economics, Rajshahi University.

Hamilton, Nora. 1982. *The Limits of State Autonomy: Post Revolutionary Mexico.* Princeton: Princeton University Press.

Haq, Mahbubul. 1963. *The Strategy of Economic Planning: A Case Study of Pakistan.* Karachi: Oxford University Press Limited.

Harrison, Selig S. 1959. "Case History of a Mistake: India, Pakistan and the U.S." *The New Republic,* August 10.

Hasan, Muyeedul. 1986. *Muldhara Ekattar* (The Main Trends 1971). Dhaka: University Press Limited.

Hawkins, H.C.G. 1965. *Wholesale and Retail Trade in Tanganyika: A Study of Distribution in East Africa.* New York: Fredrich A. Praeger.

Hay, Colin. 2002. *Political Analysis: A Critical Introduction.* Basingstoke: Palgrave.

Hertzberg, Sidney. 1954. "The Crisis in U.S. Foreign Policy," *Commentary* 18 (June).

Hopkins, Raymond. 1972. *Political Roles in New State.* New Haven: Cambridge University Press.

_____. 1977. "How to Make Food Work." *Foreign Affairs* No. 27.

Hossain, Kamal. 1979. "Political Development in Bangladesh: Promise and Reality." *Contributions to Asian Studies* Vol. XIV.

Humphrey, Clare E. 1990. *Privatization in Bangladesh, Economic Transition in a Poor Country. Westview Special Studies on South and Southeast Asia.* Boulder: Westview Press.

Huque, Ahmed Shafiqul and Muhammad Yeahia Akhter. 1989. "Militarisation and Opposition in Bangladesh: Parliamentary Approval and Public Reaction." *The Journal of Commonwealth and Comparative Politics* 27(2) July.

Hussain, Tofazzal. 1976. "The Emerging Pattern–I," *Bangladesh Observer,* May 16.

IBRD (International Bank for Reconstruction and Development). 1984. *Bangladesh: Economic Trends and Development Administration.* 2 Vols. Washington D.C.: IBRD.

_____. 1974. *Bangladesh: Development in Rural Economy,* Vol 1. Washington D.C: IBRD.

_____. 1974a. *Bangladesh Agricultural Credit Review.* Washington D.C.: IBRD.

Iliyas, Khondoker Mohammad, ed. 1979. *Bangladesher Samaj Biplobe Bangobodhur Darshan* (Bangabandhu's Philosophy in the Social

Revolution in Bangladesh, in Bengali). Dhaka: Bangabandhu Parishad.

IMF. 1992. *International Financial Statistics Yearbook 1990*. Washington D.C.: International Monetary Fund.

India Times. 2005. "Maoists: India's growing worry." February 15 at http://timesofindia.indiatimes.com/articleshow/1021286.cms.

Islam, Amirul. 1985. "Interview" in *History of Bangladesh War of Independence: Documents*, Vol 15 edited by Hasan Hafizur Rahman. Dhaka: Ministry of Information, Government of the People's Republic of Bangladesh. pp. 77-163

Islam, Major Rafiq-ul. 1983. *Ekti Phoolke Bachabo Boley* (To Save a Flower). Dhaka: University Press Limited.

Islam, Nurul. 1978. *Development Strategy of Bangladesh*. London: C. Hurst & Company.

_____. 1977. *Development Planning in Bangladesh. A Study in Political Economy*. London: C. Hurst and Company.

Islam, Syed Serajul. 1988. *Bangladesh: State and Economic Strategy*. Dhaka: University Press Limited.

_____. 1986. "The Rise of the Civil-Military Bureaucracy in the State Apparatus of Bangladesh," *Asian Thought & Society* 11(31) March.

Jahan, Rounaq. 1980. *Bangladesh Politics: Problems and Issues*. Dhaka: University Press Limited.

_____. 1972. *Pakistan: Failure of National Integration*. New York: Columbia University Press.

Jahangir, B.K. 1986. *Problematics of Nationalism in Bangladesh*. Dhaka: Center for Social Studies.

Jankantha. 2003. "British Lawmakers Criticize Clean-Heart indemnity." January 23.

_____. 2002. Editorial. December 27.

Jalal, Ayesha. 1986. "Constructing a State: The Interplay of Domestic, Regional and International Factors in Post-Colonial Pakistan," Colloquium Paper, Asia Program, Widrow Wilson International Center for Scholars, Washington D.C. April 16.

Januzzi, F. Tomasson and James T. Peach. 1980. *The Agrarian Structure of Bangladesh: An Impediment to Development*. Boulder: Westview Press.

Jatiya Samajtantrik Dal (JSD). 1976. *Sammaybad*. No. 4. February 23.

Jones, Steve. 1979. "An Evaluation of Rural Development Programmes in Bangladesh" *The Journal of Social Studies* No. 6.

Jugantor. 2003. "Those who died in the hands of the Army." January 10.

Kalecki, Michal. 1976. E*ssays on Developing Economies*. Hassock: Harvester Press.

_____. 1972. *Selected Essays on the Economic Growth of the Socialist and the Mixed Economy*. London: Unwin.

Keohane, Robert O. and Joseph S. Nye Jr. 2000. "Introduction." In *Governance in a Globalized World,* edited by Joseph S. Nye Jr. and John D. Donahue, Washington D.C.: Brookings Institution Press.

Khan, Ayub. 1967. *Friends, Not Masters: A Political Autobiography*. London: Oxford University Press.

_____. 1964. *Speeches and Statements*. Karachi: Pakistan Publications.

Khan, Azizur Rahman. 1979. "The Comilla Model and the Integrated Rural Development Programme in Bangladesh: An Experiment in Cooperative Capitalism." *World Development* No. 7.

Khan, Azizur Rahman and Mahbub Hossain. 1989. *The Strategy of Development of Bangladesh*. London: Macmillan.

Khan, Mohammad Mohabbat and Habib Mohammad Zafarullah. 1980. *Politics and Bureaucracy in a New Nation, Bangladesh*. Dhaka: Center for Public Administration.

Khan, Zillur Rahman. 1984. *Martial Law to Martial Law: Leadership Crisis in Bangladesh*. Dhaka: University Press Limited.

Khondker, Bazlul H. and Selim Raihan. 2004. "Welfare and Poverty Impacts in Bangladesh: A General Equilibrium Approach." Paper presented at the Northwest Universities Development Consortium, HEC, October 1-3, Montreal, Canada, 2004.

Kissinger, Henry. 1979. *The White House Years*. Boston: Brown and Company.

Kohli, Atul. 1987. *The State and Poverty in India*. Cambridge: Cambridge University Press.

Krasner, Stephan. 1978. *Defending the National Interests*. Princeton: Princeton University Press.

Kulkarni, V.G. 1990. "Armed Neutrality." *Far Eastern Economic Review* December 27.

Kukreja, Veena. 1991. *Civil-Military Relations in South Asia: Pakistan, Bangladesh and India.* New Delhi: Sage.

Lambert, R.D. 1959. "Factors in Bengali Regionalism in Pakistan." *Far Eastern Survey* 28(4) April.

Lewis, Stephen R. 1970. *Pakistan, Industrialization and Trade Policies.* London: Oxford University Press.

Lenin, V.I. 1964. *Collected Works*, Vol. 6. Moscow: Progress Publishers.

Lifschultz, Lawrence. 1979. *Bangladesh: The Unfinished Revolution.* London: Zed.

Mafeje, A. 1977. "Neo-Colonialism, State Capitalism, or Revolution?" In *African Social Studies,* edited by P.C.W. Gutkind and P. Waterman. London: Heinemann.

Majumdar, A. Mannan. 1978. "Village Mahajanpur." In *Exploitation and the Rural Poor,* edited by Ameerul Huq. Comilla: BARD.

Mamdani, Mahmood. 1976. *Politics and Class Formation in Uganda.* New York and London: Monthly Review Books.

Maniruzzaman, Talukdar. 1982. *Group Interests and Political Changes, Studies of Pakistan and Bangladesh.* New Delhi: South Asia Publishers.

_____. 1980. *Bangladesh Revolution and Its Aftermath.* Dhaka: Bangladesh Books International.

_____. 1973. "Radical Politics and the Emergence of Bangladesh." In *Radical Politics in South Asia,* edited by Paul Brass and Marcus Franda. Cambridge: The MIT Press.

Mann, Michael. 1986. "The Autonomous Power of the State." In *States in History,* edited by John A. Hall. Cambridge: Basil Blackwell.

Mannan, Manzurul. 1990. "The State and the Formation of a Dependent Bourgeoisie in Bangladesh." *South Asia Journal* 3(4).

Mapolu, Henry. 1990. "Tanzania: Imperialism, the State and the Peasantry." In *African Agriculture: The Critical Choices,* edited by Hamid Aït Amara and Bernard Founou-Tchuigoua. London: Zed Books. Accessed on February 21, 2004, at http://www.unu.edu/ unupress/unupbooks/uu28ae/uu28ae0h.htm#8.%20tanzania:%20im perialism,%20the%20state%20and%20peasantry.

Marx, Karl. 1974. "Eighteenth Brumaire of Louis Bonaparte." In *Karl Marx: Surveys From Exile, Political Writings*, Vol. 2, edited by D. Fernbach. Harmondsworth: Penguin.

_____. 1968. "Contribution to the Critique of Political Economy: in *Collected Works of Marx and Engels*. New York: International General.

Mascarenhas, Anthony. 1986. *Bangladesh: A Legacy of Blood*. London: Hodder and Stoughton.

Matin, Abdul. 1998. *Bangobandhu Sheikh Mujib: Koekti Prashongik Bishoy* (Bangabandhu Sheikh Mujib: Some Relevant Issues). London: Radical Asia Publications.

McHenry, Donald F. and K. Bird. 1977. "Food Bungle in Bangladesh," *Foreign Policy* 27 Summer.

Migdal. Joe S. 1988. *Strong Societies and Weak States, State-Society Relations and State Capabilities in the Third World*. New Jersey: Princeton University Press.

Miliband, Ralph. 1973. "Poulantzas and the Capitalist State." *New Left Review* 82(November-December):83-92.

_____. 1969. *The State in Capitalist Society*. New York: Basic Books.

Molla, Md Gyasuddin. 1990. *Politics of Food Aid, Case of Bangladesh*. Dhaka: Academic Publishers.

Moni, Sheikh Fazlul Huq. 1973. Post-editorial. *Banglar Bani*. September 24.

Morgan, Dan. 1974. "Dacca Aid Tied to Cuban Ban." *Washington Post*, September 30.

Morning News. 1973. List of Awami League Candidates. February 13 and February 17.

_____. 1973a. News Report. August 3.

_____. 1973b. News Report. November 5.

_____. 1972. News Report. January 18.

_____. 1972a. News Reports. February 25 and February 29.

Mortoza, Golam and Aniruddha Islam. 2005. "Bangla Bhaier Rajottye" (Under Bangla Bhai's Rule). *Shpatahik* 2000 June 4.

Muhith, A.M.A. 1978. *Emergence of a New Nation*. Dhaka: Bangladesh Books International.

Mustafa, I. 1989. "Rise of Business Groups in Bangladesh." Mimeograph. Dhaka: BIDS.

Namboodripad, E.M.S. 1973. "On Intermediate Regimes." *EPW* December 1.

National Awami Party (NAP). 1972. *Aims, Objectives, and Programs of the Bangladesh National Awami Party.* Dhaka: NAP.

Nations, Richard. 1971. "The Economic Structure of Pakistan and Bangladesh: Class and Colony." *New Left Review* 68:3-26.

New Age. 2004. "PM irked as Bangla Bhai at large." May 31.

_____. 2004a. "The fault lies in politics." Editorial, September 8.

New York Times. 1977. October 20.

Nordlinger, Eric. 1981. *On the Autonomy of the Democratic State.* Cambridge: Harvard University Press.

Offe, Claus. 1975. "The Theory of the Capitalist State and Problems of Policy Formation." In *Stress and Contradiction in Modern Capitalism,* edited by Leon L. Lindberg et al. Lexington, MA: Heath.

Osmani, S.R. and M.A. Quasem. 1985. *Pricing and Subsidy Policies for Bangladesh Agriculture.* Dhaka: Bangladesh Institute of Development Studies.

Oszlak, Oscar. 1981. "The Historical Formation of the State in Latin America: Some Theoretical and Methodological Guidelines for Its Study." *Latin American Research Review* 16(2):3-32.

Papanek, Gustav F. 1967. *Pakistan's Development, Social Goals and Private Incentives.* Harvard: Harvard University Press.

Patil, D.K. 1972. "Lightening Campaign: The Mukti Bahini." *Weekly Holiday,* December 16.

Parastatal Sector Reform Commission (PSRC). 1997. *1996/1997 Review and Action Plan for 1997/1998.* Dar es Salaam: United Republic of Tanzania.

Patnaik, U. 1972. "On the Mode of Production in Indian Agriculture - A Reply." *Economic and Political Weekly* 7(40) September.

Petras, James. 1982. "The Peripheral State: Continuity and Change in the International Division of Labor" *Journal of Contemporary Asia* 4.

Phillips, Nicola, 2004. "International Political Economy, Comparative Political Economy and the Study of Contemporary Development." *IPEG Papers in Global Political Economy* No. 8, May 2004.

Poulantzas, Nicos. 1976. "The Capitalist State: A Reply to Miliband and Laclau." *New Left Review* No. 95 (January-February): 65-83.

_____. 1976a. *The Crisis of Dictatorships.* Translated by David Fernbach. London: New Left Books.

_____. 1975. *Classes in Contemporary Capitalism.* Translated by David Fernbach. London: New Left Books.

_____. 1973. *Political Power and Social Classes.* Translated by Timothy O'Hagan. London: New Left Books.

_____. 1973a. "The Problem of Capitalist State." In *Ideology in Social Sciences,* edited by Robin Blackburn. New York: Vintage Books.

Puchkov, V.P. 1989. *Political Development of Bangladesh, 1971-1985.* New Delhi: Patriot Publishers.

Rahim, A.M.A. 1978. "A Review of Industrial Investment Policy in Bangladesh, 1971-1977." *Asian Survey* 18(11) November.

Rahim, Enayetur and Joyce Rahim. 2003. Bangladesh Liberation War and the Nixon White House 1971. Dhaka: Pustaka.

Rahman, Atiur. 1986. *Peasants and Classes.* Dhaka: UPL.

Rahman, M. 1973. "Economic Incentives and Rural Income Distribution: Some Observation in the Light of Bangladesh Experience." Unpublished paper. Dhaka: Bangladesh Planning Commission.

Rahman, Matiur and Azizul Huq. 1987. *Dhanik Shrenir Lootpater Kahini.* (The Story of the Pillage by the Rich, in Bengali). Dhaka: Ekota Prokashoni.

Raj, K.N. 1973. "The Politics and Economics of 'Intermediate Regimes.'" *Economic and Political Weekly* 8(27).

Reuschmeyer, Dietrich and Peter Evans. 1985. "Transnational Linkages and the Economic Role of the State: An Analysis of Developing and Industrial States in the Post World War II Period." In *Bringing the State Back In,* edited by Peter Evans, Dietrich Reuschmeyer, and Theda Skocpol. Cambridge: Cambridge University Press.

Riaz, Ali. 2005. "Bangladesh in 2004: The Politics of Vengeance and the Erosion of Democracy." *Asian Survey* 45(1):112-118.

_____. 2004. *God Willing: The Politics of Islamism in Bangladesh.* Lanham: Rowman and Littlefield.

_____. 1998. "Two Trends in Analyzing the Causes of Military Rule in Bangladesh". *Bulletin of Concerned Asian Scholars* 30(1):56-65.

Riaz, Ali and Zillur Rahman. 1991. *GonoObhuthyan '90* (The Mass Upsurge '90). Dhaka: Kagoj Prokashan.

Rizvi, Gowhar. 1991. "Bangladesh: Towards Civil Society." *The World Today* 47(8-9):155-160.

Rizvi, Hasan Askari. 1987. *The Military and Politics in Pakistan 1947-86.* Lahore: Progressive Publishers.

Roxborough, Ian. 1982. *Theories of Underdevelopment.* London: Macmillan Press Ltd.

Sangbad. 1979. Interview with Moudud Ahmed. November 12.

_____. 1973. News Report. March 10.

Sayeed, Abu. 1989. *Bangladesher Swadhinata Judhyeir Arale Judhya* (War Behind the Bangladesh Independence War). Dhaka: Sarif Ahmed.

Sayeed, Khalid Bin. 1980. *Politics in Pakistan.* New York: Praeger.

Schendel, Willem van. 1981. "After the Limelight: Longer-Term Effects of Rural Development in a Bangladesh Village." *Bulletin of Concerned Asian Scholars* 13(4).

Schwarz, Rolf. 2004. "State Formation Processes in Rentier States: The Middle Eastern Case." Paper presented at the fifth Pan-European Conference on International Relations, ECPR Standing Group on International Relations, September 9-11, The Hague.

Sen, Anupam. 1988. *Bamladesa, Rashtra o Samaja, Samajika Arthanitira Swarupa* (Bangladesh: The State and Society. A Socioeconomic Study). Dhaka: Shitya Samabya.

Sen, Binayek. 1988. "Bangladesher Brihat Bourgeoisie Srenir Bikash: Akti Druto Parjebekhyan" (Growth of Big Bourgeoisie in Bangladesh: An Observation). *Muktir Diganta* No. 4.

Sen, Binayek, Mustafa K. Mujeri, and Qazi Shahabuddin. 2004. "Operationalising Pro-Poor Growth: A Country Case Study on Bangladesh." Mimeograph. A Joint initiative of AFD, BMZ (GTZ, KFW Development Bank), DFID, and the World Bank, October 2004.

Sen, Rangalal. 1986. *Political Elites in Bangladesh.* Dhaka: University Press Limited.

Sengupta, A. 1971. "Regional Disparity and Economic Development of Pakistan." *Economic and Political Weekly.* 6(45) and (46):2279-2322.

Shahidullah, Muhammad. 1985. "Class Formation and Class Relations in Bangladesh." In *Middle Classes in Dependent Countries*, edited by Dale L. Johnson. Beverley Hills: Sage.

Shanin, Teodor. 1982. "Class, State and Revolutions: Substitutes and Realities." In *Introduction to the Sociology of the 'Developing Societies'*, edited by Hamza Alavi and Teodor Shanin. New York: Monthly Review Press.

SIDA/ILO. 1974. *Report on the Integrated Rural Development Programme*. SIDA/ILO

Siddiqui, Kamal. 1981. *Bangladeshe Bhumi Sngaskarer Rajnaitik Arthanity* (The Political Economy of Land Reforms in Bangladesh). Dhaka: BIDS.

Siddiqui, Kamal et al. 1990. *Social Formation in Dhaka City.* Dhaka: University Press Limited.

Singh, Kushwant. 1971. "Freedom Fighters of Bangladesh." *Illustrated Weekly of India,* December 19.

Singhal, Damodar P. 1972. *Pakistan.* New Jersey: Prentice Hall.

SIPRI. 1981. *SIPRI Yearbook 1981.* Oxford: Oxford University Press.

Shivji, Issa G. 1976. *Class Struggles in Tanzania.* New York: Monthly Review Press.

Skocpol, Theda. 1985. "Bringing the State Back In: Strategies of Analysis in Current Research." In *Bringing the State Back In,* edited by Peter B. Evans et al. Cambridge: Cambridge University Press.

_____. 1979. *States and Social Revolutions.* Cambridge: Cambridge University Press.

Slovo, J. 1974. "A Critical Appraisal of the Non-Capitalist Path and the National Democratic State in Africa." *Marxism Today* June 1974.

Sobhan Rehman. 2002. *Bangladesh in New Millennium: Between Promise and Fulfillment.* Dhaka: Center for Policy Dialogue.

_____. 1991. "Introduction." In *Debt Default to the Development Finance Institutions*, edited by Rehman Sobhan. Dhaka: University Press Limited.

_____. 1982. *The Crisis of External Dependence, The Political Economy of Foreign Aid to Bangladesh.* Dhaka: University Press Limited.

_____. 1980. "Politics of Food and Famine in Bangladesh." In *Bangladesh*

Politics, edited by Emajuddin Ahmed. Dhaka: Center for Social Studies.

_____. 1970. "Cost of a Strong Centre." *Forum* January 3.

_____. 1968. *Basic Democracies, Works Programme and Rural Development.* Dhaka: University of Dhaka, Bureau of Economic Research.

Sobhan, Rehman and Ahmed Ahsan. 1984. *Disinvestment and Denationalization: Profile and Performance.* Dhaka: Bangladesh Institute of Development Studies.

Sobhan, Rehman and Muzaffer Ahmad. 1980. *Public Enterprise in an Intermediate Regime, A Study in the Political Economy of Bangladesh.* Dhaka: Bangladesh Institute of Development Studies.

Sobhan, Rehman and Syed Akhter Mahmood. 1981. "Repayments of Loans to Specialised Financial Institutions in Bangladesh: Issues and Constraints." *Bangladesh Development Studies* 9(1).

Solaiman, M. and M. Alam. 1977. "Characteristics of Candidates for Election in Three Union Parishads in Comilla Kotwali Thana." Mimeograph. Comilla: Bangladesh Academy of Rural Development.

Spain, James. W. 1954. "Military Assistance for Pakistan." *The American Political Science Review* 48(3):738-51.

Stallings, Barbara. 1985. "International Lending and the Relative Autonomy of the State: A Case Study of Twentieth-Century Peru." *Politics and Society* 14(3):257-88.

Stein, Howard. 1985. "Theories of the State in Tanzania: A Critical Assessment." *The Journal of Modern African Studies* 23(1):105-123.

Stern, Joseph J. 1971. "Growth, Development, and Regional Equity in Pakistan." In *Development Policy II: The Pakistan Experience,* edited by Falcon and Papanek. Cambridge: Harvard University Press.

Strange, S. 1996. *The Retreat of the State: The Diffusion of Power in the World Economy.* Cambridge: Cambridge University Press.

Syeduzzaman, M. 1991. "Bangladesh's Experience with Adjustment Policies." In *Structural Adjustment Policies in the Third World,* edited by Rehman Sobhan. Dhaka: University Press Limited.

Therborn, Goran. 1978. *What Does the Ruling Class Do When It Rules?* London: New Left Books.

Thomas, Clive. 1984. *The Rise of Authoritarian State in Peripheral Societies.* New York: Monthly Review Press.

_____. 1978. "Class Struggle, Social Development and the Theory of the Non-Capitalist Path." In *Problems of Socialist Orientation in Africa,* edited by Mai Palmberg. New York: Africana Publishing Company.

_____. 1974. *Dependence and Transformation: The Economics of the Transition to the Socialism.* New York: Monthly review Press.

Tilly, Charles. 1994. "Entanglements of European City States." In *Cities and the Rise of the State in Europe, AD 1000-1800,* edited by Charles Tilly. Boulder, CO: Westview.

_____. 1990. *Coercion, Capital and European States, AD 990-1990.* Oxford: Basil Blackwell.

Time. 2004. "State of disgrace." April 12. http://www.time.com /time/asia/magazine/article/0,13673,501040412-607842,00.htm.

Trimberger, Allen Key. 1978. *Revolution from Above: Military Bureaucrats and Development in Japan, Turkey and Peru.* New Brunswick: Transaction Books.

Ulanovsky, R. 1974. *Socialism and the Newly Independent Nations.* Moscow: Progress Publishers.

_____. 1969. "Some Aspects of the Non-Capitalist Way for Asian and African Countries." *World Marxist Review* September.

Umar, Badruddin. 1980. *Towards the Emergency.* Dhaka: Muktadhara.

_____. 1979. *Bhasa Andolana O Tatkalina Rajiniti* (Language Movement and Contemporary Politics), Vol. 3. Chittagong: Boi Ghar.

_____. 1975. *Bhasa Andolana O Tatkalina Rajiniti* (Language Movement and Contemporary Politics), Vol. 2. Dhaka: Mawla Brothers.

_____. 1973a. "On Muslim Bengal." *Weekly Holiday,* May 27, June 3, June 10.

_____. 1973b. "Now there is No Opposition." *Weekly Holiday,* March 11.

_____. 1970. *Bhasa Andolana O Tatkalina Rajiniti* (Language Movement and Contemporary Politics), Vol. 1. Dhaka: Mowla Brothers.

United Nations. 1992. *Yearbook of National Account Statistics 1990.* New York: United Nations.

United Nations. 1972. Ambassador Ema Sailor's Report of High-Level UN Consultants to Bangladesh. Vol. 1. March-April. Mimeograph. New York: United Nations.

Uyangoda, Jayadeva. 1986. "Nationalism and State Formation in Bangladesh." Unpublished Ph.D. dissertation, Department of Political Science. University of Hawaii.

Vivekananda, Franklin. 1986. "Why Aid Does Not Work?" In *Bangladesh Economy: Some Selected Issues,* edited by Franklin Vivekananda. Stockholm: Bethany Books.

Venkataramani, M.S. 1982. *The American Role in Pakistan, 1947-1958.* New Delhi: Radiant.

Wahab, M.A. 1980. "The Rural Political Elite in Bangladesh: A Study of Leadership Pattern in Six Union Parishads in Rangpur District." Unpublished M. Phil. Thesis, Institute of Bangladesh Studies, Rajshahi University, Rajshahi.

Waterbury, John. 1991. "Twilight of the State Bourgeoisie?" *International Journal of Middle East Studies* 23(1):1-17.

Weekly Holiday. 1976. News report. January 18.

_____. 1974. "Why the Armed Forces Have Been Called Out." April 28.

_____. 1973. Post-Editorial. February 4.

Weekly Wave. 1973. Interview with Ziaur Rahman. March 25.

_____. 1973a. March 18.

_____. 1972. News Report. December 2.

Westergaard, Kirsten. 1985. "State and Rural Society in Bangladesh. A Study in Relationship." Scandanavian Institute of Asian Studies Mimeograph Series, No. 49. London: Curzon Press.

Wilcox, Wayne. 1965. "The Pakistan"s Coup d'etat of 1958." *Pacific Affairs* Vol. 38.

White, Lawrence J. 1974. *Industrial Concentration and Economic Power in Pakistan.* Princeton, NJ: Princeton University Press.

Wood. Geofrey D. 1997. "States without citizens: the problem of the franchise state." In *Too Close for Comfort: NGOs, States and Donors,* edited by D. Hulme and M. Edwards. London: Macmillan.

_____. 1978. "Class Differentiation and Power in Bandokgram: The Minifundist Case." In *Exploitation and the Rural Poor,* edited by Ameerul Huq. Comilla: BARD.

World Bank. 1989. *Bangladesh: Recent Economic Development and Short Term Prospects.* Washington D.C.: World Bank.

_____. 1985. *Bangladesh: Economic and Social Development Prospects*, Vol. IV (Statistical Appendix). Report No. 5409, April 12. Washington D.C.: World Bank.

Zaman, M.A. 1975. "Bangladesh: The Case of Further Land Reform." *South Asian Review* 8(2) January.

Ziemann, W. and M. Lanzendorfer. 1977. "The State in Peripheral Societies." In *The Socialist Register 1977,* edited by Ralph Miliband and John Saville. London: Merlin Press.

Index

A

N

S

Printed in the United States
37322LVS00002B/1-92